# Effective Thinking

# Effective Thinking Skills

*Preventing and managing personal problems*

Richard Nelson-Jones

CASSELL

Cassell
Wellington House
125 Strand
London WC2R 0BB

First published 1989
Reprinted 1996, 1997


**British Library Cataloguing-in-Publication Data**
A catalogue record for this book is available from the British Library.

ISBN 0-304-33828-1

Typeset by Fakenham Photosetting Ltd.

Printed and bound in Great Britain by
Redwood Books, Trowbridge, Wiltshire.

# Contents

# List of Thinksheets

# Preface

This book is intended for people who wish to think more effectively about their personal problems and decisions. Its philosophic position is that of pragmatic existentialism. You are personally responsible for *making* your own happiness and fulfilment through the quality of your choices. This is true even in adverse circumstances. Thinking skills are viewed as series of choices that may be well or poorly made. To think effectively you require a repertoire of thinking skills that you then apply to your problems and decisions. This book describes these skills and encourages you to use them.

A number of themes are stressed. First, you can support or oppress yourself by how you think. To quote Abraham Lincoln: 'most folks are about as happy as they make up their minds to be'. Second, you should use thinking skills for preventing as well as managing problems. Why land yourself in trouble unnecessarily? Third, using effective thinking skills requires courage. You affirm and define your existence by rising above your own and others' human fallibility.

The book draws heavily on the insights of the new cognitive therapies. The first two chapters focus on what thinking is and on how you initially acquire and later sustain poor thinking skills. Then follows a series of chapters on the skills of: owning responsibility for your choosing; using self-talk; formulating realistic personal rules; perceiving yourself and others accurately; realistically attributing cause for what happens in your life; predicting and creating your future; and using visual thinking. Frequently, deficient skills in these areas position you to deal ineffectively with your problems. Next come two putting-it-together chapters demonstrating how you can apply your thinking skills to making decisions and to preventing and managing specific problems. The final chapter looks at how you can gain the courage to keep thinking for yourself.

What features does this book possess? It is definitely intended as a how-to-do-it book. Ultimately no one else can do your thinking for you. There are 55 thinksheets designed to help you learn by doing. Use these thinksheets flexibly: for instance, only stay with them as long as they work for you and, if necessary, modify them to suit your needs. Additionally, there are numerous case examples covering a wide range of problems. Most of these are drawn from clients with whom I have worked. These were people who were damaging their happiness and fulfilment by making self-oppressing, as contrasted with self-supporting, thinking choices. I have tried to write in simple, clear English avoiding psychobabble. Also, I have attempted to add colour and contrast to the book with some jokes, quotations, lyrics and limericks.

I express the following appreciations. To Naomi Roth and the editorial and production team at Cassell for their work in preparing the book. To Dawn Butcher of the Royal Melbourne Institute of Technology Wordprocessing Unit for the help and courtesy in typing the manuscript. Last, but not least, to all those cognitive theorists, researchers and therapists on whose work this book is based. I have tried to acknowledge them adequately both in the text and in the bibliography at the end.

I hope that you enjoy using the book and that it helps you to think more effectively when faced with problems and decisions in your life.

Richard Nelson-Jones

# 1  Choosing How You Think

Most folks are about as happy as they make up their minds to be.

*Abraham Lincoln*

Choices, choices, choices, whenever you think you make choices. Human animals are probably unique in their capacity for thinking and choosing. Other animals operate on the basis of instincts. Humans have the capacity for self-awareness and for thinking themselves into and out of difficulty. This is a book about learning to become more able to control your thinking. It aims to help you make thinking choices that support rather than oppress you; also, where appropriate, to help others to do the same. It seeks to develop your skills of 'straight' as contrasted with 'crooked' thinking about your personal problems. It is a book about having the courage to think for yourself.

Below are a number of examples of people whose thinking choices adversely affect their happiness and level of performance.

Pam is a high school student who is shy. All the time she worries what others think of her and whether they will reject her.

Roger and Joyce are a couple in a distressed marriage. Roger has a tendency to attribute many of Joyce's actions to malevolent intentions. He omits to check the accuracy of his perceptions.

Sue and Paul have been going steady for a year. Recently, they have not been getting on very well. Sue thinks: 'If Paul loves me he should know instinctively how to make me happy, I should not have to tell him.' This thought blocks her from telling Paul what she wants.

Denis works in a clothing shop. He is about to get a new boss. He regards this as a big threat and thinks: 'I'm damn well not going to let him get the better of me'. He has still to meet his new boss.

Betty is a college student coming up to her final exams. She thinks she must get an outstanding degree. Otherwise, both she and her parents will think she is a failure. Her thinking, which ties her worth as a person to academic achievement, contributes to her severe exam anxiety.

Numerous other examples could be provided about how people, through ineffective thinking, sabotage their own happiness and fulfilment. As the saying goes, 'they are their own worst enemies'. Unfortunately, often such thinking has negative consequences for others too.

Many writers throughout the centuries have attested to the importance of thinking. In the first century A.D., Epictetus wrote: 'Men are disturbed not by things, but by the views which they take of them.' He also stated that 'the chief concern of a wise and good man is his own reason'. Shakespeare had Hamlet say: 'There is nothing either good or bad, but thinking makes it so.' Shortly afterwards, the French philosopher Descartes wrote: 'I think, therefore I am' ('*cogito, ergo sum*'). The fact that humans have the potential to think does not necessarily mean that this potential gets fully used. Jonathan Swift, the author of *Gulliver's Travels*, observed: 'an old saying and a true, "much drinking, little thinking"'. We humans do not need to take to drink to befuddle our thinking! We easily succeed without such props.

Perhaps I can use humour to illustrate further the point that our thinking can adversely influence how we feel and act. Below is a limerick in which the central character not only *causes* but *sustains* her problem through ineffective thinking.

> There was a young student from Kew,
> Whose talents for thinking were few,
> With every transgression,
> She swelled with aggression,
> Which allowed her to stew and to stew.

As Epictetus stated, negative feelings are generated less by events themselves than by the ways in which you think about them. In the above limerick, anger and self-pity were the outcomes of faulty thinking. Focusing on your thinking choices gives you a 'handle' to combat a range of unwanted feelings, including persistent anger, depression and excessive anxiety. Furthermore, if you *think* more effectively and *feel* better you are more likely to *act* in self-enhancing rather than in self-defeating ways.

**Preventing as well as managing problems**

So far I have focused on the thinking difficulties of others. Now I confront you with the observation that *you too* are likely to have areas of significant thinking difficulty that contribute to *your* personal problems. You may react: 'What me? . . . Never!' Or you may readily admit that it is a daily struggle to discipline your thinking so that you do not harm yourself and others. My position is that thinking difficulties beset us all.

Effective thinking skills can help you avoid problems as well as deal with them more effectively when they occur. Take the example of top golfers such as Jack Nicklaus, Nancy Lopez, Greg Norman or Sandy Lyle. Their aim is to go round the course in the minimum number of strokes. They use their skills in a 'preventing problems' way to stay on the fairway and out of the rough. However, reassuringly, even the best of golfers end up in the rough. Then they use their skills in a 'managing problems' way to get out.

Assuming you are rational, like the top golfers you want to go through life with the minimum number of avoidable problems. Effective thinking skills can increase your chances of staying on the fairway. For instance, if you are skilled at perceiving yourself and others accurately, you may prevent some avoidable conflict. However, inevitably all of you will find yourselves in conflicts. Here you use your thinking skills to manage these problems in the most constructive way.

**What are personal problems?**

One way of viewing personal problems is that they are difficulties that challenge you to find solutions. Personal problems, like excessive anger, relationship conflicts, shyness, loneliness, lack of concentration, test anxiety, boredom, unemployment, choosing a career and working with difficult colleagues, all challenge you to find solutions. However, in line with the analogy of the top golfers, another way of viewing personal problems is preventive. Here, whenever possible, the problem is how to avoid the problem. This view sees personal problems as often more covert than overt. Your challenge is to avoid making the thinking choices that position you for unnecessary and more visible problems.

By the end of this book I hope you possess a greater awareness of some of the thinking difficulties with which humans beset themselves, and that you possess some useful self-help skills for preventing and managing your problems and decisions of living. Let's try to keep out of the rough and to stop being 'our own worst enemies'.

**WHAT IS THINKING?**

The focus of this book is on acquiring self-help skills to overcome thinking difficulties which interfere with happiness and fulfilment. The aim is to help ordinary people think through their everyday problems of living. However, before exploring what contributes to ineffective thinking in regard to personal problems, let us briefly examine what thinking is.

There are a variety of mental processes that can be subsumed under the word thinking. Although it is far from exhaustive, Table 1.1 lists over 30 mental processes that highlight aspects of thinking. Thus thinking is a general term comprising many different processes. Furthermore, it is possible to think about the processes of thinking. Indeed, if you are to control your thinking, it is important to become aware of and influence your thinking about how you think.

Table 1.1    *Some processes of thinking*

| | | |
|---|---|---|
| Anticipating | Creating | Judging |
| Attributing | Deciding | Knowing |
| Being aware | Distorting | Memorizing |
| Being curious | Dreaming | Perceiving |
| Believing | Evaluating | Problem-solving |
| Choosing | Fantasizing | Reasoning |
| Concentrating | Forgetting | Reflecting |
| Conceptualizing | Imaging | Remembering |
| Concluding | Introspecting | Understanding |
| Considering | Intuiting | Visualizing |

## Thinking and choosing

In this book thinking is viewed from an existential perspective. Thinking is an integral part of human existence. Humans are condemned to be thinkers and choosers. We make our lives through our choices. The sum of our lives may be viewed as the sum of the consequences of our choices. Humans cannot *not* think. Choosing, or deciding from various options, is the central feature of the processes of thinking. Just as we cannot *not* think, we cannot *not* choose. As noted Viennese psychiatrist Viktor Frankl observes: 'During no moment of his life does man escape the mandate to choose among possibilities' (Frankl, 1969, p. 85). Our mental processes involve thinking choices at various levels of self-awareness and self-control. For instance, people can *choose* to observe much of their mental functioning and, if they find it is not working for them, *choose* to alter it. I do not mean to imply that this is invariably easy, but it is usually possible.

Some people's thinking processes are more effective than other people's. The late Abraham Maslow used to say that mental patients were not sick, they were 'cognitively wrong'. By that he meant that their mental processes entailed poor thinking choices that led to outcomes which were then labelled as mental illness. He stated that: 'neurosis, psychosis, stunting of growth—all are, from this point of view, cognitive diseases as well, contaminating perception, learning, remembering, attending and thinking' (Maslow, 1962, p. 189). People whose basic needs were being met were more likely to make 'growth' choices than those deficient in gratifying their basic needs.

American psychiatrist William Glasser (1984), the originator of reality therapy, also emphasizes the role of choosing in our lives. He views people as control systems in a continuous process of making choices as they attempt to control their lives. People choose the misery they feel. Better choices are available if they learn how to make them. Glasser does not explicitly mention thinking skills. Nevertheless, he clearly implies that by using better thinking skills humans can avoid much of their distress.

Albert Ellis (1962, 1980), the originator of rational-emotive therapy, is perhaps the most prominent psychologist in recent years to focus on the way people choose to think themselves into negative emotions such as anger, anxiety and depression. Ellis is very concerned to help his clients towards freedom of choice on the basis of rational thinking. Rationality consists of thinking in ways which contribute to the chosen goals of survival and happiness. Irrationality consists of thinking in ways which block or interfere with attainment of goals. In particular, Ellis focuses on the way people choose irrational belief systems with which they then persistently reindoctrinate themselves. Like a faulty record, they stay stuck in the same groove.

Perhaps enough has been said by way of introduction to indicate that the notion of people choosing to think themselves into their personal problems is very common in contemporary psychology. Ellis has written some 'rational humorous' songs to illustrate this point. With apologies to Richard Rodgers and Oscar Hammerstein, let me illustrate the point that we can choose to think ourselves into problems by parodying the lyrics of one of their most famous songs. My intention is not to belittle the misery felt by depressed and suicidal people, but rather to highlight how their thinking may contribute to this.

> Climb ev'ry mountain,
> Count every blow,
> Savour ev'ry put-down,
> Till your mood feels low.

> Climb ev'ry mountain,
> Heighten ev'ry fear.
> Wallow in self-pity.
> Till suicide feels near.

> A depression that needs all the care you can give,
> Ev'ry day of your life for as long as you live.

> Climb ev'ry mountain,
> Heighten ev'ry fear,
> Wallow in self-pity.
> Till suicide feels near.

Comedy and tragedy may not be far apart when inadequate thinking choices are considered. A large number of jokes focus on other people's thinking deficits, for instance jokes in Britain about the Irish, in the United States about the Poles, and in New Zealand about the Australians. For example, a New Zealand prime minister observed about the migration of New Zealanders to Australia that it raised the intelligence level of both populations! It is easy to poke fun at the notion of *others* being dim-witted and creating their problems. However, people in psychological pain are more to be sympathized with than laughed at. They require help to enable them to make more effective thinking choices.

## Some dimensions of thinking

Besides choosing, a number of dimensions of thinking are either apparent in or may be inferred from Table 1.1. They include the following.

- *Pictures and words*. Thinking involves visual images and fantasies as well as thoughts expressed in words, language and self-talk. Think of someone you love. Does your mind conjure up a picture about them, words, or a mixture of both?

- *Perceiving accurately and inaccurately*. Perceiving means apprehending through the mind and through the senses. Your perceptions of yourself, others and the environment may be accurate. However, certain perceptions may be either distorted or denied altogether even though you may have registered them below awareness.

- *Levels of awareness*. Thinking processes operate at varying levels of awareness. While humans are capable of accurate perception and reasoning, frequently they fail fully to use their capability. The notion of defensive thinking implies that individuals remain unaware not only of the outcomes of their defensive processes but also of the processes themselves. Further examples of unconscious thinking processes include dreaming and the well-springs of creativity. Maslow (1962) distinguishes between primary and secondary process 'cognition' or thinking. He makes a plea for acknowledging constructive as well as destructive unconscious primary thinking processes.

  Some thinking processes may be accessible to awareness rather than either conscious or unconscious. For instance, psychiatrist Aaron Beck (1976) proposes the notion of *automatic thoughts* that are influential in contributing to negative feelings like anxiety, phobias and depression. Such thoughts pass by almost unnoticed unless people are instructed to focus on them.

- *Rational and irrational thinking*. Thinking choices can lead to conclusions that are realistically and accurately drawn from testable premises. However, human thinking often strays from being based on logical reasoning. Consequently, in varying degrees it becomes irrational and self-defeating.

- *Personal experiencing and valuing.* The notion of thinking for yourself implies that each of you has a unique capacity both for experiencing inner and outer events and also for placing a value on your experiencing. Certain thinking choices are alien to your personal experiencing and valuing. These may involve treating other people's beliefs and values as if they were your own. The poet W. H. Auden wrote of the effects of the totalitarian state: 'And terror like a frost shall halt the flood of thinking'. His words are also pertinent to the ways in which your fears of others and of yourself may distance you from acknowledging, let alone stating, what you truly think.

## Thinking, feeling and action

There are many different ways in which the relationship between thinking, feeling and action may be considered. Here I present three viewpoints, albeit interrelated. Two of these viewpoints are depicted in Figure 1.1. All three are helpful in highlighting differing aspects of the relationships between thinking, feeling and action.

- *Thinking, feeling and action interacting with each other.* This is depicted in the top diagram in Figure 1.1. Thinking is often the consequence and/or accompaniment of feelings at varying levels of awareness. You may choose to regulate your feelings by altering the way in which you think about yourself, people and the environment. The connection between thinking and action is also two-way: thinking influences action and action in turn influences thinking. Likewise feelings and actions influence each other.

- *Thinking, feeling and action integrated with each other.* This viewpoint is holistic. There is no mind–body split, no dichotomy between human thinking and animality. This is the ideal position found in humanistic writers like Carl Rogers and Maslow. Rogers (1961) observes that as humans become more able to perceive their significant biological experiencing, they act more rationally and less defensively. In non-human animals the link between feeling and action is provided by their instincts. Humans differ in two significant ways from non-human animals. First, they possess relatively weak instinct remnants rather than strong instincts. Second, they possess a capacity for thinking and self-awareness which can override their instinct remnants. In varying degrees humans may then cease to think, feel and act in an integrated way.

- *Feeling and action consequent upon thinking.* This is the position advanced by writers like Ellis, Beck and the so-called 'cognitive-behaviourists'. It is based on a simple ABC framework:

    A   The activating event.
    B   Your thoughts.
    C   Your feelings and actions.

*Thinking, feeling and action interacting with each other*

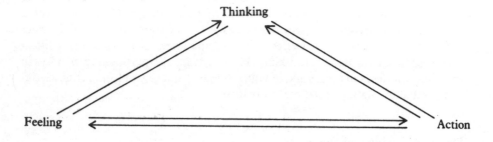

*Thinking, feeling and action integrated with each other*

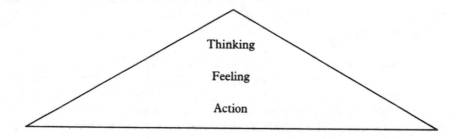

Figure 1.1    Two viewpoints on the relationships between thinking, feeling and action.

The idea is that what you feel and do at C can be either helpful or harmful. This is not so much because of what happened at A, but because of how you think at B about what happened at A. In short, your feelings and actions are heavily influenced by how you think about activating events. An extension of this ABC model is that the action and feeling consequences at C then feed back to B with the further possibility of you altering your thinking.

There is no simple answer to questions concerning the relationships between thinking, feeling and action. Also, there is no simple answer to whether changing how you act follows from changing how you think or the reverse. In reality, cognitive and cognitive-behavioural therapists sometimes intervene to change clients' behaviour first rather than their thinking. Beck, with his depressed patients, often starts by encouraging them to engage in some basic activities. By this he hopes to alter their thinking concerning their capacity to influence their environments (Beck *et al.*, 1979). Sometimes a good place to start altering your thinking may be to start changing your behaviour in real-life situations that have previously caused you difficulty. Later in the book you will be introduced to the notion of conducting personal experiments in which you change your behaviour as a means of testing the accuracy of your thinking and, if necessary, altering it.

## WHAT ARE THINKING SKILLS?

As the preceding section has shown, the verb thinking covers numerous mental processes. However, in this book the main focus is on those skills that help you to manage your problems and decisions of living better. Consequently, although there is overlap between intellectual skills and those thinking skills useful for daily living, the former do not get emphasized as such. Nevertheless, this is very much a book about using your brain!

### What are skills?

The meaning of the word *skill* includes proficiency, competence and expertness in some activity. The essential element of a skill is the ability to make and implement an effective sequence of choices so as to achieve a desired objective. For instance, if you are to be a good decision-maker you have to make and implement the choices entailed in making good decisions. The fact that thinking gets viewed in skills terms does not mean that using the skills must be mechanistic and boring. Effective thinking skills can free you to be more spontaneous and help you regulate unwanted feelings.

The concept of a skill is best viewed not as an either/or matter in which you either possess or do not possess a skill. Rather it is preferable to think of yourself as possessing skills *strengths* and *weaknesses* or a mixture of the two. If you make good choices in a skills area, for instance when making decisions, this is a skills strength. If you make poor choices, this is a skills weakness. In all thinking skills areas you are likely to possess both strengths and weaknesses in varying degrees. For example, in the skills area of making decisions, you may be good at identifying and collecting relevant information, but poor at evaluating the consequences of each alternative involved in the decision. The object of counselling, training and self-help in thinking skills is, in one or more skills area, to shift the balance of your strengths and weaknesses more in the direction of strengths. Put another way, it is to help you think about your thinking so that you become a better chooser.

### Defining thinking skills

To gain maximum happiness and fulfilment you require a *repertoire* of thinking skills. Your repertoire is the stock of skills that you are able to use when necessary. It is insufficient just to know what a thinking skill is. You have to use it as and when required. Below is a definition of *thinking skills* for the purposes of this book.

> Thinking skills are sequences of choices, across various mental processes. Your repertoire of thinking skills comprises your strengths and weaknesses in each skills area.

Effectively using your thinking skills helps you both to prevent avoidable problems and to manage unavoidable problems constructively.

**Reservations about a thinking skills approach**

Some of you may have reservations about an approach focusing on encouraging you to discipline your thinking skills. Your reservations may include the following.

- *It's too intellectual.* A focus on how you think may take you up into your head rather than help you to get in touch with your feelings and to take appropriate actions. Many clever people are very stupid in their private lives.

- *It's too mechanistic.* A thinking skills approach allows insufficient scope for individual differences, free will, intuition and creativity. Instead, people are reduced to being mechanical thinking boxes somewhat like computers.

- *It's too superficial.* People's problems of living are often the result of considerable emotional deprivations in their upbringing. As such they may require long-term counselling. Just focusing on tightening up their thinking is insufficient. Furthermore, most people's behaviour is influenced by numerous genetic and contextual considerations. These considerations include sex, age, intelligence, biochemistry, health, socioeconomic status, culture, chance, other people's behaviour and so on. To say that people can be much more in control of their lives if they think more effectively does not adequately take into account the force of these other considerations.

- *It's too hard.* What most people want is an easy life within the confines of conventional ways of viewing their world. Few people have either the desire or the capacity for genuine independent thought. It is asking too much to expect the average person to discipline his or her thinking.

Each of the above reservations is a partial truth rather than a whole truth. Focusing on thinking skills can be a counter-productive intellectual exercise. However, working on how you think can liberate you to experience your feelings more fully and to behave more effectively. Because something can be done the wrong way does not mean you cannot be successful doing it a different way. The same comment holds true for focusing on thinking skills being too mechanistic.

You can focus on thinking skills to release rather than to restrict your capacity for creativity and independent thought.

The idea that focusing on thinking skills is too superficial is again a partial rather than a whole truth. Some people require nurturing emotional relationships to lower their anxiety level to the point where they can usefully work on their thinking. Additionally, genetic and environmental considerations place parameters on everyone's control over their lives. However, there are still numerous opportunities to choose how you exist. Endeavouring to rid yourself of 'stinkin' thinkin'' and to replace it with effective thinking can help you to do this, even though sometimes you may have to make the most of poor conditions. Thinking for yourself is hard. Because it may be too hard for many does not mean that with effort it will be too hard for you. There is a difference between hard and impossible.

## BEING PERSONALLY RESPONSIBLE FOR YOUR THINKING

When you are being personally responsible you are in the process of making the choices that maximize your happiness and fulfilment (Nelson-Jones, 1984, 1988). Personal responsibility is a positive concept whereby you are responsible *for* your well-being and making your *own* choices. It contrasts with a common meaning of responsibility, namely that of responsibility *to* others, including living up to their standards. Although the process of personal responsibility is difficult, it also liberates. It frees you to concentrate on how you can be most effective. It entails neither focusing on other people's faults nor feeling that you need say 'my fault' all the time.

This book aims to help you adopt and implement a fundamental attitude of personal responsibility for how you think about your personal problems. Viewing thinking skills as sequences of choices allows you to do this. The focus is on your present and future behaviour. Your past thinking choices merit attention only to the extent that you can learn from them.

Assuming personal responsibility for your thinking does not mean only thinking about yourself. Humans are social animals and, as such, interdependent. The division between meeting the needs of self and meeting those of others is a complex one. Nevertheless, thinking effectively about your personal problems increases the possibility of synergy rather than opposition between meeting your own and others' needs. Humans have the capacity to transcend narrow self-interest both in their loving relationships and in taking a wider interest in the welfare of their species. Ineffective thinking not only releases the negative, but also restrains the positive, potential of people. In turn, effective thinking blocks the bad and encourages the good.

In his influential book *The Courage to Be*, theologian Paul Tillich (1952) wrote: 'The courage to be is the ethical act in which man affirms his own being in spite of those elements of his existence which conflict with his essential self-affirmation' (p. 3). Tillich viewed the world through a religious framework. Nevertheless, his words echo the message of this book. Rephrasing Tillich, the courage to be entails assuming personal responsibility for affirming your being through the adequacy of your thinking choices. This is despite conditions in yourself and in your circumstances that conflict with your self-affirmation. It is within your power to improve how you think about your problems. The choices are yours!

## CHAPTER HIGHLIGHTS

How you think influences how you feel and act and *vice versa*.

Thinking involves many different processes and is visual as well as verbal.

Choosing is the central feature of the processes of thinking.

To gain maximum happiness and fulfilment you require a repertoire of thinking skills.

You are personally responsible for your thinking choices and for developing and using appropriate thinking skills when faced with personal problems.

Effective and independent thinking can require courage.

# 2   Learning How Not to Think

Yet each man kills the thing he loves,
  By each let this be heard,
Some do it with a bitter look,
  Some with a flattering word.

*Oscar Wilde*

*Parenthood*. A relationship that legitimizes the older generation in passing on their anxieties and distortions of reality to the younger generation.

*Childhood*. An 18-year custodial sentence in which children acquire the vices of their elders under the guise of learning their virtues.

The aim of this chapter is to give you greater understanding of how you learned to make your present thinking choices when faced with personal problems. Here I help you to review how you attained your present level of thinking skills. In subsequent chapters I look at ways of improving specific skills. This chapter is divided into two parts: *acquiring* deficient thinking skills and *sustaining* them. As the chapter progresses you may come to see more clearly that, although in the past many others may have shaped your thinking choices, you are now responsible for them in the present and future.

## ACQUIRING DEFICIENT THINKING SKILLS

Much of this section is relevant to learning how to make good as well as poor thinking choices in your personal life. If you are to think effectively about your problems, ideally you require both a feeling of security and thinking skills. A simple equation is:

Effective Thinking = Security + Skills

By security I mean a feeling of self-worth. This is likely to lessen any debilitating anxieties that may interfere with your thinking. A repertoire of thinking skills will be presented throughout the remainder of this book. First I review some processes by which you learned your thinking skills and some ways in which you may have acquired a degree of debilitating anxiety.

## Stages in the development of thinking

The branch of academic psychology that focuses on thinking is called cognitive psychology. To date cognitive psychologists have focused more on the development of intellectual and moral thinking than on the development of thinking about personal problems, although these involve moral issues. Much of their work has focused on the development of children's thinking, for example, Piaget's (1970) developmental stages of logical thinking. However, attention has also been paid to the development of thinking in adolescents, for example, Kohlberg's stages of moral thinking (Kohlberg & Gilligan, 1971), and in young adults, for example, Perry's (1970) stages of intellectual and ethical thinking.

The work of Piaget has particular relevance to understanding how, because their capacity for independent critical thinking takes many years to develop, children are at great risk of acquiring faulty habits of thinking from adults. Piaget considered that stages of thinking have a sequential property. They appear in a fixed order of succession with each necessary for the formation of the following one. Piaget stressed that his developmental stages did not represent biological maturation alone. They also took into account children's experience of their physical and social environments.

Briefly, Piaget's three stages or periods in the development of children's logical thinking are as follows.

1.  *A sensorimotor period* (ages 0–1½). Here there is a movement from babies being creatures of automatic reflexes to the development of a primitive form of representative imagery for problem-solving.

2.  *A period of representative intelligence leading to concrete operations.* This has two sub-periods.

    (a) *Pre-operational sub-period* (ages 1½–7). This begins with the formation of processes such as language and mental imagery.

    (b) *Concrete operations sub-period* (ages 7–12). Children have developed some basic logical rules, but their thinking is still closely related to concrete objects.

3.  *Period of formal operations* (ages 12 on). Children can transcend concrete reality and think about what might be. They can operate on

propositions that are about other propositions and not just about concrete reality.

Piaget's work on the development of logical thinking, though still being refined by further research, has implications for why you may engage in faulty thinking when faced with personal problems. For instance, much significant learning about personal problem-solving is learned from parents and others before children have fully acquired the capacity for logical thinking. This may be a factor predisposing your reactions to problems in later life to be more 'automatic' than rational. Also, many people may never attain the stage of formal operations; possibly 40 to 50 per cent fail to do so. Furthermore, even those of you who have developed the capacity for logical thinking may fail to use some or all of it when experiencing the anxiety generated by certain problems.

## Learning from observation

The term social learning indicates that most learning takes place within a social context. Learning from observing others is one of the main methods of social learning. Psychologists use the term 'modelling' to describe learning from observing others. You learn from listening to and watching people, like your parents, who demonstrate behaviour, including their thinking skills. Modelling involves both an observer and a model. Modelling is more likely to be effective if: (a) the observer attends well; (b) the observer retains the material efficiently; and (c) the modelled behaviour results in outcomes that are valued.

Learning from observing others frequently differs when the focus is on thinking rather than action skills. With action skills the old saying 'monkey see, monkey do' is much more likely to apply. Thinking skills are not visual in the sense that action skills are. It is rare for thinking skills to be clearly verbalized. People seldom talk aloud about their thinking processes when faced with personal problems. More often they talk and behave in ways that assume thinking skills strengths and weaknesses. For example, parents frequently think in overgeneralized terms with a great emphasis on how they and others 'should', 'ought' or 'must' be. To the extent that they model rigid and punitive standards, they model a style of thinking that contributes to their children acquiring skills weaknesses.

Inability to observe people who think effectively about their personal problems means that a valuable source of learning has been lost. Even worse, children may acquire deficient thinking skills from poor models. Eric Berne (1972), the originator of transactional analysis, pointed out the differences in how parents think and react when something goes wrong in their families. In some families parents may react by searching for rational solutions to problems. In other families parents may get angry, feel hurt or become depressed. Thus they fail to model the thinking skills for coping adequately with personal difficulties.

There are many kinds of people who, for good or ill, may have acted as models for your thinking choices. Such people include:

- *Parents.* These include step-parents and surrogate parents.

- *Brothers and sisters.* Possibly, especially if they are older.

- *Teachers.* Contact with teachers may be both in class and in extracurricular activity.

- *Peer groups.* People of roughly your own age.

- *Famous people.* Such people may be well-known sports or entertainment personalities. Some may be historical or religious leaders.

- *Fictional people.* Characters portrayed in books, on television and in films.

- *Advertising.* People thinking and behaving in specific ways with the purpose of influencing purchasing decisions.

Generally, your parents have been the most important early influencers of your thinking. Most of you carry your parents around in your heads long after leaving home. Think of the ways in which your parents, or substitute parents, handled personal problems, be they in their own lives, with you or with other members of the family. How do you consider the thinking skills strengths and weaknesses with which you now handle personal problems may have been influenced by each of their examples?

## Learning from consequences

As children act on their environments, their environments produce consequences for their actions. When a child behaves well according to parental standards, parents are more likely to say 'good boy/girl' or 'bad boy/girl'. In each instance the parent sends a message not only about a specific piece of behaviour, but about how the child should think about that behaviour in future. Furthermore, depending on how sent, parents may be communicating either affirming or 'put-down' messages about the worth of the child.

Many parental messages may be conducive to children developing adequate thinking skills for coping with future personal problems. Earlier I mentioned Berne's observation that, in some families, parents search for rational solutions when things go wrong. Children in such families are likely to learn not only from modelling, but also from being encouraged to think rationally about their own problems. Another example is that of a child who is being teased and bullied in primary school. The child may be provided with emotional support through having his or her thoughts and feelings sensitively understood by either or both parents. Also, the child may be helped and rewarded by parents for developing realistic thinking skills for coping with the problem of being teased.

Psychologist Claude Steiner (1974) writes: 'When problem solving is discouraged by parents, children develop a reaction of mindlessness, stupidity, passivity, and incapacity to think in the face of difficult situations' (p. 151). Such 'training in mindlessness' may include providing negative consequences for the use of skills involving awareness, intuition and rationality. Unfortunately, as the following limerick illustrates, some parents' own insecurities and thinking difficulties get in the way of their capacity to help their children think effectively.

> There are parents regardless of season,
> Who won't let their kids use their reason,
> They rule them with fear,
> No objections can bear,
> For to think for yourself is high treason.

Above I focused on parents providing positive and negative consequences that develop or retard their children's acquisition of effective thinking skills. However, parents are not alone in providing such consequences. Teachers, friends, relatives and many others do so too. The peer group can exert particularly strong pressure on young people to gain approval by thinking in conformist ways rather than by thinking for themselves.

There may be differences in the kinds of thinking skills you are encouraged to acquire depending on whether you are a girl or a boy. Skills involving intuition and sensitivity to the needs of others may be more encouraged in girls than in boys. Skills involving being analytical, independent, willing to take a stand, and willing to take risks may be more encouraged in boys.

Traditionally, the role of the woman has been that of the social harmonizer in the home. Furthermore, women tend to be more disclosing and to form closer friendships than men. Consequently, males even more than females may have received negative consequences when trying to develop the thinking skills required for close personal and family relationships. Conversely, the possibility exists that women more than men may manifest thinking skills weaknesses outside the home, e.g. in business. However, the thinking that sustains traditional gender roles is currently being strongly challenged, but not universally so. In Western countries, the proportion of women both in the workforce and in higher education has increased markedly. In sum, the consequences for the development of thinking skills are becoming less related to gender than in the past.

## Acquiring inadequate concepts and information

It is a great help in thinking about personal problems if you possess a realistic conceptual framework within which to understand them. The late George Kelly, a noted personality theorist, is reputed to have said that asking a psychologist to describe a problem without the concept of anxiety was like asking a jockey to win a race without a horse! If you do not possess a reasonable understanding of the concept of anxiety, you are disadvantaged in understanding both yourself and others. Every major counselling and personality theory offers a language and set of concepts for comprehending human behaviour. Clients and people in general also require realistic conceptual frameworks to guide their thinking, feeling and action choices.

In all probability most of you grew up with conceptual frameworks that both helped and hindered you in effectively thinking about your problems. This book attempts to provide a more adequate conceptual framework. In general there is little systematic training in the home or the school in how to think through personal problems. Instead most people are left to pick it up as best they can.

Children often grow up with considerable gaps in information about essential aspects of life. However, if you are to think realistically about personal problems, you require as much relevant information as is necessary to make good choices. Sometimes with the best and sometimes with the worst of intentions, children are subjected to lies, half-truths and omissions of truth. All of these blunt their awareness of life. For instance, parents are dishonest some, if not much, of the time. They engage in impression management. They may conceal information that differs from how they want their children to see them. Also, they may be too embarrassed to talk about how children are born, their own sexuality or their financial position. Furthermore, their own anxieties about subjects like death may mean that their children get fobbed off with euphemisms rather than gently, yet honestly, confronted with reality. Governments, education services and the media may also present, or fail to present, information in ways that restrict people's awareness of reality.

## Acquiring high anxiety

The ancient Roman poet Horace wrote: 'At the rider's back sits dark Anxiety'. The same topic is approached in a humorous way by comedian Mel Brooks, who claims to suffer from high anxiety. Anxiety is a part of our animal nature. Just as you cannot avoid choosing and thinking, you cannot avoid your potential for anxiety. Ultimately the fear of death, non-being or destruction is the underlying fear from which all other anxieties are derived. I prefer the term survival anxiety. Anxiety has a survival value in that it alerts you to realistic dangers to your existence. Unfortunately, all people suffer in varying degrees from what I, like Mel Brooks, term high anxiety. Sometimes anxiety can be high because of actual threats to your existence. However, the importance of high anxiety here is that it is higher than that required to cope efficiently with life's challenges, either general or specific. As such it is disproportionate and debilitating rather than facilitating.

There is a two-way relationship between high anxiety and thinking skills. People who are highly anxious may block their awareness of the information they require to think effectively. For instance, they may have 'tunnel vision' in which they rigidly focus on only a few considerations in a complex situation. Additionally, they may block their awareness of their own thoughts and feelings, or lack an adequate sense of themselves against which to evaluate inner and outer information. However, poor thinking skills not only result from, but may also contribute to high anxiety. Poor thinking skills about personal problems may generate negative outcomes which in turn may engender lack of confidence and anxiety.

There is a close connection between feelings of security and feelings of anxiety. Perhaps a good definition of feeling secure is that you are relatively free from debilitating anxieties. Feelings of insecurity both manifest and engender anxiety. Below are some of the behaviours whereby parents are likely to help their children feel secure and worthwhile. For each item, behaving in the opposite way may create insecurity and high anxiety.

- *Showing commitment.* Children need to feel that their parents are dependable in their commitment to them. They require a secure base from which to explore and learn.

- *Expressing affection.* Warmth and prizing need to be clearly demonstrated, including by touch.

- *Understanding thoughts and feelings.* Children need to feel that parents are emotionally accessible and understand their feelings and thoughts.

- *Acknowledging separateness and difference.* Parents require sufficient security to respect their children as separate and different from themselves.

- *Direct communication.* The sending of messages needs to be as clear as possible with an absence of 'hidden agendas', 'power plays' and 'put-downs'.

- *Openness.* Parents reveal themselves as three-dimensional human beings and admit their fallibility. There is a minimum of impression management, lies, omissions of truth and half-truths. Reality is acknowledged rather than denied or distorted.

- *Working through problems.* Being prepared to work through family problems as they arise on the basis of mutual respect.

- *Providing suitable learning opportunities.* Helping children feel and become more competent by providing them with learning opportunities geared to their stage of development. This includes provision of relevant information.

- *Encouragement.* Encouraging children rather than discouraging them as they learn skills and competencies, including thinking skills.

- *Modelling personal responsibility.* Helping children learn from parental example that ultimately each person is responsible for making the choices that create their unique happiness and fulfilment.

Parents are not alone in helping young people acquire feelings of security and insecurity. Everybody with whom the young person grows up is capable of making a contribution for good or ill.

Some people's feelings of insecurity and of high anxiety are very pronounced. They may require a long-term counselling relationship. At first the emphasis may be on providing a corrective emotional experience focused on nurturing and healing before they are taught how to think through their problems. In practice, the division between nurturing and teaching is seldom clear-cut.

## SUSTAINING DEFICIENT THINKING SKILLS

Nearly 300 years ago British philosopher John Pomfret wrote: 'We live and learn, but not the wiser grow'. Pomfret's message has been given a more contemporary expression by Albert Ellis (1985) in the lyrics of his rational-humorous song based on 'Beautiful Dreamer'.

> Beautiful hang-up, why should we part,
> When we have shared our whole lives from the start?

A useful distinction is that between *acquiring* deficient thinking skills and *sustaining* them. The past cannot be relived. If you are to overcome your thinking skills weaknesses your focus must be on how they are sustained in the present. Often they are well-developed habits acquired many years before and sustained since then. Eric Berne (1972) developed the notion of scripts. By this he meant that people's lives are pre-ordained from early on by a script which they then follow faithfully. I see following a life script more in terms of how you sustain poor and good thinking skills. Poor thinking skills constrict choice and thus give people's lives the appearance of the acting out of a script.

There is an important difference of emphasis between acquiring and sustaining deficient thinking skills. In acquiring deficient thinking skills the main emphasis is on what others did to you. In sustaining them the main emphasis is on what you do to yourself. Although environmental considerations play a part, you have now internalized your deficits and risk perpetuating them with further poor choices.

### What you do to yourself

What are some of the processes by which you may sustain your thinking skills weaknesses? Below are some suggestions.

- *Inadequate conceptual framework.* Because thinking effectively about personal problems is rarely systematically taught, there may be gaps in your conceptual framework. This may include not possessing the overall concept of thinking as a set of skills. Also, you may have gaps in your knowledge about specific skills.

- *Faulty self-perceptions.* Your view of yourself may be that you are always a rational human being. Such a view of yourself may block you from acknowledging incoming information that differs from it. Your perceptions of yourself are what you regard as 'I' or 'me'. Your self-picture reflects your feelings of security and of competence to cope with life. The more insecure you are, the more you are likely to have rigid self-perceptions that are not amenable to change through feedback. Instead of having what Rogers (1961) terms openness to your experiencing, both inner and outer, you deny and distort information that differs from your picture of yourself. Such information may cause high anxiety in insecure people. To retain your self-perceptions and sense of security, you may engage in defensive 'security' operations. One result of these security operations is that you retain deficient thinking skills since they remain unexamined. Another result is that you stay insecure.

- *Self-reindoctrination.* Much of your thinking takes the form of self-talk. The self-talk of many people when faced with personal problems is highly repetitive. Their thinking resembles a record player that is stuck in the same groove. Ellis (1962) points out that people retain their emotional disturbance through their illogical self-verbalizations. Repetitively self-verbalizing your illogical beliefs both represents and sustains deficient thinking. Counterproductive self-reindoctrination is more likely to take place if your self-perceptions allow little room for the adequacy of your thinking to be challenged.

- *High anxiety.* High anxiety can continue to interfere with your thinking in the ways mentioned earlier. It may block your awareness of both your thoughts and your feelings. Also, it erodes your sense of self so that you lack a sound inner base for evaluating inner and outer information. High anxiety can cause you to feel unnecessarily threatened by feedback that differs from your self-perceptions. These feelings of threat may trigger off security operations whereby you 'operate' on the feedback to reduce its threat. These security operations take place beneath conscious awareness. Thus you may sustain your illusion of security at the price of relinquishing some of your hold on reality. Below I have rewritten the lyrics of the first verse of Cole Porter's song 'High Society' to illustrate this point.

> Just dig our problems mounting high,
> They're now approaching beyond the sky,
> We've been for years fleeing reality,
> My goodness gracious now we are going to be,
> In high, high, high anx-ie, high anxiety.

High anxiety also makes you fearful of change. Maslow's (1962) distinction between safety and growth choices is relevant here. You may prefer the safety of your existing thinking skills, however deficient, to the growth entailed in changing the way you think and, in turn, act.

- *Secondary gains and pay-offs.* In this context secondary gains and pay-offs are the inner rewards you get for keeping your deficient thinking skills. For instance, angry Annie blames everybody but herself for her misfortunes. If she is going to attain the real gain of accurately attributing responsibility for her misfortunes, she will have to relinquish the secondary gain of being able to blame others all the time. This is an easy and convenient habit that stops her from the work of having to change *her own* thinking and behaviour. Ellis acknowledges that sometimes people's resistance to change may stem from pleasurable pay-offs. However, he considers that people's resistances very frequently 'stem from low frustration tolerance: their stubborn refusal to go through immediate pain to get future gain. Their main payoff is instant comfort, which undramatically and insidiously prevents them from working at therapy and surrendering their disturbances' (Ellis, 1980, p. 11). Ellis's observation has relevance for people outside as well as inside therapy.

- *Insufficient awareness of personal responsibility.* One of the main factors contributing to many people sustaining their deficient thinking is that they possess insufficient awareness of their personal responsibilities for making the most of their lives. The fact that sustaining thinking skills deficits has a large element of 'what you do to yourself' rather than either 'what others have done in the past' or 'what your environment does to you' means that changing deficient thinking skills is closely associated with the degree to which you assume personal responsibility for making it happen. In general being personally responsible is much easier said than done.

**What your environment does to you**

The earlier section on *acquiring* deficient thinking skills focused mainly on external influences. Many of these external influences may still persist, thus helping you *sustain* deficient thinking skills. These negative influences are briefly mentioned below.

- *Deficient modelling.* People who have modelled poor thinking skills in the past may continue to do so. For instance, a parent who demonstrates perfectionist standards for achievement continues to do so. Many men may continue to be afraid to show feelings of vulnerability and caring. Many women may continue to think retiringly and passively. The media, through demonstration, continues its relentless pressure on you to think like a good consumer and also to value youth, success and sex.

- *Inappropriate consequences.* Thinking skills deficits may persist because of their positive consequences. For instance, you may be able to manipulate people into believing they are persecuting an innocent victim such as yourself when the reverse may be the case. Getting angry and the thinking that accompanies it may get you what you want. However, this may be at the expense of mutual respect and learning to develop the thinking skills to manage your anger better. Just as using poor thinking skills may have positive consequences using good thinking skills may have negative consequences. For instance, however well you present your ideas, thinking for yourself may threaten others. This may make it harder for you to think independently.

- *Lack of information and opportunity.* You may continue to lack the opportunity to acquire a realistic conceptual framework with which to think about your problems. Significant people in your environment may continue to fob you off with impression management, lies, omissions of truth and half-truths. Additionally, having acquired deficient thinking skills, you may not have access to people, such as skilled counsellors, to help you overcome them. What some people require is a relationship in which the counsellor offers not only support and understanding, but also confrontation and education. Frequently such relationships are not readily available.

In this chapter I have stressed that the way in which you think mainly reflects your learning history. Furthermore, your good and poor thinking choices have been learned in the first place, but then may be being sustained for good or ill. The fact that they are mainly sustained by inner considerations heightens the need for you to take control of your thinking. Undoubtedly, you already do this to some extent. I will now turn to some of the specific skills for improving your thinking when faced with personal problems.

## CHAPTER HIGHLIGHTS

Your thinking skills strengths and weaknesses have been learned.

Both maturational and social learning factors influenced the development of your thinking.

You learned your thinking skills strengths and weaknesses from: observing others; the consequences provided for you; the adequacy of the concepts and information you received; and from how secure you were helped to feel.

Once they were learned, you have sustained many of your thinking skills strengths and weaknesses.

You yourself sustain your deficient thinking through: possessing an inadequate conceptual framework; having faulty self-perceptions; self-reindoctrination; high anxiety; giving way to secondary gains and pay-offs; and possessing insufficient awareness of your personal responsibility for authorship of your life.

You are helped by others and the environment to sustain deficient thinking skills through: deficient modelling; inappropriate consequences; and persistence of lack of information and opportunity.

You can learn to take more control of your thinking.

# 3 Owning Responsibility for Choosing

I choose, therefore I am.

*Adaptation from Descartes*

To make the growth choice instead of the fear choice a dozen times a day is to move a dozen times a day towards self-actualization.

*Abraham Maslow*

People who are effective at coping with their problems and decisions of living possess the skill of owning their responsibility for choosing within the constraints of reality. Those who are ineffective add their denials and distortions to existing reality constraints. The poet T. S. Eliot once wrote: 'Human kind cannot bear very much reality'. Frequently, humans choose to follow what I facetiously call the Nelson-Jones' Reality Principle, namely, 'if you can't accept reality, create it!' However, the price of creating your own reality can be high. It sows the seeds of alienation from yourself, others and the environment.

In this chapter I focus on four interrelated skills of owning responsibility for choosing to make your life within the constraints of reality: choice awareness, responsibility awareness, existential awareness and feelings awareness.

## CHOICE AWARENESS

Here is a vignette of a woman who has just come for counselling.

Katie is in her early 40s, the mother of four children with ages ranging from 4 to 16. Six months ago her husband Peter left her to set up house with his secretary Penny. Katie is furious with him for 'abandoning' her and the children. Additionally, Katie is now having a difficult time with her eldest daughter Sandra, age 16, who has decided for the time being to live with her father. Katie, who used to have a good relationship with Sandra, is now very angry with her and says that she has become 'selfish' and 'hard'. Her relationship with her other children is deteriorating too, not least because they see her pushing and shoving Peter when he comes round unannounced to visit them. Katie has a huge chip on her shoulder and feels herself very much the victim of others' bad behaviour. She feels angry, anxious, depressed, confused and powerless.

Katie is similar to many people of both genders who come for counselling. They feel that their lives are out of their control. They have relinquished, temporarily at least, their capacity to make effective choices within the constraints of reality. Even assuming that her husband Peter has behaved very badly, in the final analysis Katie is *choosing* to allow her emotions to be controlled by his bad behaviour rather than *choosing* to work to free herself from his negative influence. Furthermore, she has probably *chosen* to allow her relationship with Sandra to deteriorate. An important part of counselling with people like Katie is to help them become more aware that: (1) they are always choosers; (2) their choices always have costs and consequences; (3) within the constraints of reality, they can learn to increase the probability of the consequences of their choices being for good rather than for ill.

## Three areas of choosing

There are three main areas in which humans are choosers: in relation to themselves, others and the environment. These areas overlap. In each, people as choosers are confronted with existential conflicts between themselves and the 'givens' of their existences. Central to all areas of choosing is the conflict between freedom and responsibility. Sartre (1956) has described humans as being condemned to freedom. However, the price and challenge of this freedom is the responsibility for making your life.

- *Choosing in relation to yourself.* Choosing in relation to yourself encompasses choosing how you feel, think and act. Although physical reactions may be involuntary and outside your control, psychological reactions are potentially within your control. Much of this book is devoted to helping you understand that how you choose to feel is related to how you choose to think and act. I hope to help you enter your inner world to explore not only the surface choices, but also the underlying or *under-choices* that you make. These under-choices frequently block your truly owning your life and fulfilling your potential.

● *Choosing in relation to others*. In any relationship, for instance between Katie and Peter, there are at least four relationships: each participant's relationships to themselves and also to each other. Furthermore, since people exist in social networks of family, friends, community leaders and others, there may be numerous other contextual relationships in which the relationship between Peter and Katie exists. Human beings are programmed to need each other as well as to be threatened by each other through fears such as engulfment and abandonment. Choosing in relation to others extends beyond personal relationships to work and leisure relationships. However, not all work and leisure relationships require others.

   Choosing in relation to others confronts you with some of your boundaries as a chooser. First, you are confronted with your isolation. Ultimately, human existence is solitary. For instance, no one can die your death for you. Second, and related to your ultimate isolation, you are confronted with the boundaries between 'me' and 'you'. To a large extent you can *control* how you choose in relation to yourself. However, with others, the most that you can hope to do is to *influence* how they choose to think, feel and act in relation to themselves and to you. This can be a hard limitation for many to accept.

● *Choosing in relation to the environment*. Choosing in relation to the environment involves your relationship with the natural order. Death, fate and meaninglessness are three of the boundary situations that confront all people in relation to nature. The paradox of life is that, while living, we die. Although death is biologically inescapable, psychologically many erect defences against awareness of their own mortality. The fact that the natural order can be capricious and that life can involve inescapable suffering is another boundary situation that confronts all people. Additionally, the natural order does not provide much of a structure for meaning beyond the survival instinct. Maslow (1970) has observed that humans have 'weak, subtle and tender instinctoid needs' that are at risk of being 'overwhelmed by the tougher, more powerful culture, rather than the other way about' (p. 82). Thus if humans are not condemned to search for meaning in face of an indifferent universe, they are close to this state.

## Consciousness-raising concerning choosing

Throughout the remainder of this book you are provided with thinksheets designed to develop your thinking skills by giving you the opportunity to apply them. It may seem ironic that, on the surface, the first of these focuses on body language. However, its underlying purpose is to raise your consciousness about how you may be failing to exercise fully your capacity to choose.

**Thinksheet I    Choosing your body language**

*Instructions*
This thinksheet is in two parts.

1.  *Describing, being aware, choosing*
    (a)   Either on your own or to a partner spend a minute or two *describing* what the concept of body language means to you. Your partner should either remain silent or 'reflect' what you say.

    (b)   Now spend a minute or two doing a gestalt-type awareness exercise in which you say, either to yourself or to a partner, 'Now I am *aware* . . .', before mentioning each aspect of your body language that enters your awareness, e.g. 'Now I am aware that my arms are folded'.

    (c)   Then spend a minute or two in which you say 'I *choose* to . . .' in relation to each aspect of your body language that you choose to have. For instance, if your arms are folded, say 'I choose to fold my arms', or if you change your seating position, say 'I choose to . . .', and then add how you have chosen to move your body.

    (d)   How did you experience going through this describing, being aware, choosing sequence? If you are with a partner tell him or her, then reverse roles.

2.  *Yes/no: confronting your conditioning*
    People in Western cultures have been taught to shake their head up and down when they says 'yes' and side to side when they say 'no'. Hold a conversation either with yourself or, preferably, with a partner, in which each time either of you says 'yes' you shake your head from side to side and each time you say 'no' you shake your head up and down. How do you experience doing this and what does it tell you about how you have learned to make choices?

I frequently start my workshops with the exercises contained in Thinksheet 1. With the describing, awareness, choosing sequence most people, when they get to choosing, *choose* to move their body into a position that is more comfortable for them. They feel empowered and freer to make, albeit in a simple way, some choices which work for them. The exercise succeeds even in New York French restaurants! I demonstrated it in one to Sheenah, a former student, who is now a highly successful Park Avenue psychotherapist. She was *aware* that her arms were tight and there was tension in the back of her legs. When she moved on to *choosing*, she leaned back, opened her posture and uncrossed her arms. In brief, she had an 'aha' experience. The yes/no part of the exercise helps some people become aware that many of the constrictions on their choices are learned habits of which they are unaware until they are confronted with them. This applies to many of the thinking skill weaknesses that interfere with choosing.

---

**Thinksheet 2    Choosing the reverse response**

This thinksheet is designed to help you become more aware that you can choose how you think about and respond to others. The idea is to get you thinking and responding in the opposite way to your initial inclinations.

*Instructions*

1.  Think of someone who makes you feel angry, then imagine going out of your way to do something that makes that person feel happy. How might he or she react?

2   Think of someone who makes you feel inhibited, then imagine yourself talking and relating to that person in a relaxed and outgoing way. How might he or she react?

3.  Think of someone you want to avoid, then imagine going up to that person and initiating a conversation in a friendly way. How might he or she react?

4.  Think of someone with whom you have had an argument, then imagine going up to that person and acknowledging the rightness of their position. How might he or she react?

5.  Think of someone from whom you may take more than you give, then imagine giving them something they would really like. How might he or she react?

---

Thinksheet 2 was designed to raise your consciousness of yourself as a chooser. However, it also has some relevance to the handling of personal problems. Often you may get some insight into how you could approach a problem by reviewing it in the completely opposite direction to how you currently view it. Was this the case for you in any of the areas covered in Thinksheet 2?

## RESPONSIBILITY AWARENESS

In recent years the concept of causal attribution has been one of the most researched and written about areas in psychology. Attribution refers to the ways and processes by which people attribute causes and meanings to their own behaviour, to others' behaviour and to environmental events. The aspect of causal attribution that I focus on here is the extent to which people choose to assume rather than avoid responsibility for their lives. This is broken down into two overlapping areas: acknowledging responsibility for the authorship of your life, and acknowledging responsibility in your everyday problems and decisions.

## Responsibility for authorship of your life

The psychoanalytic, behavioural and humanistic positions are each prominent in contemporary psychology. However, each contains a major assumption that supplies a 'cop-out' for not choosing to assume personal responsibility for authorship of your life. With the psychoanalytic position you can attribute your difficulties to unconscious and instinctual determinants of behaviour. With traditional behaviourism, the 'cop-out' attribution is that of environmental determinism. With the humanistic position, as represented by person-centred therapy, the 'cop-out' attribution is that parental and cultural influences have been stronger than your self-actualizing tendency. Fortunately, counsellors and psychotherapists from these theoretical positions tend not to practise literally what they preach. Instead, they also assume the existential insight that people are responsible for *making* their lives through the adequacy of their choices.

This book aims to help you develop the fundamental thinking skill of assuming an attitude of personal responsibility for your life. To the extent that you have been condemned to freedom, you have also been condemned to the responsibility to fashion your life out of that freedom. Are you always responsible for your choices? The answer is 'yes', but with qualifications. In the previous chapter, you saw how your learning may have interfered with your capacity to be an effective chooser. You also saw that there was a maturational lag in that your capacity for reasoning developed later than your need to make some of the choices that would help you live most effectively. However, a distinction was made between 'what others did to you' that helped you acquire your deficient thinking skills and 'what you do to yourself' that helps sustain them. Thus the burden of responsibility comes back to you.

Many social factors may work against your assuming personal responsibility. Adverse conditions, like poor housing, unemployment, poverty, racial discrimination and lack of educational opportunity, may make it difficult for you to learn to make initially and then to keep making the choices that, despite such adversities, serve you best. However, remove these adverse social conditions and problems of personal responsibility are still likely to be rife, if less uncomfortable. Even in the most appalling conditions, people still have choices regarding the quality of their inner and outer lives. In his inspiring book *Man's Search for Meaning*, Viktor Frankl (1959) relates how, in Nazi concentration camps, some individuals could choose to scale personal heights by turning their tragedies into triumphs of the human spirit.

Earlier in this chapter a distinction was made between choosing in relation to yourself, others and the environment. All three strands are drawn together in the following personal responsibility *credo*.

---

### PERSONAL RESPONSIBILITY CREDO

I am personally responsible for my choices regarding how I think, feel and act in relation to myself, others and the environment.

Within the realistic limitations of my existence, I make my life through my choices.

I am always a chooser.

My choices always have consequences for good or ill.

My choices always have costs.

The sum of my life is the sum of the consequences of my choices.

---

### Responsibility in everyday problems and decisions

It is one thing to accept your overall responsibility for making your life, yet another to transmit this goal successfully to your daily problems and decisions. Here it is important that you attribute responsibility and cause accurately. Two of the main faulty choices you can make are to attribute either too much or too little responsibility to yourself.

- *Attributing too much responsibility to yourself.* Some people choose to attribute too much responsibility to themselves. This can contribute to sustaining feelings of depression. Beck and his colleagues observe that this is a common pattern among depressed patients (Beck *et al.*, 1979). To counteract this, he advocates a 'reattribution' technique. Together with his patients he reviews the relevant evidence to make appropriate attributions of responsibility.

  Unemployment is another area where maladaptive internal attributions of responsibility may contribute to low self-esteem and depression. Here a useful distinction is that between responsibility for the cause of the problem and responsibility for its solution. Some unemployed persons may feel failures because they wrongly attribute their being made unemployed to personal inadequacy rather than to structural and technological changes outside their control. Furthermore, these feelings of failure may be prolonged if they wrongly attribute their difficulty getting re-employed to personal inadequacy rather than to the realities of their job-getting situation. Here I do not mean to imply that there are not other instances where internal attributions for becoming and staying unemployed may be realistic.

- *Attributing too little responsibility to yourself.* There is a widespread tendency among humans not to notice their own contributions to their distress and to attribute responsibility elsewhere. This can be illustrated by a joke concerning a psychological researcher who had trained a frog to jump when he said 'jump'. One day he decided to extend his research by cutting off one of the frog's rear legs and then saying 'jump'. The frog jumped sideways. Then he cut off the second rear leg and said 'jump'. The frog did not move. The psychologist concluded that the frog had suddenly gone deaf! He was not the sort of person who would accept his own responsibility for what he had done.

    Johanna Watson (1986) reviewed the attributions of 70 Australian married couples referred for psychiatric assistance. Her findings of their attributions about the causes of their children's emotional disturbance indicate that parental defensiveness is alive and well 'Down Under'. Parents commonly saw the child's behaviour as being caused by something within the child, such as the child's 'nature' or 'just the way he or she was born'. Eighty-nine per cent of fathers and 76 per cent of mothers did not see themselves as being of either primary or secondary importance in their child's level of adjustment. Watson observed that of the fathers who attributed their child's disturbed behaviour to the family, 65 per cent said their wives were the major contributors, usually considering them to be too 'soft' with the child. Thirty-nine per cent of the mothers attributing the disturbed behaviour to the family attributed the problems to their husbands, usually citing their lack of time for or of interest in the child.

As the above research suggests, a common pattern in relationship conflicts is that either or both partners make a convenient leap in logic and start by blaming the other rather than by looking at their own behaviour. Psychiatrist Thomas Szasz (1973) has written: 'In the animal kingdom, the rule is eat or be eaten; in the human kingdom, define or be defined' (p. 20). Unfortunately, all too much of this kind of defensive thinking takes place in marriage and family conflicts: hence the high casualty rate among both adults and children. However, the carnage does not stop there. Children frequently repeat in their own families the thinking, feeling and action skills weaknesses of their parents.

---

Thinksheet 3   Exploring accurately owning responsibility in others' lives

*Instructions*
For each of the following excerpts write down

1.   Whether the main character or characters are choosing to attribute too much or too little responsibility to themselves and why you choose to think this.

2.   How they might change their thinking so that they can behave more effectively in future.

*Excerpts*

(a)  Brett is a 17-year-old who is shy with girls. He never makes a first move, but expects a girl to demonstrate clearly her interest in him before he will consider asking her out.

(b)  Tony is a married man with two daughters aged 15 and 13. Recently he struck Joy, the 15-year-old, because 'she made me so mad'.

(c)  Sally is a 50-year-old spinster who, until recently, was secretary of a charitable organization. A month ago she resigned after a row at a board meeting. She went out of her way to tell her friends, 'I had no choice but to resign'.

(d)  Tina is furious with her 16-year-old daughter Tanya for going to the house of her boyfriend Keith one lunchtime when no one else was there. Tina is afraid of Tanya having an unwanted pregnancy. The two are currently not on speaking terms.

(e)  Arthur is a lazy teacher who is quick to notice when other teachers are being lazy. He thinks: 'Why should I bother when others are getting away with it?'

---

**Thinksheet 4    Exploring accurately owning responsibility in your life**

*Instructions*

1.   Write down the extent to which you consider you accurately own responsibility for your thoughts, feelings and behaviour when faced with personal problems and decisions.

2.   Describe a specific situation in which you consider you recently succeeded in accurately owning responsibility when faced with a personal problem or decision.

3.   Describe a specific situation in which you consider you recently failed in accurately owning responsibility when faced with a personal problem or decision.

4.   Review whether you have a tendency to attribute too much responsibility to yourself, or too little, or a mixture of the two.

---

## EXISTENTIAL AWARENESS

> Either he's dead or my watch has stopped.
> *Groucho Marx* (feeling a patient's pulse)

The report of my death was an exaggeration.

*Mark Twain*

Awareness of your mortality is the aspect of existential awareness on which I focus here. You are responsible for your choices within your life span. Although the exact length of your life is uncertain, your awareness that it is finite highlights your responsibility for its quality.

Western cultures have problems with the notions of ageing and death. Youth and sexual attractiveness often appear valued more than wisdom and maturity. Death is surrounded with euphemisms like 'passing away' and 'going to one's maker' rather than openly acknowledged as an integral part of life. Death threatens people with their own anxieties over non-being.

### Diminished existential awareness

There are a number of ways in which people exhibit insufficient existential awareness concerning their mortality.

- *Death can be postponed*. Some people lead their lives as though they had unlimited time. Kassorla (1984) calls them people with 500 year plans. The first 100 years is for doing things for their parents, the second for their neighbours, the third for their children and families, the fourth for some other pressure group that they value, and by the fifth 100 years they might get round to doing something for themselves. Since they feel no urgency, many opportunities for choosing to live more fully get squandered. Such people are asleep to the existential realities that they have only one life, it is taking place *now*, it is limited and it is 'ticking away' all the time. They have not grasped the existential truth that to live is to die, so they had better make the most of their lives.

- *Death cannot happen to me*. The illusion of immortality may be more a feature of younger than of older people, but not always so. Many young people have gone off to wars in the past buoyed up by images of glory and patriotism rather than images of their deaths and suffering. Many young males take unnecessary chances with their lives on the road. The AIDS epidemic provides another example of lack of existential awareness. Although many homosexuals engage in 'safer' sex, there are still others who allow themselves to be sexually penetrated by strangers without condoms.

- *Death is transient*. Some people fail to realize the permanence of death. An example of this, from one of my former clients, follows.

Jack, aged 17, felt that his whole life proved he was a failure. His alcoholic father had left home when he was 10. He had frequent rows with his mother. He left school aged 16 and started drinking heavily. He agreed to see me after a serious suicide attempt in which, in a drunken rage, he slashed his wrists with a knife. In counselling he mentioned that before his suicide attempt he had wondered what being dead was like and thought that this might be an interesting experience. After this experience he thought he could return to life.

● *My reward is in heaven.* One of the prime functions of most religions is to help people handle their anxieties about death and dying. Some people's motivation to do something about their present lives on earth is weakened by the prospect of compensatory benefits in their future lives. This point was made by Karl Marx in his observations that 'religion ... is the opium of the people'. The prospect of rewards in heaven has been held out to soldiers in 'holy wars' throughout the centuries, including in this century by leaders such as Ayatollah Khomeini.

### Advantages of existential awareness

That an awareness of death can heighten awareness of life is illustrated in Yalom's (1980) case study of Eva. She was a 45-year-old deeply depressed patient with advanced ovarian cancer. Her father had died many years ago of lingering cancer, about which no one had dared tell him. Eva, however, confronted her physician and demanded all available information about her cancer. Furthermore, acting on the basis 'existence cannot be postponed', she led as full a life as possible, including making a much-desired trip to Africa.

Yalom observes that many patients with cancer report that they live more fully in the present. They no longer postpone living until some time in the future. Furthermore, many become more able to count their blessings. Thus awareness of death can not only heighten people's need to make the most of their lives, but can also help them experience more deeply many of the gifts of living previously taken for granted.

Viktor Frankl, the founder of logotherapy, also emphasizes the importance of people acknowledging their 'responsibleness' for their choices within life's finiteness. He writes that the categorical imperative of logotherapy is: 'So live as if you were living already the second time and as if you have acted the first time as wrongly as you are about to act now!' (Frankl, 1959, p. 173). He observed that in Nazi concentration camps some people behaved like swine and others like saints. All had the potential for both within them, but which one became actualized depended less on the conditions than on their personal *decisions*.

Existential awareness involves not only an awareness of non-being, but also an awareness of being. You can be physically alive and psychologically deadened. Rather than making direct contact with yourself, others and the environment in the *present*, you may be dwelling on the *past* or fearful about the *future*. The degree to which you can make effective thinking choices is a major determinant of your ability to exist fully in the present.

## Consciousness-raising concerning death, dying and finiteness

There are many ways that helping-service professionals try to raise people's consciousness concerning death, dying and finiteness. These include the following:

- *Imagining your death.* Here you are encouraged to imagine the process of dying and your death. You may also be encouraged to explore the impact your death might have on others. This kind of imagining exercise forms part of the training for AIDS counsellors in San Francisco's Shanti Project (shanti meaning 'inner peace').

- *Reminiscing about contacts with death and dying.* People can be encouraged to share their experiences and feelings about their contact with people who were dying. They should be helped to make links with their thoughts and feelings about their own deaths.

- *Contact with dying people.* Arrangements may be made for people to interact with the dying. Three approaches to this are: (1) arranging for a visit to a hospice; (2) observing meetings of a group of terminally ill patients; and (3) introducing people with terminal illnesses into everyday groups.

Thinksheet 5 is designed to raise your awareness of your finiteness, the passage of time and your responsibility for being an effective chooser in the remainder of your life.

---

**Thinksheet 5   Confronting your finiteness**

*Instructions*
1.  Your past: milestones
    Draw a line down the centre of one or more pages. Go down the page(s) drawing a line outwards for every five years of your life to date. The first line goes to the left representing 0–5 years, the second line goes to the right representing 6–10 years, the third line goes to the left representing 11–15 years and so on. Under each of these lines write down what you consider were the main personal milestones that had meaning for you in influencing the sort of person you are today.

2.  *Your present: physical signs of ageing*
    (a)   Write out a list of any physical signs of ageing that you can recognize in yourself, for instance, greying hair, scaly skin, increasing deafness, etc.

(b)    What is your attitude towards these signs of your mortality?

3.    *Your future: how much time do you have?*
    (a)    To what age do you expect to live? Give reasons for this prediction.

    (b)    Get a pocket calculator and work out:
    ● how many hours there are in a year
    ● how many minutes there are in a year
    ● how many days you expect to live
    ● how many hours you expect to live
    ● how many minutes you expect to live.

(c)    What are your thoughts and feelings now that you have confronted yourself more precisely with the time you may have left on this earth?

---

## FEELINGS AWARENESS

Much of this book emphasizes how you can influence how you feel through how you choose to think and act. However, another skill is that of learning to acknowledge and be aware of your feelings. Central to your ability to think effectively is your ability to become aware of and own your significant feelings. This does not mean that you are encouraged always to express them; rather, feelings tend to be the parents of choices. You can decide whether to develop them, to regulate them or to treat them as unimportant.

There are two aspects of feelings awareness dealt with here: listening to your body and listening to your inner valuing process. Both involve you in becoming aware of your bodily sensations, although the first might be viewed as more physical and the second more psychological. However, the notion of a simple mind–body split is erroneous.

### Listening to your body

Listening to your body is an extension of the existential awareness discussed in the previous section. There you were confronted with one aspect of the natural order: the inescapability of death. Here you are confronted with another aspect of the natural order: namely, that you are a human animal. Many people who think ineffectively are also out of touch with significant physical sensations, for instance, their need for relaxation and their sexuality. On the other hand, people who live effectively are frequently healthy animals. Not only may they have been initially endowed with good health, but their animality has not been seriously interfered with by psychological difficulties. Maslow (1970), in reporting the findings of his study of self-actualizing people, observed that they tended to be good animals who ate and slept well and enjoyed their sexual lives without inhibition.

If you are truly to own your responsibility for choosing, you have to be aware not only of your physical death but also of your physical life. You are centred in your body and your physical capacities provide many of the significant boundaries of your existence. Although Thinksheet 6 cannot convey the full extent of the importance of your animality, it may help sensitize you to the fact that responsible choosers acknowledge that they are grounded in a physical and not just a psychological existence.

---

**Thinksheet 6   Listening to your body**

*Instructions*
This thinksheet is best done on your own before being discussed with another or others.

1.  Sit in a quiet place with your eyes closed and for the next three to five minutes focus on the sensations of your breathing.

2.  Sit in a quiet place, close your eyes for about five minutes and try to tune into your bodily sensations. Focus on the flow of what your body is feeling rather than on what you are thinking. In other words, focus on physical sensations.

3.  Sitting in a quiet place with your eyes closed, focus on the physical sensations in each of the following parts of your body for about a minute:

    *   your head
    *   your arms
    *   the trunk of your body
    *   your legs.

4.  List the ways in which your physical sensations (for instance, fatigue) may influence how you think. Be as specific as possible.

---

## Listening to your inner valuing process

Carl Rogers viewed virtually all humans as, to a greater or lesser degree, out of touch with their inner valuing process. Since this valuing process represents the person's essence or core, this distancing makes it difficult for them to make choices that reflect what they truly feel rather than what they have been taught they should feel. The main thrust of his person-centred therapy was to reunite clients with those parts of their inner valuing processes from which they were alienated. Rogers' view was that the inner valuing process was not just reactive. It was also active. It represented people's 'actualizing tendency' to maintain and enhance themselves, which he considered to be the central human motivating drive (Rogers, 1980).

An important part of owning responsibility for your choosing is that your wants and wishes are representative of you as a unique individual rather than 'borrowed' to please others, such as your parents or partner. At times you may be fully aware that you are making choices to please others rather than yourself. Sometimes this may be entirely rational; you know what you want for yourself, but decide to take others' wishes into consideration. At other times it may indicate lack of assertion; you know what you want, but are too afraid to go for it. There are other occasions where the position is less clear. For instance, you may find it difficult to discover what you truly want or you may think you know, but a nagging feeling of discomfort persists. Also, there are some people so out of touch with their valuing process that they deny many of their feelings altogether.

Assuming responsibility for choosing involves you in being emotionally responsive both to yourself and to others. Frequently your wants and wishes emerge as feeling fragments, that you may glimpse if you are attentive, rather than as full blown emotions. You need to develop the skill of inner listening and of sorting out the 'wheat from the chaff' of your feelings. Many of the thinking skills discussed in this book are aimed at the removal of blocks to your acknowledging your true feelings. Some of you may choose to seek professional counselling. This may be for 'remedial' or 'growth' purposes or for a mixture of the two. For instance, you may come to acknowledge that you are very unaware of your feelings and have little identity of your own. Alternatively, you may consider that you are reasonably emotionally responsive, but want to be even more so.

Thinksheet 7 is designed to help you become aware of the importance of listening to your feelings and intuition when faced with problems and decisions of living. The thinksheet focuses only on accessing your feelings. Ideally, in real life, you act on considered judgement which takes your feelings into account. Learning to be emotionally responsive can be a long and arduous process. For some of you, Thinksheet 7 may raise more issues than it answers.

---

Thinksheet 7    Listening to your feelings

This thinksheet is best done on your own before you discuss your experiences with another or others.

I.   *Your past: learning emotional responsiveness*
     Write down your answers to the following questions.
     (a)   Take a piece of paper, draw a line down the centre, at the top of the left hand column write *Harmful messages* and at the top of the right hand column write *Helpful messages*. In each column list messages you received while you were growing up which harmed or helped your becoming aware of your feelings, intuition and wants and wishes. These

messages were received either from observing others or from the consequences of your behaviour.

(b)   How aware do you think you *now* are of your feelings, intuition and wants and wishes? Give reasons for your answer. In what ways, if any, do you wish to change?

2.   *The present: focusing on your feelings*
(a)   Take a problem or decision that has been bothering you recently.

(b)   Both physically, in terms of absence of distractions, and psychologically clear a space whereby you can focus in on what you are feeling in relation to that problem or decision.

(c)   Spend from five to ten minutes 'quiet time' with your eyes shut just experiencing what you *feel* in relation to the problem or decision. Do not try to analyse or think your way through the problem. Instead just experience the flow of your feelings.

(d)   At the end of your 'quiet time' assess whether you think and feel any differently about the decision or problem, than you did at the start.

---

Owning responsibility for your choosing is a complex area. In this chapter I have presented four dimensions of relevant awareness: choice, existential, responsibility and feelings. Subsequent chapters focus on other thinking skills choices that, if rightly made, may position you to achieve your goals. However, if wrongly made, they may position you for further faulty choices. Sometimes these choices are obvious, but frequently they operate below awareness. Becoming more aware of these thinking choices is a step in the direction of making them work for rather than against you. Although Shakespeare might have paid more attention both to deficient learning and to environmental deprivations, there is still much truth in the following quotation from *Julius Caesar*:

> Men at some times are masters of their fates:
> The fault, dear Brutus, is not in our stars,
> But in ourselves, that we are underlings.

## CHAPTER HIGHLIGHTS

You make choices in relation to three main areas: yourself, others and the environment.

Many people have insufficient awareness of themselves as choosers.

You are responsible for the authorship of your life.

You are responsible for your choices in everyday problems and decisions and for attributing responsibility accurately rather than attributing too much or too little responsibility to yourself.

You may possess insufficient awareness of your existential finiteness.

Developing a realistic awareness of death can heighten your quality of living.

You are a human animal and, as such, need to acknowledge and understand your physical sensations and limitations.

You need to be sensitively attuned to your inner valuing process and not distort or deny any significant feelings.

# 4 Using Self-Talk

People who talk to themselves are not crazy. It is what they choose to keep telling themselves that determines this.

The ways in which you choose to talk to yourself can significantly influence how you feel and act. For instance, Sally, a single woman in her early thirties, is a salesperson for a kitchen manufacturer. At the start of her second session of counselling she related how anxious she is at having just received an invitation to a ball on the following Saturday. She described her fears in the following words, relating them to her experiences at sales seminars.

> I think that this is my main problem at the moment because it has always been a big problem. Every seminar I go to I always think on the coffee breaks I'm going to have nobody to talk to and I can't mingle . . . and that's my biggest problem—mingling . . . and I always think no one likes me so nobody wants to talk to me.

Although Sally was emotionally deprived while growing up, her current negative self-talk about nobody liking her and nobody wanting to talk to her sustains her problem of meeting suitable men. A feelings consequence of Sally's self-talk is her high anxiety in social situations. A behavioural consequence is that in company she oscillates between inhibition and loudness.

People talk to themselves even when they remain silent. This is illustrated by the psychoanalyst who had a client who remained silent for three sessions, for each of which he was charged 100 dollars. Half-way through the fourth session the client requested permission to ask a question and said: 'Do you by any chance need a partner?' In other words, his self-talk was: 'This analyst is in on a good racket. Let's see if I can get in on it too!'

## WHAT IS SELF-TALK?

### Defining self-talk

Self-talk is the verbal aspect of thinking. It goes by numerous other names. These include:

- Self-dialogue

- Inner monologue

- Inner dialogue

- Inner speech

- Self-verbalization

Basically, self-talk is what you say to yourself during your waking hours. Although images or pictures may accompany self-talk, they are not the same. Sometimes you are aware that you talk to yourself when confronted with a problem or decision of living. On other occasions, you may be less aware or unaware of what you say to yourself. You may become more aware of your 'hidden' sentences if you go into counselling, join a thinking skills training group or work through a book such as this.

### What is the self?

With all this talk about self-talk, what is the self? Your self is what you call 'I' or 'me'. It is the centre of your personal universe. Your self has three major components.

- *Your natural self.* Each person possesses a fundamental inner nature or inner core of genetic aptitudes, drives, instincts, instinct remnants and human potentialities. This represents your animal nature. Some of your animal nature is the same across the human species: for instance, needs for food, shelter, physical safety, belonging and love. Some of your animal nature is unique to you: your individual aptitudes, inner valuing process and drive to realize yourself. This inner nature or inner core of your personhood I call your 'natural self'.

- *Your learned self.* This self is the product of your social learning history. It includes the ways you have been taught to view yourself and your skills strengths and weaknesses. In Chapter 2 I reviewed some of the processes through which you acquired your thinking skills. In an ideal world, your learned self would be in accord with your natural self. It would give you the skills of fulfilling your nature within the constraints of reality. However, in the real world, most of you have learned ways of thinking about yourself that block you from attaining your human potential. Your learned self can be for good or ill and is usually a mixture of the two.

- *Your choosing self.* Whereas your natural self represents your genetic endowments and your learned self reflects your past learning history, your choosing self represents your capacity to *make* your life through your choices in the present and future. Thus you not only have a self, but also are in the constant process of creating your self. A great advantage of having a choosing self is that it provides you with the capacity to choose to discard the habits of thinking and self-talk of your learned self that block your fulfilling the inner core of your nature or natural self. Another advantage of having a choosing self is that you can choose aspects of your natural self that you wish to develop. This may be particularly important for the development of social interest and concern for others that goes beyond immediate self-interest.

### Self-support or self-oppression

You can use self-talk for self-support, self-affirmation and for realizing your human potential or for self-downing and for blocking your growth as a person. In everyday language you can choose to be either 'your own best friend' or 'your own worst enemy'.

In each of you, in varying degrees, there is an inner conflict between the self-talk that affirms your natural self and the self-talk of parts of your learned self. Here you may use self-talk against yourself in ways that lead to negative emotions and to self-defeating actions. If you win the conflict or make progress in it you are likely to lead a freer, happier, more spontaneous and more fulfilled life. The costs for those who are losing the struggle can be high. These costs include: increased strife, alienation and escape into alcohol, drugs, promiscuous sex, violence and even suicide. There are also far too many people leading lives of quiet despair.

### Choice points

All the thinking skills presented in this book involve self-talk. My aim is to help you become more aware of how you currently use self-talk for good or ill, and to show you where your choice points are for altering your self-talk in your own best interests. In Chapter 1 I mentioned the simple ABC framework used by writers like Ellis (1980) and Beck & Greenberg (1974) to show that feeling and action are influenced by how you think. This framework is (again):

A   The activating event
B   Your thoughts
C   Your feelings and actions

At B you have a choice about what you choose to say to yourself or think. By learning the appropriate use of self-talk, you can learn how best to think about your thinking. By making the right thinking choices at critical choice points you can assume more control of how you feel and act. Focusing on your self-talk helps you work from inside to outside. By altering your inner environment of thinking choices you lay the groundwork for dealing effectively with your outer environment of people and external events. In this chapter, much of the emphasis is on coping self-talk. However, all the other thinking skills in their different ways also involve both self-talk and helping you to cope better with your problems and decisions of living.

## USING 'I' SELF-TALK

Thomas Gordon (1970), the author of *Parent Effectiveness Training*, suggests that parental requests are much more likely to be listened to by children if they are sent as 'I' messages that own thoughts and feelings ('I'm feeling tired. Please play elsewhere.') than if they are sent as 'you' messages ('You are a naughty boy/girl.') that put them on the defensive. The notion of 'I' messages or 'I' self-talk can usefully be applied to your inner self-talk as well as to your outer talk. By 'I' self-talk I mean using words and phrases starting with the personal pronoun 'I' in ways that help you to assume rather than to avoid personal responsibility for your thinking choices. Below are some ways in which 'I' self-talk may help you to support rather than to oppress yourself.

*Avoiding putting yourself down with 'you' self-talk.* Just as 'you' messages can put others down, when used as self-talk they can put you down. For instance, when Fran, who is taking a three-hour essay examination, notices that she has started to answer one of the questions incorrectly she faces a thinking choice point. On the one hand, she could use 'you' self-talk, such as: 'You idiot. Why did you make such a stupid mistake? You have really screwed it up.' On the other hand, she could use 'I' self-talk, such as: 'I've made a mistake. What can I do to put it right in the time available?' This latter kind of self-talk is more likely to help her than the former.

*Using verbs that acknowledge your responsibility as a chooser.* It is possible for you subtly to box yourself in with your use of verbs and so to relinquish some of your freedom to choose. For instance, your self-talk may include verbs like 'can't, must, ought, should, have got to' and so on, that imply less choice than you may actually possess. Alternative verbs that acknowledge you have a choice include 'won't, want to, prefer to and choose to'.

*Owning your feelings, thoughts and actions.* In your self-talk just as in your outer talk you may make statements starting with words like 'you, people, we and it', that camouflage your acknowledgement of your feelings, thoughts and actions. Here are some examples:

*Owning a feeling.* You have a colleague whom you find difficult at work.

'Non-I' self-talk: 'He is a horror.'
'I' self-talk: 'I feel hurt by his criticism.'

*Owning a thought.* You have doubts about the effectiveness of a political leader.
'Non-I' self-talk: 'Nobody seems to think she is doing a good job.'
'I' self-talk: 'I do not think she is doing a good job for the following reasons . . .'.

*Owning an action.* You have left yourself very little time in which to complete an assignment.
'Non-I' self-talk: 'It always happens that I'm pushed to meet deadlines.'
'I' self-talk: 'I've made a mistake in not leaving myself enough time to do the job properly.'

When reading the above examples you may have observed a trend. All the 'non-I' self-talk statements locate the source of your feelings, thoughts and actions outside of yourself. All the 'I' self-talk statements locate control of your feelings, thoughts and actions with you. In each instance there has been a choice point regarding how you talk to yourself.

*Avoiding unnecessarily rigid self-perceptions.* Your self-picture is a unique collection of many different self-perceptions that constitute your way of describing and defining yourself. Areas in which you have self-perceptions include your body, sexuality, style of relating, feelings and emotions, tastes and preferences, academic prowess and achievement, work and leisure abilities and interests, and philosophy and values. Some self-perceptions, for instance 'I have blue eyes', are tied to your genetic endowment. For other self-perceptions, you have more choice. For instance, people who say: 'I am a poor letter writer' or 'I am an indifferent cook' may both make accurate statements about how they now perceive themselves but also inaccurate inferences about how they need to be in future, since they may choose to change. The risk here is to describe aspects of yourself as though they are unalterable parts of your heredity when they are not.

---

**Thinksheet 8   Using 'I' self-talk**

*Instructions*
Write out your answer to the following questions.

1.   What does self-talk mean to you? What does using 'I' self-talk mean?

2.   To what extent do you consider you oppress or restrict yourself by using 'I' self-talk insufficiently in the following areas? Where possible, illustrate with specific examples.

(a)   Putting yourself down with 'you' self-talk.
(b)   Using verbs not acknowledging choice.
(c)   Not being open about your feelings, thoughts and actions.
(d)   Having rigid self-perceptions.

3.   If necessary, set yourself specific and realistic goals for improving your use of 'I' self-talk.

---

## COPING SELF-TALK

Coping self-talk is a skill that has been used for a range of problems and with many different groups. The problems include managing stress, anger, test anxiety, shyness, impulsiveness and pain. The groups of people trained in coping self-talk include nurses, teachers, police officers, probation officers and athletes.

Top athletes face considerable stress when they compete. Below are examples of possible negative and coping self-talk, provided by Dr Peter Fricker, a psychologist at the Australian Institute of Sport, for a swimmer who is standing on the starting block at a major international competition.

> Negative self-talk might go as follows: 'If I don't win this, there goes endorsement, there goes family pride, national limelight. I won't get a telegram from the Prime Minister.'

> Coping self-talk might be: 'I know how to swim and to swim fast because I've been doing it twice a day for the past 10 years. All I have to do is to get in there. Okay, my technique means I've got to concentrate on getting my right arm in the water at that angle and a nice movement in the water under my body. That's all I've got to think about. If I just get in and do that as well as I can and as fast as I can I'll be right. That's the process of swimming.' (Fricker, 1987, p. 1)

Put simply, negative self-talk focused on the possible *outcomes* of the race while coping self-talk focused on the *processes* of swimming fast. The goal for negative self-talk was glory. The goal for coping self-talk was 'doing as well as I can'.

### What is coping?

The term coping in relation to a personal problem means to grapple successfully with it. Coping involves thinking, feeling and action. To cope effectively you need to be able to draw on your repertoire of thinking skills, including coping self-talk, to manage the stress or problem at hand. Your use of thinking skills has two main objectives: reducing the feelings of distress associated with the problems and taking appropriate actions to change the situation. Thus *coping* self-talk contains two major elements: *calming* self-talk and *coaching* self-talk. The former helps you calm your anxieties while the latter keeps you focused on the processes of the task at hand. Staying focused on the task, rather then engaging in self-talk that is irrelevant to it, also contributes to calming your anxieties.

Coping self-talk is about *coping* or 'doing as well as I can' rather than about *mastery* or 'being perfect' and 'having no anxiety'. Coping is a much more realistic goal than mastery. Altering your goal from mastery to coping is likely to increase your self-support and to decrease your self-oppression. You now possess an attainable standard towards which to strive. This is likely to increase what Stanford University psychologist Albert Bandura (1977) calls your self-efficacy, your conviction that you can successfully execute the behaviour required to produce a given outcome.

The notion of coping is also relevant to learning and implementing thinking skills. Mastery self-talk about the learning process would be that you make steady progress all the time. There is no room for or tolerance of set-backs and failure. Coping self-talk about learning is that difficulties and mistakes are an inevitable part of the process. You cope with these as best you can and learn from your mistakes. With coping rather than mastery self-talk you are more likely to persist since you tell yourself that mistakes are learning experiences rather than failures. Furthermore, once you have learned the thinking skills and are implementing them in your daily life, using coping self-talk is an important way in which you can encourage rather than discourage yourself to keep using them.

## Awareness, choice and action

It is now time to focus on how you can apply coping self-talk to your problems. I present this in three stages: awareness, choice and action. Awareness entails your becoming more aware of your current use of self-talk and identifying where it is more harmful than helpful. Choice involves focusing on the thinking choice points of whether to use either negative or coping self-talk and also on how to talk to yourself. Action means building up your skills of using coping self-talk to help you influence your feelings and also act more effectively when faced with actual problems.

## Awareness of your self-talk

### Becoming aware of self-talk

The Canadian psychologist, Donald Meichenbaum (1977, 1983, 1985, 1986) has perhaps been the most prominent advocate of focusing on people's self-talk to help them cope better with their problems. It is unlikely that you consciously or deliberately tell yourself various things when confronted with problems. Making unhelpful self-statements may have become an ingrained style of thinking, similar to the way you think automatically when you drive a car.

Before we look at specific ways in which you may use negative self-talk, try Thinksheet 9, which is designed to increase your awareness of the fact that you use self-talk when faced with stressful situations and problems in your life. The object of this thinksheet is to heighten your awareness that you actually use self-talk rather than to analyse whether it is negative or coping.

---

**Thinksheet 9**   Becoming aware of using self-talk

*Instructions*
1.  *Self-talk about a past situation*
    Think of a specific situation in your recent past that you experienced as anxiety-evoking and stressful. Close your eyes and visualize the scene. Just replay the events in slow motion and try to access your thoughts and feelings as you faced the situation. What thoughts did you have or, put another way, what were you telling yourself in the situation? When you open your eyes, write down as much of your self-talk as you can remember.

2.  *Self-talk about a future situation*
    Think of a specific situation in your near future that you anticipate experiencing as anxiety-evoking and stressful. Close your eyes and picture the scene. Visualize in slow motion what you anticipate happening in the situation and try to access your thoughts and feelings in regard to it. What thoughts did you find you were having or, put another way, what were you telling yourself about the situation? When you open your eyes, write down as much of your self-talk as you can remember.

---

There are a number of methods by which you can stimulate both your recall and your anticipation of your self-talk. Thinksheet 9 used visualization, or what Meichenbaum (1985) terms imagery-based recall. Other methods include keeping a self-monitoring diary and conducting 'personal experiments' in which you actively place yourself in difficult situations with the purpose of collecting self-talk data.

*Perceiving the relevance of self-talk*

As with any other thinking skill, you are more likely to use coping self-talk if you perceive it as relevant to overcoming a problem that you face than if you do not. You need to see that your thinking influences how you feel and act and also that your lack of coping self-talk has contributed to your sustaining a particular problem.

The fact that you choose to use coping self-talk for a problem does not preclude your using other thinking skills as well. For instance, shy people may also need to alter self-oppressing personal rules which involve the demanding of acceptance from everyone. Additionally, they may need to acquire better skills at acting on the environment: for instance, improving their conversational skills, voice quality and amount of eye-contact. In sum, you are more likely to see coping self-talk as relevant if you regard it as a necessary *part* of rather than as a sufficient *whole* of your approach to a problem.

*Characteristics of negative self-talk*

The two main characteristics of negative self-talk are that it is neither calming nor coaching, although these characteristics overlap.

Various skills weaknesses can contribute to your self-talk raising rather than lowering your anxiety. Characteristics of self-talk *contributing to rather than calming emotional distress* include the following.

- *Emphasizing mastery rather than coping*. Here you set your standards unrealistically high and hence lower your expectation that you can be successful. Roger is a good student except when it comes to exams. Then he tells himself: 'If I don't get all A grades, I have as good as failed.'

- *Catastrophizing*. This involves you in making out that, if you do not get what you want, it is a catastrophe. Marcia is a woman returning to the workforce after raising a family. Before her first job interview she thinks: 'If I don't get this job it will just prove that I am unemployable and that will be a catastrophe'.

- *Adversely reacting to your physical symptoms*. You can convert your feelings of anxiety into panic attacks by what you tell yourself about your physical symptoms once you start getting anxious. Although not going as far as full-blown panic attacks, many people heighten their anxiety and apprehension by adversely reacting to their body sensations. These sensations can include tension, nausea, breathlessness, palpitations, choking, hot and cold flushes and sweating. Bob, a bedding salesman, is afraid of speaking in public. His sales director has asked him to give a presentation to a group of buyers from a large bedding chain store. When the time comes Bob thinks: 'I can feel the tension in the pit of my stomach and my throat feels dry. This means that it is obvious that I am going to have difficulty in managing. At worst, things may get out of control and I will blank out totally.'

- *Being overly self-conscious about what others think*. You can freeze yourself by talking to yourself as though you are the centre of other people's universes. The dress Eartha wanted to wear to a party did not come back from the cleaners on time. Consequently she wore another dress which was not quite as good and thought: 'People can notice that I'm not looking my best. If only I had that other dress I could relax and enjoy myself.'

- *Putting yourself down*. You many talk to yourself in a way you 'wouldn't even talk to a dog'. Julian is learning a new game of cards. He gets increasingly angry that he is not catching on as quickly as the others and tells himself: 'You fool. You oughtn't to be so stupid. Why do you always have to mess things up.'

- *Focusing on setbacks and not owning successes.* This deficit may be more one of what you do not tell yourself than what you do. Maria and Marge have been good friends for some years. Recently Maria has felt that Marge has been taking less interest in her and that their friendship is in difficulty. Both women have experienced tension in their relationship. Maria tells herself about all the problems in it. She omits to tell herself that they still have good times together, such as last Saturday when they played tennis and swam.

The second main characteristic of negative self-talk is that it does not help you give yourself coaching self-instructions. Three of the ways in which you *hinder coaching yourself effectively* are as follows:

- *Not setting yourself clear goals.* Because you have not clarified in your own mind what you want to achieve, you are unable to tell yourself the steps necessary to achieve it.

- *Not breaking tasks down.* You may have set yourself clear goals, but failed to break the task or problem down into incremental smaller steps more easily achieved. Consequently you experience difficulty in talking yourself through the specific steps necessary to achieve the subgoals and, thus, the overall goal.

- *Not concentrating on the task at hand.* In the earlier example of the competitive swimmer, success was more likely to come if the swimmer's self-talk focused on the processes of fast swimming rather than on glory.

---

**Thinksheet 10    Exploring your negative self-talk**

*Instructions*
1. With regard to *either* your overall style of self-talk when faced with personal problems *or* with regard to a specific situation in your recent past that you experienced as anxiety-evoking and stressful, identify whether you use or used any of the following characteristics of negative rather than coping self-talk.

   (a)  Characteristics increasing emotional distress:
   - emphasizing mastery rather than coping
   - catastrophizing
   - adversely reacting to your physical symptoms
   - being overly self-conscious about what others think
   - putting yourself down
   - focusing on setbacks and not owning successes.

   (b)  Characteristics decreasing performance effectiveness:
   - not setting yourself clear goals
   - not breaking tasks down
   - not concentrating on the task at hand.

2.  Summarize what you perceive to be your current style of self-talk when faced with personal problems.

---

### Thinking choices in coping self-talk

*Cues to use coping self-talk*

There are a number of cues or triggers for when it may be appropriate to use coping self-talk. These are choice points for you. Coping self-talk is best engaged in before, during and after anxiety-evoking situations. Consequently, one of the cues to use coping self-talk is when you have a difficult situation coming up. Another cue is if you become aware that you are using any of the characteristics of negative self-talk described above. Other cues are when you experience persistent negative feelings and engage in self-defeating actions. Coping self-talk need not be restricted to anxiety-evoking situations. The coaching element of coping self-talk has a wider application.

*Calming self-talk*

When you use coping self-talk you tend to intersperse calming with coaching self-talk. Here each is mentioned separately before examples are given in which they are combined. Calming self-talk involves both the presence of supporting and the absence of negative self-talk. Characteristics of negative self-talk likely to contribute to emotional distress have already been reviewed. Here the emphasis is on the 'dos' rather than the 'don'ts' of calming self-talk.

Two important areas of calming self-talk are as follows.

- *Telling yourself to stay calm.* Sample self-statements include: 'keep calm, slow down, relax and just take it easy'. Additionally, you can instruct yourself to 'take a deep breath' or 'breathe slowly and regularly'.

- *Telling yourself you can cope.* Sample self-statements include: 'I can handle this situation, my anxiety is a signal for me to use my coping skills, and all I have to do is to cope'. Additionally, if you have coped with a situation better, acknowledge this: 'I used my coping skills and they worked'.

*Coaching self-talk*

Coaching self-talk is no substitute for possession of the action skills of actually achieving a task. However, coaching self-talk can help you to cope with anxiety-evoking and stressful problems in the following ways.

- *Clarifying your goals*. Be specific. For instance, if you have purchased a faulty record, your goal might be: 'On Tuesday afternoon I will return the record to the shop and ask for it to be replaced'.

- *Breaking tasks down*. Here you need to think through a step-by-step approach to achieving your goal, including how you might handle setbacks. Once your plan is clear, you then need to be able to instruct yourself through the steps of implementing it.

- *Concentrating on the task at hand*. While keeping your goal in mind, you focus on talking yourself through the processes of the steps involved in attaining it. You are like a pilot who talks himself or herself through to a difficult landing. You concentrate on the task at hand and discipline yourself not to think extraneous thoughts.

### Examples of coping self-talk

Coping self-talk may be used before, during and after anxiety-evoking and stressful situations. Often calming and coaching self-instructions are combined, for instance: 'Calm down. Just take one step at a time.' You need to think through the self-instructions that work for you. Below are examples of possible before, during and after self-talk for coping with shyness, anger, test anxiety and a job interview.

- *Coping with shyness*. Coping self-talk for a stressful social situation might be as follows.

  (a)  Before:
       'Now calm down. Think of some things I can talk about.'
       'I can cope with this situation if I take it steady.'

  (b)  During:
       'Relax. Everybody is not looking at me.'
       'My anxiety is manageable. I know I can cope.'

  (c)  After:
       'Well done. I managed to control my negative ideas.'
       'I'm pleased that I'm making progress in handling social situations.'

- *Coping with anger*. Coping self-talk for an anger-provoking encounter might be as follows.

  (a)  Before:
       'Remember, stick to the issues and avoid put-downs.'
       'I can cope with this encounter if I don't let my pride get in the way.'

  (b)  During:
       'My anger is a signal telling me to keep task oriented.'

'Calm down. I can feel in control so long as I keep my cool.'

(c)  After:
'Though we did not resolve anything, at least I handled myself well.'
'I'm learning to cope better without getting aggressive.'

- *Coping with test anxiety*. Coping self-talk for taking a test might be as follows.

(a)  Before:
'I don't have to be perfect. All I have to do is as best I can.'
'What are the specific skills I need to take this test effectively?'

(b)  During:
'Now calm down, relax, and take some slow, deep breaths.'
'Read the test instructions carefully and plan my time accordingly.'

(c)  After:
'I survived. I did not feel so bad after all.'
'When I control my self-talk, I can control my fear.'

- *Coping with a job interview*. Coping self-talk for a job interview might be as follows.

(a)  Before:
'Let's think through how I can best present my case.'
'Relax. Even if I do not get the job it is not the end of the world.'

(b)  During:
'Speak firmly and calmly and answer the questions asked.'
'It's OK to be anxious. I know I can manage these feelings.'

(c)  After:
'I did it. I managed to contain my negative ideas and got the job.'
'Even though I didn't get the job, I did well to be selected for the interview and I'm doing better each time I use my coping self-talk.'

Thinksheets 11 and 12 are designed to build your skills at formulating coping self-talk and using it when faced with personal problems.

---

**Thinksheet 11**   Formulating your coping self-talk

*Instructions*
Write out your answers to the following questions.

1.  What is the difference between *calming* self-talk and *coaching* self-talk?

2.  Give two specific examples each of:
    - calming self-talk

- coaching self-talk
- coping self-talk that combines calming and coaching self-instructions.

3.  The examples of coping self-talk in the text focused on shyness, anger, test anxiety and a job interview. Refer back to the text and, for each of these problem areas, provide one additional self-instruction for before, during and after. For example, in coping with shyness provide one coping self-instruction each for before, during and after a stressful social situation.

---

**Thinksheet 12    Applying coping self-talk to a personal problem**

*Instructions*
Write out your answers to the following questions.

1.  Identify a problem for which you consider coping self-talk might be appropriate.

2.  Set yourself clear goals for what you want to achieve.

3.  Take three index cards, one each for before, during and after. One side of each card is for negative self-talk and the other side for coping self-talk. At the top of one side of your before card write *Negative self-talk before* and at the top of the other side write *Coping self-talk before*. Label your during and after cards the same way.

4.  On each of your before, during and after cards write out at least two negative self-talk instructions and two coping self-talk instructions in relation to your problem. Read your coping self-talk instructions at least twice daily for a week.

5.  What do you think might be the emotional and behavioural consequences of using your coping self-talk instructions in contrast to your negative self-talk instructions for managing your problem?

6.  What other skills might you require to manage your problem most effectively?

---

## Coping self-talk and action

So far I have attempted to increase your awareness and to clarify some of your thinking choices when using coping self-talk. Here I focus on building a bridge between knowing what to do and doing it in practice.

*Taking a gradual approach to learning*

One way of learning and consolidating your coping self-talk skills is to go from the simple to the more difficult. You can gradually learn to use coping self-talk either within a problem area or across problem areas: for example, starting with using coping self-talk for a less anxiety-evoking job interview before using it for a more anxiety-evoking test taking situation. The principle of graduated learning and practice is the same for both approaches. You build up your confidence and skills by practising and succeeding at less anxiety-evoking before moving on to more difficult challenges. One way of distinguishing the more from the less difficult tasks is to give each a rating on a difficulty scale of 1 to 10. You can then rank the tasks into a hierarchy.

*Rehearsal*

If you have access to other people, you may be able to rehearse coping self-talk as you role-play situations with them. However, many of you are likely to be working on your own. Here using coping self-talk during visualized rehearsal can be an effective method of learning. For instance, Vince, a shy teenager, can imagine himself before, during and after anxiety-evoking social situations. As he visualizes progressively more difficult scenes he employs coping self-talk. Before moving on, Vince replays each scene until he considers his coping self-talk has helped him manage his anxiety and stay focused on the task. He also develops coping self-talk for handling setbacks: for instance, 'I am a learner and I'm not going to succeed all the time'.

*Practice*

Throughout this chapter I have tried to convey that you use self-talk all the time. You may need to practice hard at relinquishing your oppressing self-talk and replacing it with supporting self-talk. In Thinksheet 12 you identified a specific problem in your life where using coping self-talk might help you. If you consider that this is too difficult a problem on which to start, identify a less difficult problem in which you have a reasonable chance of a successful outcome if you use coping self-talk as you alter your behaviour. Be open to modifying your coping self-talk if you are uncomfortable with it and it does not work for you. As mentioned earlier, genuine learning rarely occurs without setbacks and difficulties. Use coping self-talk to encourage yourself in handling these. Also use coping self-talk to acknowledge your successes, thus motivating you to persist.

---

Thinksheet 13   Transferring coping self-talk into action

*Instructions*
Either for the problem you worked on in Thinksheet 12 or for a less difficult problem:

1. Draw up a hierarchy of two situations, one more anxiety-evoking and one less so, for which coping self-talk might be appropriate.
2. Formulate two each of before, during and after coping self-instructions for each situation on your hierarchy.
3. Rehearse using your coping self-instructions as you visualize each situation on your hierarchy. Replay the scenes as much as is necessary. Do not move on to the second situation until you feel that you have managed your anxiety and stayed focused on the task when coping with the first situation.
4. Try using your coping self-talk as you deal with each situation on your hierarchy in real-life. Modify your coping self-talk if necessary. Reward yourself with praise when you improve at controlling your anxiety and keeping focused on the task.

---

Since you use self-talk all the time, it is important that you start increasing your *coping* self-talk and decreasing your *negative* self-talk NOW. Remember, it is not whether you talk to yourself but what you choose to keep saying to yourself that makes you crazy!

## CHAPTER HIGHLIGHTS

Self-talk is the verbal aspect of thinking.

Your self has three major components: your natural self, your learned self and your choosing self.

You can choose to use self-talk either to support or to oppress yourself.

'I' self-talk is generally preferable to 'you' self-talk.

Coping self-talk contains two major interrelated elements: calming self-talk and coaching self-talk.

Calming self-talk helps you manage the emotional distress associated with anxiety-evoking and stressful situations.

Coaching self-talk helps you instruct yourself in the successful execution of the different steps involved in a task.

Negative self-talk involves thinking in ways that contribute to self-defeating emotions and actions.

You need to become aware of how you currently use negative self-talk.

You can choose to replace your negative self-talk with coping self-talk.

You may need to use additional thinking and action skills when faced with personal problems.

When learning to use coping self-talk for your problems, take a gradual approach, rehearse and practise.

Start using more coping self-talk NOW.

# 5 Choosing Your Personal Rules

The Golden Rule is that there are no golden rules.

*George Bernard Shaw*

Human beings govern themselves with rules. In this chapter my main focus is on your inner rules. Wessler & Hankin-Wessler (1986) call these rules by which people live 'personal rules of living'. Here I modify their term slightly and call them personal rules *for* living or, more briefly, personal rules. These personal rules are principles or guides *for* conduct, be this of yourself, others or the environment.

The concept of directives is closely related to that of personal rules. Directives are the internal orders or commands that you give to yourself. While this chapter's main focus is on your personal rules, attention is also paid to your pressurizing and inhibiting directives. These directives are manifestations of your personal rules.

Personal rules and their accompanying self-talk can be used for self-oppression or for self-support. The poet W. H. Auden once wrote: 'Weep for the lives your wishes never led'. Sometimes you may allow your natural self to be inhibited by restrictive rules from your learned self. Your personal rules underlie how you approach specific problems. In Chapter 4 examples of coping self-talk were provided for managing shyness, anger, test anxiety and a job interview. However, associated with the negative emotions and actions present in each of these situations were some underlying self-oppressing personal rules: for example, for shyness, 'I *must* be liked by everyone'; for anger, 'others *must* treat me the way I want'; for test anxiety, 'I *must* achieve at a high level'; and for a job interview, 'I *must* get the job'. Reasons why personal rules like these are self-oppressing rather than self-supporting are presented later.

Personal rules go beyond being relevant to specific problems to include being relevant to a problem central to all people, namely the conflict between your past and traditions and your present need to assert and define yourself as a unique individual. Goethe once stated: 'What thou has inherited from thy fathers, acquire it to make it thine'. The past can have benign or harmful influences. Its ghosts are pervasive. The learnings handed down by parents and others are not to be rejected entirely. Instead, parental and traditional rules are best reviewed by your choosing self and then owned, lived up to, discarded or reformulated.

Personal rules are central to your ability to define and assert yourself in the present. Your personal rules can help or hinder you in resisting pressures on you to conform against your interests, whether to friends, family or wider social groupings. This can be an area of particular importance to members of socially stigmatized minority groups. For instance, homosexual people may have to handle their own lack of acceptance of their sexual preference. Additionally, they may have rules that leave them open to putting themselves down further if rejected by others because of it.

Personal rules are of fundamental importance to ethical and social living. They relate to the potential conflict between self-interest and social interest. Although conscience can also be applied to how you treat yourself, an important part of conscience relates to your personal rules regarding how you treat others. Conscience may seem an old-fashioned term in an age where the pursuit of hedonism, be it short-term or longer term, is so highly valued. Conscience is a concept that does not feature prominently in contemporary applied psychology. However, I regard developing your conscience as a vital part of developing your full humanness. Working with your personal rules is not restricted to working through the harmful 'voices in your head' from your past, but also about developing your human potential for social living.

The remainder of this chapter is divided into four main sections: what are personal rules?; combating your self-oppressing personal rules; combating your self-oppressing directives; and listening to and developing your conscience.

## WHAT ARE PERSONAL RULES?

Your personal rules are the 'dos' and 'don'ts' by which you lead your life. Each of you has an inner rule-book that guides your living. You may be aware of some of your rules, but there are others of which you are unaware. Some of these latter personal rules are moderately easily accessible to your awareness. However, others may be more threatening and anxiety-evoking. Consequently, you may have more difficulty acknowledging them.

Most people in Western cultures possess what might be termed an *illusion of autonomy* whereby they see their behaviour as predominantly the result of their free choice. Frequently, this is erroneous. Many humans are governed by others' rules which they act on *as if* they were the result of their free choice. British psychiatrist R. D. Laing (1969) uses the metaphor of people acting as if hypnotized: not only do they follow instructions but they also remain unaware that they have been given these instructions in the first place.

Personal rules represent a form of self-talk, much of which goes on below awareness. They are the filters, structures or templates that form some of the *underchoices* that influence your feelings, thoughts and actions. For instance, Martin, a college student, has an underlying personal rule that: 'I must always receive approval'. Consequently when he meets Ann, a warm and attractive fellow student, and considers asking her out for a date, he perceives her as a threat and tells himself that he cannot handle the chance of being rejected. Throughout all of this, Martin remains unaware of his basic underlying personal rule concerning approval.

Another aspect of personal rules is that they are your standards for judging your own and others' behaviour. If your rules are self-supporting they can motivate you and help you to attain realistic goals. However, if your rules are self-oppressing, they leave you open to a triple dose of self-downing. For instance, Steve sets himself an unrealistically high goal of winning a tennis tournament. The first dose of self-downing is because he has not won. The second dose of self-downing is because he becomes anxious and depressed because he has not won. The third dose of self-downing is because he now starts devaluing not just his tennis playing ability but himself as a person both because he has not won and also because he is getting anxious and depressed about it.

## COMBATING YOUR SELF-OPPRESSING PERSONAL RULES

I use the term combating deliberately because self-oppressing personal rules tend to be deeply ingrained habits of relating to yourself, others and the world. You usually have to fight hard both to lessen their influence and to avoid losing the gains you have made. There is no concept of cure in overcoming self-oppressing rules. Albert Ellis suggests that practically all humans have a strong biological predisposition to think irrationally and thus disturb and continue disturbing themselves. Because of this even those humans helped by the most efficient forms of psychotherapy find it virtually impossible to achieve and maintain good mental health. Ellis (1987) regards most of his clients as 'natural resisters who find it exceptionally easy to block themselves from changing and find it unusually hard to resist their resistances' (pp. 370–1).

Combating self-oppressing personal rules involves three elements: awareness, choice and action. First, you increase your awareness both that they exist and also of your specific faulty rules. Second, you learn to dispute your thinking and to reformulate self-oppressing into self-supporting rules. Third, you work hard at integrating changed rules with changing your actions.

### Increasing your awareness of self-oppressing personal rules

*Inappropriate feelings and actions as signals*

How do you know if you possess self-oppressing personal rules? This can be difficult given that the rules are so much a part of you that you are unaware of many of their existences. As when observing puffs of smoke at the Vatican on the election of a Pope, you have to understand the signals.

Persistent inappropriate feelings can signal that you possess a self-oppressing personal rule. The dividing line between appropriate and inappropriate feelings is not always clear. Life can be difficult, so appropriate feelings cannot simply be equated with 'positive' feelings like happiness, joy and accomplishment. Some 'negative' feelings, like sadness, grief, fear and anger, can be entirely appropriate for the contexts in which they occur. You have to ask yourself questions like: 'is this feeling appropriate for the situation?', 'is keeping feeling this way helping or harming me?' and 'am I taking responsibility for my feelings or allowing them to be determined by others' behaviour?'

Inappropriate feelings and actions are interrelated. If you feel excessively angry you may act violently and worsen rather than help your position. Again appropriate questions are: 'are my actions helping or harming me?' and 'am I taking responsibility for my actions or allowing them to be determined by others' behaviour?'

If you are uncomfortable with the way you feel or act, your self-talk can take the form of 'I feel this way because . . .' or 'I act in this way because . . .'. These self-statements can initiate your search to become aware of the relevant personal rule or rules contributing to your distress. I do not suggest that on every occasion you backtrack from inappropriate feelings and actions to looking for self-oppressing personal rules. Life is too short. It is a useful self-help skill for when you experience persistent and/or major distress.

*Mustabatory and absolutistic rules*

Masturbation is probably the most common form of human sexual activity and I do not wish to give it a bad name. Nevertheless, Albert Ellis has coined the term 'mustabation' to refer to rigid personal rules characterized by 'musts, oughts and shoulds'. He has identified three major clusters of irrational beliefs or personal rules that 'create' inappropriate feeling and action consequences (Ellis, 1980).

1. I absolutely *must* do well and win approval for all my performances, or else I rate as a rotten person. Illustrative irrational rules are:
   'I must always have total love and approval from others.'
   'I must always perform all important tasks outstandingly and perfectly well.'

2.  Others absolutely *must* treat me considerately and kindly, in precisely the way I want them to treat me; if they do not, society should severely blame and damn them. An illustrative irrational rule is:
    'Others must always go out of their way to treat me perfectly considerately and fairly.'

3.  The conditions under which I live absolutely *must* be arranged so that I get practically everything I want comfortably, quickly and easily, and get virtually nothing that I do not want. An illustrative irrational rule is:
    'The conditions of my life must always be easy, safe and comfortable.'

Some of the *main characteristics of self-oppressing personal rules* include the following.

● *Demandingness*. Thinking of your wants and wishes as demands rather than as preferences.

● *Perfectionism*. Putting pressure on yourself and others to be perfect. Nobody's perfect.

● *Overgeneralization*. Making rules for *all* situations rather than allowing flexibility for specific situations.

● *Self-rating*. Rating yourself as a person and not just how functional your specific characteristics are for achieving your goals.

● *Catastrophizing*. Thinking that it is or will be absolutely awful if you, others or the environment are not as they should be.

● *Low tolerance of frustration*. Telling yourself that you cannot stand the anxiety or discomfort arising from you, others or the environment not being as they should be.

Ellis has grouped the disturbances caused by humans making absolute demands on self, others and the environment into two major categories: ego disturbance and discomfort disturbance. Ego disturbance refers to the disturbances created by self-downing and discomfort disturbance relates to the emotional discomforts, such as anxiety, that people feel when their demands are not met. He advocates self-acceptance and high tolerance of frustration as fundamental to rational living.

Below are some examples of self-oppressing personal rules set within the ABC framework: A is the event, B is the personal rule and C is the consequences.

Leona is a prominent scientist.
A   I give an uncharacteristically poor public speaking presentation.
B   I must perform perfectly well at public speaking at all times.
C   I feel inadequate and anxious because I have given a poor talk. I try to make out to others that my presentation was not too bad.

Tricia is a woman in her mid-thirties.

A    A man I accepted a date with rapes me.

B    There must have been a perfectly right way I should have behaved that would have avoided me being raped.

C    I blame myself and feel anxious, depressed and guilty. I have stopped going out with men.

Charles, a college student, is a talented musician who has enrolled in a business studies course.

A    I fail my first year in business studies.

B    I must always please my parents.

C    I feel alienated and depressed. I decide to repeat the year in business studies to see if I can do better.

Carol is a mother of a teenaged daughter.

A    My daughter and I have constant fights.

B    I must control what my daughter does.

C    I feel a failure as a mother and am consequently depressed and anxious. My daughter is increasingly rude to me.

An issue in detecting self-oppressing personal rules is the degree to which there are certain central themes that occur again and again. Ellis has suggested on different occasions 10, 11 or 12 central irrational beliefs that fall into his three major headings. Beck & Emery (1985) consider that their patients' maladaptive assumptions often focus on one of three major issues—acceptance, competence and control.

Rules can be held about what is the appropriate way to conduct intimate relationships. Eidelson & Epstein (1982) state that five dysfunctional relationship beliefs are: disagreement is destructive; mindreading is expected; partners cannot change; sexual perfection is necessary; and the sexes are different. A further major dysfunctional relationship belief is that conflicts must be handled competitively rather than collaboratively.

Thinksheet 14 has been designed to help make you more aware both that you have self-oppressing personal rules and what these may be in one or more problem area(s) of your life. It is based on a worksheet developed by British psychologist Windy Dryden (Dryden & Ellis, 1986).

---

**Thinksheet 14**    Becoming aware of your self-oppressing personal rules

*Instructions*

1.  Select a problem that you wish to work on.

    A (the event)   Describe the situation that contributed to your upset.

C (the consequences)   Describe how you felt and acted. Do you consider any of your feelings and actions to have been inappropriate?

B (your personal rule(s))   Looking for 'musts, oughts, shoulds, have tos, got tos', list any demands you made or might make of:
yourself
others
the situation.

If the worst happened or were to happen, list any negative evaluations or ratings that you made or might make of:
yourself
others
the situation.

2   If you wish, repeat the above ACB exercise for another problem situation in your life.

---

### Choosing to dispute and reformulate your self-oppressing personal rules

In the previous section you may have become aware that your underlying self-talk contains some self-oppressing personal rules. You may also have gone some way to identifying them. Disputing and reformulating these personal rules are two skills that can help you move towards self-supporting rules.

#### Disputing

Ellis (1980) considers the technique of disputing to be the most typical and often used method of his rational-emotive therapy (RET). Disputing involves your challenging the false assumptions that you hold about yourself, others and the world. Take the earlier example of Leona, the prominent scientist whose personal rule was: 'I must perform perfectly well at public speaking at all times'. Questions that Leona might ask herself to dispute her self-oppressing personal rule include those following.

What evidence exists for the truth of my personal rule?

What evidence exists for the falseness of my personal rule?

What are the worst possible things that might happen to me if I gave a less than perfect public presentation?

In what ways can't I stand failing to give a perfect public presentation?

Do I demand the same standards in making public presentations of other people as I require of myself?

In what ways does giving a less than perfect public presentation make me worthless as a person?

What are the costs and consequences for me of my demand that I must always give a perfect public presentation?

To what extent does my wanting to give a perfect public presentation represent my past learning history rather than the reality of my present situation and wishes?

You may need to dispute the same self-oppressing personal rule again and again. This is because you have well-developed habits of reindoctrinating and recontaminating yourself.

### Reformulating

Reformulating involves substituting self-supporting for self-oppressing characteristics in specific personal rules. Some of the *main characteristics of self-supporting personal rules* include:

- *Expressing preferences rather than demands*. You distinguish clearly between your non-absolutist preferences, wishes and likes and your absolutist demands, needs and requirements.

- *A coping emphasis*. Managing or coping with situations rather than being perfectionist in regard to them.

- *Being based on your own valuing process*. Your rules are not just rigid internalizations from others.

- *Flexibility*. Where appropriate, being amenable to change.

- *Absence of self-rating*. Your rules lead to a functional rating of specific characteristics according to whether they are useful for survival and fulfilment rather than to a global rating of your personhood.

Let me illustrate with some possible self-supporting reformulations for the four earlier examples of Leona, Tricia, Charles and Carol.

Leona
Self-oppressing personal rule: 'I must perform perfectly well at public speaking at all times.'
Self-supporting personal rule: 'Though my preference is always to give a polished talk, I may not always do so. If I give a less than perfect talk it is something I can cope with, not a catastrophe, and I may learn something from it.'

Tricia
Self-oppressing personal rule: 'There must have been a perfectly right way I should have behaved that would have avoided my being raped.'
Self-supporting personal rule: 'Nobody's perfect and there are rarely any perfect solutions. I did my best under the circumstances and just because I have been devalued by another person is no reason for me to devalue myself.'

Charles
Self-oppressing personal rule: 'I must always please my parents.'
Self-supporting personal rule: 'I would like to please my parents. However, it is more important that I assume responsibility for developing myself as an independent human being even if this means pursuing a career in music rather than business studies. I can stand the discomfort of their disapproval.'

Carol
Self-oppressing personal rule: 'I must control what my daughter does.'
Self-supporting personal rule: 'While I would prefer that my daughter does what I want, she is an independent person whom I can only influence rather than control. Her not doing what I want does not make me a failure as a person.'

The outcome of disputing and reformulating self-oppressing personal rules is ideally that you feel and act better. In the ABC framework, by choosing at B to discipline your thinking about A you have new and better consequences at C. Thinksheet 15 has been designed to help you build your self-help skills of disputing and reformulating self-oppressing personal rules.

---

Thinksheet 15   Disputing and reformulating self-oppressing personal rules

*Instructions*
1.   Select a problem situation in your life. This can be either the situation that you worked on in Thinksheet 14 or another situation, in which case you will need to complete Thinksheet 14 again before proceeding.

2.   Dispute each of the demands you made or might make in the situation.

3.    Dispute each of the ratings you made or might make in the situation.

4.    Reformulate one or more of your important self-oppressing personal rules into a self-supporting personal rule(s).

5.    What do you consider the effects of your new self-supporting rule(s) might have been or might be on your feelings and actions?

---

### Changing your actions along with your personal rules

Changing your personal rules may make it easier for you to act effectively. In turn, acting effectively is perhaps the most powerful way of generating evidence with which to dispute self-oppressing personal rules. When you are integrating changes in your thinking choices with changes in how you act, a basic guideline is *practise, practise, practise*.

Using visualization is one way in which you can create a bridge between changing your personal rules and your actions. For instance, Leona might engage in visualized rehearsal. Here she visualizes herself before, during and after an upcoming public speaking engagement and disputes and reformulates any self-oppressing rules that she detects. Leona may also choose to use coping self-talk. If you have altered the underlying personal rules upon which it is based, you are more likely to maintain your coping self-talk.

Ultimately there is no substitute for real-life practice. Psychologists differ as to whether practice is best approached gradually, from the least to most difficult tasks, or 'floodingly', by going straight to a difficult assignment. Ellis encourages his clients to do their practice assignments repetitively and floodingly. He considers that clients, by going in at the deep end and keeping on going in, more quickly learn that the worst they have feared rarely happens except in their imaginations. For instance, an individual afraid of riding on a bus would be encouraged to take bus rides many times a day. Other psychologists advocate taking a more gradual approach, for instance a person afraid of public speaking might be encouraged first to give an easy talk to a few people before a more difficult one to many people. Some of you do not have much choice. A difficult talk or an important exam is the imminent reality with which you are faced.

The support of a group can be helpful to those wishing to alter personal rules and actions. In recent years, women's groups and homosexual groups have tried to alter the consciousness of their members concerning self-oppressing rules and behaviour so that they think, feel and act in more self-supporting ways. Earlier I indicated that you may use other thinking skills, for instance coping self-talk, as you change both your personal rules and the way you act. Additionally, you may need to develop your action skills, for example, projecting your voice better when you speak in public or using your time better in exams.

---

**Thinksheet 16    Changing your actions along with your personal rules**

*Instructions*

1.  Select a problem situation in your life, preferably the one you worked on in Thinksheets 14 and 15.

2.  Specify realistic goals for changing the way you act in this situation.

3.  Visualize yourself acting as you would like before, during and after the situation. As you detect any self-oppressing personal rules, dispute and reformulate them.

4.  Face the situation in real life and change how you act as well as you can. As you detect any self-oppressing personal rules, dispute and reformulate them.

5.  Practise, practise, practise.

6.  Use coping self-talk to recognize and reward yourself for any gains you make.

---

## COMBATING YOUR SELF-OPPRESSING DIRECTIVES

There is much overlap between personal rules and directives. I find working with both concepts useful. Some of you may find the concept of self-oppressing directives easier to apply to yourself than that of personal rules.

The term directives is derived from Eric Berne's approach to counselling, psychotherapy and living, called transactional analysis. Berne (1972) developed the concept of a person's script, a preconscious life plan which is the product of parental programming plus the decisions made in response to this parental programming. Berne saw people as having an illusion of personal autonomy. However, more often than not they were unthinkingly driven by script directives. Script directives could come from either parent. They might be consistent or, in varying degrees, contradictory.

### Increasing your awareness of self-oppressing directives

Diverging from Berne's terms, self-oppressing directives fall into two major categories: *pressurizers* and *inhibitors*. The difference is that your pressurizers *drive you to act against* your interests and your inhibitors *block you from acting in* your interests.

Some possible self-oppressing *pressurizer directives* that you may have internalized include the following.

*   *Achieve at all costs.* You do not realistically take your interests, abilities and

opportunities into account but overstrive. At worst this leads to death from something like a heart attack.

- *Amass material goods*. Your self-worth as a person is related to the amount of money, goods and chattels that you accumulate.

- *Be liked*. You need to be liked by people whether or not you find them likeable. Your self-worth is related to the degree that people like you.

- *Be in control*. You have strictly to control your own and others' thoughts, feelings and actions and your environment.

- *Hurry up*. Time is always to be used rather than to be enjoyed or, even worse, wasted.

- *Be active*. You are only living if you are actively doing things. There is no room for experiencing people or nature in a reflective and receptive way.

- *Be masculine/feminine*. Act out your gender role. You should be dominant, strong and assertive if you are male and pretty, gentle and accommodating if you are female.

- *Be selfish*. Life is basically highly competitive and no one is going to look after you if you do not always 'look after number one'.

Inhibitor directives can be the inverse of pressurizer directives. Some possible *inhibitor directives* are the following.

- *Don't think*. Other people's thoughts are better than your own. Do not take the risk of thinking for yourself.

- *Don't trust*. People are highly untrustworthy. If you trust someone you are likely to be taken advantage of.

- *Don't feel*. Acknowledging your feelings is a risk for yourself and for others. It is better to anaesthetize them.

- *Don't be sensual*. Do not have a relaxed and comfortable attitude towards your own and others' sexuality.

- *Don't enjoy yourself*. This prohibition is summed up in the remark about the Protestant ethic: 'you can do anything that you want, as long as you don't enjoy it'.

- *Don't be different*. Your value is in what others think of you. Do not risk losing this source of emotional support.

- *Don't take risks*. Stick to the known and safe ways. You can never tell what the outcomes of change may be.

- *Don't acknowledge death*. The inescapable fact of your death is better avoided than faced.

You not only have pressurizers and inhibitors that affect you as an individual, but you take them into your relationships. Thus, in any partner relationship, both partners bring in the directives from their parents. These different 'family of origin' directives may be a source of considerable conflict.

---

**Thinksheet 17   Identifying your self-oppressing directives**

*Instructions*
1.  For your life as a whole:
    (a)   Take a piece of paper, draw a line down the middle, at the top of the left hand column write PRESSURIZER DIRECTIVES and at the top of the right hand column write INHIBITOR DIRECTIVES.

    (b)   In the relevant columns, list your self-oppressing pressurizer and inhibitor directives.

    (c)   Assess the impact of these directives on the quality of your life.

2.  For a specific problem:
    Repeat the above exercise, but this time focus on a specific problem area for you, for instance, sex, self-disclosing, anger, conflict. When focusing on a specific problem, try to list as many relevant directives as you can that you have internalized.

---

### Choosing to challenge and to change your self-oppressing directives

There are a number of ways that you can choose to challenge and change your self-oppressing directives. The three to be reviewed here are disputing, understanding their origins and granting yourself permissions.

#### Disputing

Disputing your directives is similar to disputing your personal rules. For instance, if you have a pressurizer directive like 'hurry up', questions that you might ask to dispute this directive include the following.

Where is the evidence that I must always hurry up?

What are the costs and consequences to me of always hurrying up?

What might happen to me if I did not always hurry up? Would this be so awful?

Do I think it is realistic to make the same demand on others to hurry up that I make on myself?

What are the ways in which I can approach time other than pressurizing myself always to hurry up?

The directive 'hurry up' is not as innocent as it might seem on the surface. It can contribute to all sorts of stress-related problems, both psychological and physical. For instance, psychologically it can contribute to your feeling anxious, under pressure and irritable. Physically you may suffer ailments such as hypertension, migraines, peptic ulcers and heart attacks.

*Understanding their origins*

Understanding the origins of your pressurizers and inhibitors can help you to realize that, although they may have had a purpose in the past, they have long outlived their usefulness. Take the pressurizer directive of 'hurry up'. While you were growing up either or both of your parents may have made a similar directive that they applied to themselves as well as to you. Thus not only were you being constantly told to hurry up, but also either or both of them were demonstrating a hurry up lifestyle to you. Because of the potency of your parents both as examples and as purveyors of rewards to you, your childhood decision to hurry up may have been realistic under the circumstances. Understanding the origin of your hurry up decision and the fact that you have unthinkingly internalized it since then may make it easier for you *now* to re-decide to hurry up only when it suits you. Your changed thinking enables you to behave flexibly rather than compulsively.

*Permissions*

Permissions give you leave to give up the power of your pressurizers and inhibitors. They come from your choosing self in support of relinquishing the negative elements of your learned self and also of releasing positive elements of your natural self. They are a form of self-talk which supports rather than oppresses you.

Below are some examples of *permissions replacing pressurizer directives*.

Pressurizer: Achieve at all costs.
Permission: It's OK to please myself regarding what standards I achieve.

Pressurizer: Hurry up.
Permission: It's OK to go at my own pace and only hurry up when necessary.

Pressurizer: Be masculine/feminine.
Permission: It's OK to express those parts of my being that I want to, regardless of whether the culture labels them masculine or feminine.

Below are some examples of *permissions replacing inhibitor directives*.

Inhibitor: Don't think.
Permission: It's OK to use my full mental capacities and to think for myself.

Inhibitor: Don't feel.
Permission: It's OK to listen to my feelings and to act on them if I choose.

Inhibitor: Don't be different.
Permission: It's OK to be myself and to support my development as a unique person.

As with many of your thinking choices, it is one thing to verbalize to yourself that you have granted yourself a permission and another to integrate it into your daily living. This issue will be raised again shortly.

---

**Thinksheet 18    Challenging and changing your self-oppressing directives**

*Instructions*
1. Select one or more significant *pressurizer* directives in your life. For each of these pressurizer directives:
   (a)  dispute them
   (b)  try to understand their origins
   (c)  replace them with an appropriate permission.

2. Select one or more significant *inhibitor* directives in your life. For each of these inhibitor directives:
   (a)  dispute them
   (b)  try to understand their origins
   (c)  replace them with an appropriate permission.

3. To what extent do you consider that you:
   (a)  restrict yourself through pressurizers and inhibitor directives?
   (b)  might free yourself to be happier and more fulfilled by granting yourself more permissions?

**Changing your actions as well as your directives**

Your pressurizer and inhibitor directives can be powerful 'voices in the head'. Much of the section on changing your actions along with your personal rules is relevant here. You have to practise, practise, practise behaving differently. You can use visualization to help you picture and rehearse a different way of being. You may either go right in at the deep-end and change your behaviour in a difficult situation or take gradual steps towards being different. Additionally, the help of a like-minded group may make it easier for you to relinquish self-oppressing directives.

Although self-oppressing directives are frequently difficult to change, some of them may also be policed by anxiety and guilt. An example is that of exclusively homosexual people, whether female or male, who gradually come to the recognition that they will not have a heterosexual lifestyle. They then have a choice either to inhibit their sexuality as much as possible or to express it homosexually. Although attitudes towards homosexuality are becoming more tolerant, it is still probable that most people in Western cultures are brought up with a strong prohibition against homosexual wishes and behaviour. Thus at each stage in the coming out process—to themselves, to other homosexuals and to the wider community—homosexual people may experience anxiety and guilt which is a residue of their earlier parental and social programming.

Anxiety and guilt can be associated with the process of relinquishing many other directives. For instance, people with a 'don't enjoy yourself' inhibitor can feel anxious and guilty about time and money spent enjoying themselves. Consequently, when changing your actions along with your directives, you may need to engage in coping self-talk to help manage the associated anxiety. You also need to change your actions at a pace you can handle.

## LISTENING TO AND DEVELOPING YOUR CONSCIENCE

> Labour to keep alive in your breast that little spark of celestial fire, called conscience.
>
> *George Washington*

> Conscience is the inner voice that warns us that someone may be looking.
>
> *H. L. Mencken*

So far I have mainly focused on loosening, freeing up and humanizing your personal rules and directives. Working through your self-oppressing internalizations of others' rules is an important way of possessing a self-supporting personal rule-book. Another way of viewing your personal rule-book is that it is your conscience. Your conscience is your awareness of what is right and wrong. Existential psychiatrist Rollo May (1953) observes: 'Conscience, rather, is one's capacity to tap one's own deeper levels of insight, ethical sensitivity and aware-ness, in which tradition and immediate experience are not opposed to each other but interrelated' (p. 215). Where your conscience represents your own valuing process, it is possible to experience anxiety and guilt not for failing to live up to others' rules, but for acting in ways that violate your human potential. Conse-quently, another way of possessing a self-supporting rule-book is to choose to live up to those rules that protect your happiness and fulfilment.

A further way of viewing your personal rule-book takes into account your relationship to the wider human community and species. Developing a wider social conscience might be viewed as a third way of possessing a self-supporting rule-book. If you possess a humane conscience in relation to yourself, you are likely to have more positive energy to direct outside yourself. You will not be so bogged down in your own negative agendas. Then you may further develop social interests beyond immediate self-interest. The more that people do this, the better are the chances for safeguarding rather than annihilating the human species.

### Listening to your conscience

There is a body of thought among some psychologists that says that human disturbance is less the result of failure to live up to others' unrealistic rules than of failure to live up to your own realistic rules (for example, Mowrer, 1964). For instance, if you want to be respected by other people you need to behave in ways that generate respect. If you want to be happy, you need to choose not to engage in escape behaviours like taking toxic drugs and excessive amounts of alcohol. In short, you may already possess self-supporting rules but then fail to support yourself by living up to them.

In this view, anxiety and guilt are not negative emotions telling you that you have self-oppressing personal rules. Rather they are appropriate or positive emotions signalling that you need to alter your behaviour to live up to self-supporting rules. Here guilt is what Maslow (1962) terms 'intrinsic guilt' result-ing from the betrayal of one's own inner nature. The self-disapproval rather than being unjustified is justified. Therefore you have the responsibility for disciplin-ing your thinking and behaviour.

Although there are numerous reasons why partners have extramarital affairs, 'cheating' on your spouse maybe an instance where you damage yourself by not listening to your conscience and living up to your rules.

> Brian is a married man with three children, aged 5, 9 and 13 years. He is the managing director of a ceramics company and a lay preacher in his church. Over the past two years he has worked very hard, often staying late in the office. During this period he has had an affair with Debbie, his secretary. He realizes that there is no long-term future in the affair and that there is a good chance of saving his marriage and

family life if he works on it. This is what he says he wants, both in a positive sense and also to ease the anxiety and guilt he feels through not living up to his own freely chosen standards. However, he is in considerable turmoil since he still has strong feelings for Debbie.

Thinksheet 19 is designed to make the point that listening and living up to your conscience may benefit you in many instances. I do not imply that this is always easy. Sometimes it involves much inner conflict and pain. You may also require skilled outside support.

---

**Thinksheet 19    Listening to and living up to your conscience**

*Instructions*
1.  Select one or more areas in your life where you consider that you experience anxiety and guilt for not living up to your conscience or personal rule-book.

2.  State your relevant self-supporting personal rules as clearly as possible.

3.  Make the case for why these rules are self-supporting. State the costs and consequences to yourself and to others of not living up to your self-supporting personal rules.

4.  Develop a step-by-step plan for bringing your actions more into line with your self-supporting personal rules.

5.  Work hard to implement your plan.

---

## Developing your social conscience

Men are rewarded and punished not for what they do, but for how their acts are defined. This is why men are more interested in better justifying themselves than in better behaving themselves.

*Thomas Szasz*

Since the focus of this book is on applying thinking skills to personal rather than social and species-wise problems, this section is a brief postscript to the chapter. Earlier I mentioned that developing a social interest that went beyond immediate self-interest was a third element of a self-supporting rule-book. This position is based on a number of assumptions. First, higher levels of human development entail listening to and building on the pro-social elements of your human nature. Self-oppressing personal rules may be egocentric rules that restrict you from awareness of your full humanity. In his famous study of self-actualizing people, Maslow (1970) observed that they 'have for human beings in general a deep feeling of identification . . . . Because of this they have a genuine desire to help the human race' (p. 165). Second, you may feel more fulfilled if, some of the time at least, you can live up to personal rules that transcend narrow self-interest. Third, enlightened self-interest may help you to develop a more caring attitude to others who share the same planet. The risks of conventional or nuclear wars are ever present.

All individuals are likely to have their own reasons for why they perpetrate their current balance (or imbalance?) between self-interest and sane social interest. Below are a few illustrative self-oppressing rules that may act as a defence against assuming a wider social interest.

- I must be appreciated. My acts are not worth doing in themselves, only for the public approval they bring.

- I must not be taken advantage of. Helping others has the risk that I may be taken advantage of. This would be terrible.

- I must help everyone. Because I cannot do everything, doing anything is not worth doing.

- I must wait for others. If it becomes the customary thing among my friends and associates to take a wider social interest, then, but not until then, will I do so too.

- Others must help themselves. All individuals have a responsibility for looking after themselves and I may only weaken their resolve if I help them.

You can dispute and reformulate personal rules that block enlightened social interest on your part. You may also try changing your behaviour in accord with your changed rules. This may involve starting with small steps, but not necessarily so. Visualizing the outcomes of your changed behaviour might strengthen your resolve. For instance, if you give money to a charity you can find out and then visualize how it is being used to benefit others. Additionally, mixing with like-minded people, either in religions or in lay groups, may further help you to develop your social conscience.

## CHAPTER HIGHLIGHTS

Personal rules are your guides for the conduct of yourself, others and the environment; they can be either self-oppressing or self-supporting.

Inappropriate feelings and actions signal that you may have underlying self-oppressing personal rules.

Self-oppressing personal rules frequently contain absolutistic 'musts, oughts and shoulds', facetiously termed 'mustabation'.

A major skill of changing self-oppressing personal rules is that of disputing their irrational assumptions.

Self-oppressing personal rules also need to be reformulated into language that is self-supporting.

Changing your actions along with your personal rules can be difficult and involve significant personal struggle.

Changing your actions is helped by practice, visualized rehearsal and group support.

Directives are closely allied to personal rules and are the orders or commands that you give to yourself.

Two major categories of self-oppressing directives are pressurizers and inhibitors.

Ways of changing self-oppressing directives include disputing, understanding their origins and granting yourself permissions.

Changing your actions along with your directives can be difficult and can involve working through anxiety and guilt.

Your existing personal rules can be self-supporting, in which case you support yourself best by listening and living up to them.

Developing your social conscience may help you attain more of your human potential and is important for the human species as well.

# 6   Choosing How You Perceive

People see only what they are prepared to see.

*Ralph Waldo Emerson*

Castles in the air—they're so easy to take refuge in. So easy to build too.

*Henrik Ibsen*

Think of yourself as an information-processing machine. All your waking hours you are bombarded with internal and external stimuli. This bombardment even takes place when you are asleep and dreaming. However, unlike when you sleep, during your waking hours you have a choice regarding how you perceive these stimuli. If you perceive them accurately, you have a better information base for living effectively. However, if you distort, deny or misinterpret significant information, you lessen your chances of avoiding inappropriate feelings and actions.

That different people can perceive the same event differently is easy to understand. Here is a humorous example. After the October 1987 stockmarket crash a previously wealthy man came home to his wife and said: 'We've just lost most of our money on the stockmarket. Perhaps we should fire the cook and you had better learn how to cook.' His wife, not to be outdone, replied: 'Well, perhaps we should fire the chauffeur and you had better learn how to make love!'

That you yourself can often perceive the same event differently may be less obvious. Take the example of someone treading on your toe. Among the different perceptions that you might choose from are that it was accidental, careless, done in anger, done because the other person was pushed, or your foot was in the way, to mention but some. You may choose the first perception that crosses your mind rather than say to yourself, 'Stop . . . think . . . what are my perceptual choices?' and then choose the most appropriate one in context. How you react is also likely to be influenced by your personal rules. For instance, if you have a rule, 'no one must ever invade my personal space', you may react the same way whether your toe was trodden on by accident or in anger.

This chapter explores how you may be choosing to perceive sometimes, if not much of the time, in self-oppressing rather than self-supporting ways. It is divided into four main areas: influencing your feelings; perceiving yourself more positively; letting go of defensiveness; and perceiving others more realistically.

## INFLUENCING YOUR FEELINGS

Since the early 1960s, Aaron Beck of the University of Pennsylvania has been particularly prominent in the area of helping people influence their feelings through choosing more realistic perceptions (Beck, 1976, 1987; Beck *et al.*, 1979; Beck & Emery 1985). In particular, he has focused on the intervening thoughts that precede depression, anxiety disorders and phobias. However, you do not need to be psychiatrically ill to benefit from the self-help skill of influencing your feelings through challenging and altering your distorted perceptions and perceptual processes. Such faulty perception is widespread.

### Awareness of the influence of perception on your feelings

Imagine that you are awakened in the night by the noise of a window banging. If you perceived that the window was banging because a burglar had entered your home you might feel very frightened. If, on the other hand, you remembered that you had earlier been looking out of the open window, got distracted by a phone call, and then forgot to close it, you might feel irritation and annoyance, but probably not fear. In each instance, your feelings were influenced by your perceptions.

In the above illustration my assumption was that you were aware of what you were thinking. However, Beck (1976) observes that frequently you are unaware of the thoughts and perceptions that influence your emotions. Instead you have what he terms *automatic* thoughts. Either you are not fully conscious of these thoughts and images or it does not occur to you that they warrant special scrutiny. Beck collaborates with his patients in the scientific or detective work of exploring and identifying these self-defeating perceptions or 'what you tell yourself'.

Below are a few simple examples based on the ABC framework.

A    Kathryn's boyfriend Abe is 15 minutes late.
B    Kathryn perceives that Abe is showing her disrespect because of this.
C    She sulks and gets angry with him when he arrives.

If at B Kathryn had thought: 'Abe usually is not late. Why don't I ask him what happened?', at C, on asking him without being aggressive, she would have found out that he was unavoidably held up by a car accident. Thus, she would have escaped her negative feelings and behaviour.

A   Eric is sitting with a group of friends and his best friend Ron is deep in conversation with Carolyn.
B   Eric perceives that Ron is bored with him.
C   Eric feels lonely and depressed.

If at B Eric had perceived that Ron's attraction to Carolyn had no negative implications for his relationship he might even have been happy for his friend.

There is a connection between self-oppressing perceptions and self-oppressing personal rules. For example, Eric may have had a personal rule that 'I absolutely must always receive approval from my friends'. This personal rule may have predisposed him to look for any negative signals in Ron's behaviour. Similarly Kathryn may have possessed a rigid personal rule about time-keeping which led to self-downing when the rule was unavoidably broken.

How do you monitor the upsetting or self-oppressing perceptions that influence your feelings? Ideally, they should be monitored as they happen. However, for this you need to develop the skill of listening to the self-talk that accompanies your inappropriate feelings. Setting aside some time each day to build up the skill of monitoring and recording your upsetting perceptions is another approach. Thinksheet 20 is designed to help you do this.

---

**Thinksheet 20   Monitoring and recording your upsetting perceptions**

*Instructions*
Below is a format for monitoring and recording your upsetting perceptions.

| A.   The situations (include date and time) | C.   Your feelings | B.   Your perceptions |
|---|---|---|
|  |  |  |

1.   Make a thinksheet similar to the above. Then for the next 24 hours monitor and record the ABCs either of a single category of negative feelings or of any significant negative feelings. In particular focus on identifying at B the thoughts and perceptions immediately preceding and accompanying your inappropriate negative feelings.

2.   What have you learned about the relationship between your perceptions and your feelings by completing the above thinksheet?

3.   Repeat the exercise until you consider that you have developed some lasting self-help skills

for recognizing your self-oppressing perceptions that contribute to inappropriate negative feelings.

---

## Common perceptual errors

### *Facts or inferences?*

Your perceptions of the world are your subjective facts. They are the points on the map by which you steer your course through life. However, subjective facts do not necessarily correspond to the objective facts of reality. Your perceptions may be based on inferences rather than fact. For instance, a favourite illustration of one of my Stanford University professors was: 'All Indians walk in single file, at least the one I saw did'. That I saw one Indian is fact; that they all walk in single file is inference. Facts are the true data of experience; inferences are deductions and conclusions drawn from the data. Inferences may be useful as long as the assumptions on which they are based are recognized and accurately evaluated. However, all too often inferences are mistaken for facts. This distances you from accurate information on which to base further thoughts, feelings and actions.

Inferences can be about yourself, others or the environment. They can be positive or negative. They are of varying degrees of accuracy in the factual data on which they are based. Below are some examples of the differences between facts and perceptual inferences. You may remain unaware of the leap in logic that has taken you from fact to inference.

| Fact | Inference |
|---|---|
| This evening I left home a couple of times briefly to run errands. | My mother did not phone me at home this evening. |
| I do not immediately understand the question on an exam paper. | This is a very difficult paper that I am bound to fail. |
| I get feedback from a couple of students on how my teaching could be improved. | I am a lousy teacher. |
| I get a high grade on an essay. | The teacher did not read it properly. |
| I win at gambling after a series of losses. | I will be lucky in future too. |

I stress the distinction between fact and inference because it is a theme that underlies most perceptual errors. You may jump to conclusions and remain unaware that you have taken the leap. Illusion then becomes your reality, in whole or in part.

*Specific perceptual errors*

Below are some specific perceptual errors that may contribute to your having inappropriate negative feelings.

● *Negativeness*. This involves overemphasizing negative aspects of yourself, others and the environment and minimizing positive aspects.

● *Personalizing*. A tendency to perceive yourself as more the centre of attention than is warranted. For instance: 'If I go to a dance, everyone will be staring at me and realize that I am a poor dancer.'

● *Overgeneralizing*. Drawing a broad conclusion from a specific observation. For example: 'The fact that Pat turned me down for a date means that all other girls will too.'

● *Magnifying and minimizing*. Distorting the significance of events when there is no basis for such gross errors of perception.

● *Black and white thinking*. Perceiving in either/or terms. For example: 'Either Stan is totally in love with me or he does not love me at all.'

● *Self-rating*. Going beyond a functional rating of a specific characteristic to devalue yourself as a person and your competence to live effectively.

● *Misattributing*. Failure to make accurate assignments of cause and responsibility for your own and others' behaviour. For instance, Eve is separated from her husband Eric and perceives: 'If Eric does not admit how badly he has treated me, I'm unable to break loose from him emotionally.'

● *Tunnel vision*. Focusing on only a limited amount of the available information in a situation rather than taking into account all significant information.

In addition to the perceptual errors listed above, there are many that come under the category of perceiving defensively. These will be explained and listed later in the chapter.

## Choosing to question your perceptions by logical analysis

The goal here is to achieve appropriate flexibility in how you perceive rather than to oppress yourself needlessly with automatic and rigid perceptual patterns. When you become aware that you are feeling and acting, or at risk of feeling and acting, in inappropriate ways, it is a good idea to check the accuracy of your information base. The computer saying 'garbage in, garbage out' applies to people as well.

Choosing to question your perceptions by logical analysis involves you in self-talk that includes trying to answer the following questions.

Stop . . . think . . . what are my perceptual choices?

Are my perceptions based on fact or inference?

If they are based on inference, are there other ways of perceiving the situation that are more closely related to the factual evidence?

If necessary, what further information do I need to collect?

Does my way of perceiving the situation involve any of my characteristic perceptual errors?

What is the perception that I could choose that represents the best fit to the factual evidence?

When questioning your perceptions you conduct a logical analysis of the accuracy with which you construe your experiences. This involves both analytic and creative skills. The latter now become our focus.

*Generating different perceptions*

One of the ways in which you may disturb yourself is by being a 'stick in the mud'. In this context, this means unnecessarily sticking in the mud of the first perception that you have rather than being more creative and flexible. An important defect of many people is that they lack the skill of generating different perceptions to understand better the reality of the situations they face. You can often be much more effective if you sharpen up your inferring to correspond more closely to the available facts. Below is an example of the generation of different perceptions taken from my private practice.

A   Katie's 16-year-old daughter Sandra decides to live with Katie's estranged husband Peter and has not contacted her for a couple of weeks.

B   Katie's perception of Sandra: 'She is selfish and hard'. Katie's perception of herself: 'I am a failure as a mother'.

C   Katie makes no effort to contact Sandra and feels angry, anxious, depressed, confused and powerless.

When I first asked Katie whether there were other ways of perceiving Sandra's behaviour, she said she could not think of any. Using a whiteboard (a useful adjunct to doing this kind of work, either in counselling or for self-help), Katie and I then set about generating alternative perceptions. Here are a few of them.

Sandra has her year-end exams coming up. She is anxious about these and finds it easier to study at Peter's place without the distracting interruptions of my 13-year-old daughter and two boys, aged 5 and 3.

Sandra currently has a lot of conflict with her 13-year-old sister Betsy and by living with her dad she can avoid this conflict.

Sandra is confused and upset over Peter's and my separation and needs time to think things through.

I tend to be hard on Sandra. For instance, the other day she went home in the school lunch hour with her boyfriend Rick when nobody was in the house. I was furious with her.

Sandra was never that fond of her dad and may be unhappy there.

These were just some of the different perceptions that Katie and I generated. Each of them contained some truth in explaining Sandra's behaviour. They also contributed to helping Katie stop labelling Sandra as 'selfish' and 'hard' and move towards seeing her as a three-dimensional teenager with strengths and vulnerabilities. Furthermore, Katie gained the insight that Sandra felt threatened by her 'aggression'. This helped Katie change her own behaviour to attain her goals. The development of this story was that, soon after her exams, Sandra came home. She wanted to have a good talk with her mum. Katie, instead of scolding her for how she had behaved, listened to her sympathetically and said how glad she was to have her home. Sandra now gives Katie support, for instance, taking some of the domestic load off her when Katie is tired. In this example I was not only working with Katie to help her perceive her way through this particular problem, but also developing her self-help skills of generating different perceptions.

*Evaluating different perceptions*

Perceptions, once generated, require evaluation to see which ones best fit the factual evidence. In the example of Katie, she evaluated each of the different perceptions mentioned above as having some validity. This was in terms of her knowledge, partly based on facts, of how Sandra thought about and coped with her world.

Below is another example from my private practice in which Louise, a former prostitute and manager of an escort agency, generated and evaluated different perceptions.

A    At the end of a social gathering, Louise walks past Karl and Anna talking in a parking lot and Karl sees her but goes on talking to Anna.

B    Louise perceives: 'Karl does not like me.'
C    Louise feels depressed and thinks that she is unattractive.

I won't go into great detail, but one different perception that Louise generated was: 'Karl has the "hots" for me, but is afraid to show it'. She laughed about this, but considered that there was no evidence in her previous contact with Karl to justify this happy thought. A further perception that Louise generated was: 'Karl was deeply engrossed in his conversation with Anna and his reverting his eyes to her did not mean anything negative about me'. She evaluated this as a realistic perception based on the evidence of their contact together.

Thinksheet 21 aims to give you practice in identifying your perceptual errors and in generating and evaluating different perceptions.

---

**Thinksheet 21    Identifying your perceptual errors and generating and evaluating different perceptions**

*Instructions*
Below is a format for completing this thinksheet.

| A.    The situation | B.    Your feelings (before and during) | C.    Your perceptions (before and during) | D.    Different perceptions you generate |
|---|---|---|---|
|  |  |  |  |

1.    Make a thinksheet similar to this, but with more space in the columns.

2.    Think of a situation where you think a 'stick-in-the-mud' perception may have contributed to your inappropriate negative feelings. Write the situation in column A, the inappropriate feelings in column B and your faulty perceptions in column C. Also in column C, write any perceptual errors, e.g. overgeneralizing, that you consider your perceptions contained.

3.    In column D generate at least five different perceptions relevant to the situation. Evaluate each perception to assess how closely each corresponds with the available facts. Then put a star (*) next to the perceptions that you consider best fit the facts.

4.  Repeat this exercise until you consider that you have developed some lasting self-help skills in identifying your perceptual errors and in generating and evaluating different perceptions.

---

### Choosing to question your perceptions by conducting personal experiments

Sometimes the sequence is that you change your perceptions through logical analysis, behave differently and then get feedback that confirms your changed perceptions. For instance, Katie changed her perceptions about Sandra and improved her listening skills. Consequently, when Sandra came back home she was much more rewarding for Sandra, which in turn made it easier for Sandra to behave in ways that were not 'selfish' and 'hard'.

On other occasions, changes in perception may follow from the carrying out of personal experiments. For instance, even if Katie remained unconvinced that Sandra was not selfish and hard, she might still choose to behave differently and see what happened. Katie could be encouraged to think of this as setting up an experiment to test the hypothesis that *if* she behaved differently in specified ways towards Sandra *then* Sandra would be more caring towards her. Assuming that Sandra then became more caring, Katie's perception of Sandra would alter in light of this feedback. In short, instead of logically analysing *existing* evidence, you change your behaviour to see if it generates *new* evidence to test the accuracy of your perceptions.

Below are some perceptions that might lend themselves to reality testing through appropriately designed personal experiments.

I'm too shy to smile and initiate conversations with people I don't know well.

I'm too nervous to phone and ask for information.

I cannot speak in public without making a fool of myself.

I can't change the tyre on my car.

I might not enjoy myself if I join a karate club.

Now I am separated, my friends will not enjoy coming over and being entertained by me as a single person.

I cannot go on holiday by myself.

He/she is an unfriendly person.

People will reject me if they find out I failed a test last year.

There are a number of considerations when designing, carrying out and evaluating personal experiments.

● Be as clear as possible about your 'If . . . then . . .' hypothesis. You may state your hypothesis either in the positive, e.g. 'If I join a karate club, then I will enjoy myself', or in the negative, e.g. 'If I join a karate club, then I will not enjoy myself'.

● Set yourself clear and realistic goals. Do not try to take on too much.

● Consider a gradual approach, using intermediate personal experiments, if attaining your ultimate goal is difficult.

● Avoid self-rating. The object of the exercise is to collect information that confirms or disconfirms your hypothesis.

● Give yourself a thorough opportunity to implement your different behaviour.

● Use coping self-talk as necessary.

● Use and develop other skills as appropriate.

● Endeavour to evaluate accurately the information generated from your experiment by being sensitive both to the difference between fact and inference and to specific perceptual errors.

● Make sure you change your perceptions to take into account any new evidence from your experiment and remain open to future new evidence.

---

**Thinksheet 22**   Testing the reality of your perceptions by conducting a personal experiment

*Instructions*
Think of a situation in which you perceive you are currently unable to act effectively to meet your needs. Conduct a personal experiment to test the reality of your perception. Go through the following steps.

1.   Clearly state your hypothesis in 'if . . . then . . .' terms.

2.   Make a careful plan of how you intend to go about changing your behaviour.

3.   Implement your plan.

4.   Assess the consequence of your changed behaviour for yourself and for others. Do they merit altering your perceptions?

5.   Clearly state any changed perceptions you have resulting from the findings of your personal experiment.

6.   Practise the self-help skills of conducting personal experiments to test the reality of your

perceptions in other situations where your perceptions may be oppressing rather than supporting you.

---

## PERCEIVING YOURSELF MORE POSITIVELY

Possibly the world's best-known psychology self-help book is Norman Vincent Peale's *The Power of Positive Thinking* (Peale, 1953). Peale's message is simple: negative thinking produces negative results, positive thinking produces positive results. Your perceptions of yourself are a crucial area in which you may be choosing to oppress rather than to support yourself. You can use labels to devalue yourself and lower your confidence. Negative self-labelling is a symptom, cause and effect of severe depression. It is also associated with both moderate and mild feelings of depression and with more minor 'lows'. In varying degrees, negative self-labelling is a characteristic of virtually all humans. It is paradoxical that, despite preferring to have others' approval, many people are extremely reluctant to approve of themselves. At varying levels of awareness you may be engaging in harsh self-criticism that interferes with your happiness and fulfilment.

### Becoming aware of your negative self-labels

Negative self-labels are unrealistically negative perceptions either of your specific characteristics or of yourself as a person. They are overgeneralized perceptions rather than functional ratings that help you attain your goals. For example, negative self-labels that you may apply to your intelligence include: stupid, dumb, an idiot, a fool, slobbish, moronic, thick or a drongo (Australian slang for a 'no hoper', derived from a race horse called Drongo who always managed to come last!). You may apply negative self-labels to other areas, including your body, your sexuality, your social skills, your feelings and emotions, your tastes and preferences, your leisure pursuits or your study and work habits.

You may also perceive yourself as possessing negative traits that are global. You rate yourself negatively as a person. In a study on vulnerability to depression, British researchers Teasdale & Dent (1987) selected the following self-devaluing adjectives from a list of words associated with depression:

| | |
|---|---|
| deficient | stupid |
| failure | unloved |
| inadequate | unwanted |
| incompetent | useless |
| inferior | weak |
| pathetic | worthless |

Another way of looking at negative self-labelling is that you construct a picture or personification of yourself. This personification is your subjective reality. However, as shown earlier, subjective and objective reality do not always correspond. You may be making inferences about yourself that do you less than justice. My experience as a practising counselling psychologist is that most clients' personifications are unrealistically negative. They are much better at listing what is wrong than what is right with themselves. This perceptual deficit of ignoring resources and focusing on failings perpetuates feelings of anxiety, depression and diminished confidence and vitality. Thinksheet 23 encourages you to become more aware of your negative self-labels so that you may challenge and change them.

---

**Thinksheet 23  Becoming aware of your negative self-labels**

*Instructions*
A   Monitoring your self-labelling.

   1.  Take a small note-pad and, for a 24-hour period, jot down the negative and positive perceptions of yourself that enter your awareness. The emphasis is on **your** perceptions so only include feedback from others if you agree with it.

   2.  At the end of the 24-hour period, transfer your perceptions on to a master sheet with NEGATIVE SELF-PERCEPTIONS in one column and POSITIVE SELF-PERCEPTIONS in the other.

   3.  Put a star (*) by each self-perception that you consider may be a negative self-label rather than a realistic assessment of yourself.

   4.  Evaluate what you have learned about yourself.

B   Become aware of your negative self-labelling in different areas.

   1.  Write down your negative self-perceptions in all of the following areas that are relevant to you:

      your body
      your sexuality
      your intelligence
      your study habits
      your occupational life
      your leisure life
      your social life
      your marital life
      your parenting
      your global view of yourself as a person

   2.  Put a star (*) by each self-perception that you consider might be a negative self-label rather than a realistic assessment of yourself.

3.  Evaluate what you have learned about yourself.

---

## Choosing more positive self-perceptions

A number of the skills discussed so far are relevant to altering your negative self-labels to more positive perceptions. You can use questioning, logical analysis, understanding their origins and reality testing through personal experiments. You can also use coping inner speech when dealing with specific situations. Additionally you may develop specific skills, for instance study or relationship skills, that help you to counteract your negative self-labels.

### Reducing negative self-labelling

Below are some further skills that may stop your tendencies to negative self-labelling.

● *Thought stopping*. When you catch yourself in an unproductive negative train of thought, shout to yourself 'stop!' Try to stifle your negative self-labels as soon as you become aware of them. The thoughts are likely to return, but you then repeat the procedure again and again as necessary.

● *Mental vacuuming*. This is a visualization skill advocated by Kassorla (1984). She gets her clients to visualize a tiny toy-like vacuum cleaner sweeping across their foreheads vacuuming up all their negative words and images.

● *Thought switching*. When you find yourself ruminating on negative self-labels, you replace them with positive perceptions and appreciation of positive experiences. For instance, if you feel lonely and inadequate you can switch to thinking of your friends and possibly even contact one. If you perceive that you rarely achieve anything, you can switch to thinking of an achievement that had personal meaning for you. If you dwell on something unpleasant in the future, you can switch to thinking of a positive future event. Thought switching can be combined with thought stopping and mental vacuuming. When negative self-labels creep up on you: (a) instruct yourself to 'stop!'; (b) mentally vacuum the negative self-label away; and (c) switch to a positive self-label or appreciation of a positive experience.

### Increasing positive self-perceptions

Why wait for negative thoughts before you switch to positive thoughts? Be ready to own your positive attributes. If anything the insecurity that leads to conceit comes from unrealistic negative self-labelling rather than from owning realistic positive perceptions. With some of my underconfident clients I negotiate a simple homework assignment in which for a week they stand in front of a mirror for five minutes each day and affirm their worth as a person by saying: 'I'm Joe/Jane Doe and what I think and feel is of value'. Some of you with confidence problems may wish to try this for yourself. It may be artificial, but some clients find that it starts getting the message across to them.

You may need to search for ways of perceiving yourself positively. Leading counselling psychologist Allen Ivey and his colleagues consider that positive asset search is an important and sometimes neglected aspect of counselling and psychotherapy (Ivey *et al.*, 1987). It is also an important and frequently neglected aspect of living. You may dwell on your failures and fail to own your resources. As such you oppress rather than support and affirm yourself.

Here is a vignette, drawn from one of my teenage clients, in which we searched for his resources.

Ben, aged 16, told his life story with dignity, despite the considerable psychological abuse he had suffered, especially from his alcoholic father. His mind went blank when I asked him to state something positive about himself. In one of our early sessions I used a whiteboard and together we searched for and listed his perceived strengths. These included the following:

*Relationships*
I am caring.
I like helping others.
I get on well with my age group.
I am attractive to some girls.
I am strongly heterosexual.
I have a girlfriend.

*Work*
I am willing to learn.
I am good with colleagues and customers in the shop where I work.
I like practical as well as 'head' tasks.

*Leisure*
I like disco dancing.
I like going out with my friends.
I like listening to soft rock music.

Ben required the emotional and practical support of long-term counselling to become more in control of his life and his thinking. Nevertheless, he did much of the work for himself. He managed increasingly to own his positive attributes and, with his growing success, to discard much of his negative self-labelling.

Thinksheet 24 encourages you to identify and own your resources. Remember that habits of negative self-labelling tend to be deeply ingrained, so you may have to work hard to learn and maintain the skill of supporting yourself with honest self-affirmations.

---

**Thinksheet 24    Searching for and affirming your resources**

*Instructions*

1. Search for and write out a list of what you genuinely consider to be your strengths or resources as a person. Start each item with the words 'I am ...' or 'I like ...'. Looking at the list of Ben's perceived resources may help you to get started. Add to your list every day for the next week, if not longer.

2. Every day for a week stand before a mirror and, in a confident voice, read out loud your list of resources at least once.

3. During the day, when you label yourself negatively, instruct yourself to 'stop!' and switch to affirming your resources.

4. Practise, practise and practise to build up the discipline of supporting and affirming yourself with honest positive perceptions of your resources.

---

## LETTING GO OF DEFENSIVENESS

There is an old British saying: 'There's nowt so queer as folk'. Perhaps this refers to the human animal's huge capacity for perceiving defensively. 'Defence mechanisms', 'defences' and 'security operations' are other terms for the ways in which people 'operate' on incoming information in order to reduce high anxiety. Their objective is to maintain consistency in their personifications of themselves and others. All of you, in varying degrees, have vestiges of childish ways of handling reality that have now become habits which oppress rather than support you. These defensive processes and perceptions reflect your lack of mental development when, as a child, you needed to protect yourself against a stronger and sometimes frightening world. Since defensive processes and perceptions distance you from reality, they may have serious consequences for yourself and others. The greater your deficits in this area, the less likelihood there is that you will perceive your defensive processes. You do it to yourself and then forget that you have done it.

## Ways of perceiving defensively

The following are some ways in which you may be protecting your picture of
yourself by perceiving defensively. All of them involve diminishing your awareness to make your life more psychologically comfortable in the short-term.

- *Denial*. Denial involves totally blocking off from conscious awareness
something regarded as too frightening or threatening. This might be some
socially stigmatized or undesirable aspect of yourself, such as homosexual
tendencies or hypocrisy.

- *Distortion*. Distortion in this context incorporates all the ways in which you
'operate' on incoming information to maintain your picture of yourself. You
may distort positive feedback to maintain a negative self-picture or negative
feedback to maintain a positive self-picture, or a mixture of the two.

- *Misattribution*. This includes all the various ways in which you attribute
cause so as to protect yourself from assuming full responsibility for your life;
for example, by blaming others needlessly.

- *Rationalization*. Rationalizations are ways of excusing behaviour that causes
anxiety. They differ from excuses in that you do not have full insight into what
you do. In short, you deceive yourself as well as others.

- *Projection*. Projection involves externalizing something which is internal; for
example, having difficulty controlling your sexual urges and setting yourself
up as a guardian of public morality. This seems to have been a problem for
certain American television evangelists.

- *Reaction formation*. You form reactions that are the opposite of what you
really feel; for instance, repulsion masking sexual attraction or love masking
intense anger.

- *Avoidance*. Avoidance is a common manifestation of denial; for example, by
remaining unaware that you avoid a difficult person or situation.

- *Defences against the good*. Blocking off or diluting both the awareness of and
the manifestation of positive qualities such as generosity and concern for
others.

- *Attack*. You attack and intimidate others who provide or might provide
unwelcome feedback to you; going for their jugular vein. As an example,
imagine what Hitler's reaction would have been to being told he was a mass
murderer.

- *Defensive lying*. This involves making up stories about yourself and others
which are intended to make you seem in the right and the other person seem in
the wrong. You give way to the Nelson-Jones Reality Principle, 'if you can't

accept reality, create it!' Defensive lying differs from deliberate lying in that you believe the distortions of reality contained in your dishonesty.

## Choosing to give up your defensive processes

Relinquishing your defensive processes can be difficult. You may want to hold on tenaciously to your version of reality. There is a joke about a psychiatrist who worked unsuccessfully for three months with a patient who thought he was dead. Finally, in frustration, the psychiatrist asked the patient, 'Do dead men bleed?', to which he replied, 'No'. The psychiatrist pulled out a scalpel, slashed the patient's forefinger and held it up to his face. In amazement the patient observed: 'Well, blow me doc, dead men *do* bleed!'

Letting go of childish ways of thinking can be hard for a number of reasons. You may have an illusion of rationality. You may not know what processes to look for. These processes may be partially or totally submerged below your awareness. Relinquishing defensive perceptions reveals a different you. This may be highly threatening, sometimes even if the new information is positive.

The first step in giving up your defensive processes is to realize their existence in almost all people, including yourself. The second step is to know what the various processes are. The third step is to review and monitor your behaviour to see if you possess any of these processes. Since they are rarely fully in your awareness, you may only get glimpses of them. For instance, if you catch yourself reacting sharply to criticism, you may question the justification for your reaction. When you calm down, you may realize the criticism was accurate, although you did not wish to hear it. You may then become aware that attack is one of your defensive ways of maintaining your picture of yourself. If you catch yourself blaming other people for characteristics you are unhappy with in yourself, then you may become aware that projection is one of your defensive processes.

Once you have become aware of a defensive process, tell yourself: 'I can get by without this childish way of thinking'. Then work hard to identify the triggers for your defensiveness and to catch it early on. For instance, if you know that you have a tendency to get defensive when someone questions whether you behave consistently, calm down, acknowledge your tendency to over-react, and think about the most appropriate response given the available evidence. Use your skills of distinguishing inference from fact and of evaluating the realism of your inferences. Additionally it is much easier for you to acknowledge and fight against your defensive processes if you can overcome certain self-oppressing personal rules. These mustabatory rules include: 'I *must* be rational at all times; I *must* be perfect; I *must* never make mistakes; others *must* think me rational at all times; others *must* agree with my picture of myself'.

Defensive processes, once identified, require constant guarding against. They represent well developed ways of distorting reality. Sometimes they may perform a benign self-protective function in allowing you to acknowledge information at a time and rate that you feel strong enough to process it. Most often your defensive processes are self-oppressing. Additionally, they can be incredibly painful for others; for instance, you may act dishonestly towards them, then attack them for noticing that you have acted dishonestly and then further attack them for reacting negatively to your attack. The fact that you may have identified and overcome a defensive process once does not mean that you are immune to it recurring. The probability is that it will and that you will have to work and practise to keep on top of it.

Thinksheet 25 has been designed to help you start exploring your defensive processes in the hope that you choose, and keep choosing, to fight against them and to think more rationally.

---

**Thinksheet 25    Letting go of your defensive processes**

*Instructions*

1.  Make out a thinksheet in which you list the following defensive processes. Do this at the left-hand margin and leave a space under each.

    denial
    distortion
    misattribution
    rationalization
    projection
    reaction formation
    avoidance
    defences against the good
    attack
    defensive lying

2.  Write out your assessment of the extent to which you engage in each of these defensive processes. Where possible, cite specific examples of how you do it.

3.  Spend some time every day for the next week reviewing your thinking and behaviour on that day and seeing if you can add information to your thinksheet about your defensive processes.

4.  Develop and implement a plan to let go of each of your defensive processes.

5.  Work hard to relinquish your defensive processes in your daily life, both now and in the future.

---

## PERCEIVING OTHERS MORE REALISTICALLY

Two-thirds of what we see is behind our eyes.

*Chinese proverb*

The way you choose to perceive others can support or oppress others as well as you. You may negatively label them in ways that have unwanted repercussions for both of you. Close relationships tend to go through cycles of alienation and affection. Persistently labelling your partner negatively is a sure way of decreasing affection and increasing alienation, possibly to breaking point. Here I briefly look at ways in which you may bring perceptual distortions into your dealings with others. Although I focus on close personal relationships, the discussion has relevance for less intimate work and personal contacts.

## Becoming aware of your perceptual distortions of others

When you develop a close relationship each of you brings a learning history of strengths and weaknesses in how you perceive. When you first meet you may have little information about each other, then gradually you each develop a fuller picture. However, the course of true love rarely flows smoothly. Here I focus on three perceptual roadblocks to genuine intimacy: personifying your partner inaccurately; misperceiving your partner's power; and misperceiving your partner's intentions and behaviour.

### *Personifying your partner inaccurately*

Two people in a relationship relate to their personifications of each other and of themselves. These are of varying degrees of accuracy. You may think: 'I'm living with him/her all the time . . . I know him/her like the back of my hand.' However, this is frequently not the case. There are two main reasons why you may have an inaccurate picture of your partner: lack of information and your perceptual errors.

*Lack of information.* As people get to know each other they discover more in both breadth and depth. Breadth refers to the number of topic areas you discuss, such as sport, money or sex. Depth refers to the intimacy level of your disclosures and the degree to which each of you is prepared to take the risk of being esteemed less by the other because of your disclosures. Many relationships get stuck at a level of self-disclosure that falls short of genuine intimacy. Since partners tend to match each other's behaviours, this consolidates the stuckness.

There are many reasons why you may know less than you think about your partner. Your partner may lack 'talking about myself' skills. You too may lack disclosing skills, which in turn makes it more difficult for your partner to open up. Additionally, you may possess weaknesses in your listening, understanding and showing understanding skills. Thus, rather than encouraging your partner to reveal himself or herself by being safe to talk to, you might be perceived as threatening and unsafe.

*Perceptual errors.* You can use many of the perceptual errors you use to oppress yourself to oppress others too. These errors include: overemphasizing their negative aspects; overgeneralizing, by drawing broad conclusions from specific observations; black and white thinking, such as that your partner either cares for you or does not care at all; and rating them as persons, for instance, 'If my partner does not remember our anniversary he/she is a rotten person'. Additionally, your defensive processes may interfere with the accuracy of your vision. 'My view of me' needs to be sustained by your fulfilling 'my view of you', however inaccurate both these personifications may be.

### Misperceiving your partner's power to control you

The balance of power in your relationship may be unequal. For instance, a husband may have more power over financial resources than his wife, thus putting her at a disadvantage. However, you may also misperceive your partner's power. In particular I refer to the perceptual tendency to misperceive the extent of their power over how you think, feel and act. Although they may influence you they cannot control you. The need for accurate attribution of responsibility for your choices and for owning your thoughts, feelings and actions has already been mentioned.

Here is an example of not owning responsibility for feelings, thoughts and actions. At an American Psychological Association Convention in New York a family therapist showed a video of his work with a rigid American-Greek husband who was justifying battering his wife, 'because her behaviour makes me so angry'. Eventually the therapist confronted and visibly stunned him with the question: 'You're not going to let her keep controlling your behaviour like that are you?' There was applause in the audience. It was an 'aha' experience for the husband to start realizing how he had misperceived his wife's power to control his behaviour. Instead of seeing himself as the victim, he now had the opportunity to accept responsibility for his behaviour.

### Misperceiving your partner's behaviour and intentions

There is a joke about a husband who picked up a woman in a bar, then took her to a motel where they made mad, passionate love until the early hours of the morning. Just before he left the motel, he took out a piece of chalk and made a few chalk marks on his cuff. On his return home his wife asked: 'Where have you been?' He replied: 'I cannot tell a lie. I'm late because I've been making mad, passionate love in a motel with a woman I picked up in a bar.' His wife, spotting the chalk marks, triumphantly replied: 'What do you mean you cannot tell a lie? You've been playing pool all night!' The moral of this story is that the meaning of your intentions and behaviour may not be the same for your partner as for you.

There are a number of research studies that have found that people in distressed marriages are more likely than people in stable marriages to perceive their partner's negative attributes as the cause of their marital problems (for instance,

Jacobson *et al.*, 1985). Distressed couples are quicker to ascribe malicious intent to each other. Other negative attributions they may make are that their partner neither loves nor cares for them and that their partner's personality is flawed. In some instances the negative attributions may have been accurate all along. In other instances, the negative attributions are self-fulfilling prophesies. They were initially inaccurate, but generated the responses that made them accurate. In still other instances, they are consistently inaccurate.

Here is an example of a wife who oppresses both herself and her husband by wrongly inferring a lack of caring from a relationship skills deficit.

> Celia thought that Andrew did not care for her. She wanted him to verbalize and demonstrate his positive feelings for her more. When she did not get the desired demonstrations of love, she became increasingly demanding and aggressive, saying that Andrew 'just did not understand women'. The reality was that Andrew had grown up in a strict family where expressions of feeling were discouraged and sometimes punished. He cared for Celia but lacked the confidence and skills to show it. Celia's misperception of his behaviour and her aggressive demandingness were only making matters worse for both of them.

Inferring negative characteristics to your partner is more likely if you possess certain self-oppressing personal rules. Some rules that lay the groundwork for marital dissatisfaction include: 'I *must* always win in a conflict; my partner *must* always fulfil my demands; my partner *must* never challenge my fantasy of myself'.

## Choosing to change your perceptions of others

How can you get greater accuracy into your perceptions of others? People can blossom and be much more cooperative if they feel appreciated. Consequently, you can support both yourself and them by working hard to counteract your destructive negative perceptions of others that are not based on reality. Although the focus here is on close personal relationships, the skills listed below are also relevant to how accurately you perceive others in many contexts.

● *Collecting more information.* By using good listening and self-disclosing skills, you make it safe for your partner to reveal more. Are you leading unnecessarily secret lives with each other? If so, try to be more open and supportive of each other.

● *Understanding the origins of your partner's behaviour.* Get to know the influences that have shaped your partner. What rules and directives were received from her or his family or origin and from other sources? What struggles and disappointments has he or she had and how well have they been coped with? A fuller knowledge of your partner's background may make it easier for you to forgive any perceived transgressions.

● *Correcting your specific perceptual errors*. Try to identify what they are and then choose not to let them interfere with the quality of your relationship.

● *Owning more responsibility for your problems*. Do not erroneously attribute the power to control your thoughts, feelings and actions to your partner. You are responsible for choosing how you perceive both others and yourself.

● *Using logical analysis*. When you start getting persistent negative feelings about your partner, say to yourself: 'Stop . . . think . . . what are my perceptual choices?' Use your skills of distinguishing fact from inference and also of assessing the validity of your inferences.

● *Conducting personal experiments*. Try altering your behaviour to see if your negative perceptions of your partner are as much a function of your behaviour as they are of his or hers. Just as partners tend to match negative behaviours, they also tend to match positive behaviours. There may be realistic opportunities for you to behave differently and so lessen your negative perceptions of each other.

● *Altering oppressing personal rules*. Try to become aware of the mustabatory demands you make on others. Question these oppressing rules and reformulate them into rules that are more supportive of others. Work hard to stop laying 'heavy trips' on others in terms of how you expect them to behave.

● *Improving specific relationship skills*. You may need to develop further certain relationship skills; for instance, your managing anger and conflict skills.

There are no easy solutions to clearing up how you perceive your partner. Some people's negative perceptions of their partners reflect their own deep insecurities. If so, they may require professional counselling. Even if you are not deeply anxious, you still have to work hard to discipline your thinking. This is especially likely when you are in conflict or under great stress.

---

Thinksheet 26    Choosing to perceive others more realistically

*Instructions*
Answer the following questions.
1.  Regarding either your partner or some other person of your choice, assess the extent and ways in which you:

    (a)  personify them inaccurately

(b)   misperceive their power to control you

(c)   misperceive their behaviour and intentions.

2.   If you consider some of your perceptions either of your partner or of some other person are inaccurate, assess the extent to which each of the following might help you to perceive him or her more realistically:

(a)   collecting more information

(b)   understanding the origins of his or her behaviour

(c)   correcting specific perceptual errors of yours

(d)   owning more responsibility for controlling your behaviour

(e)   using logical analysis

(f )   conducting personal experiments

(g)   altering oppressing personal rules

(h)   improving specific relationship skills.

3.   Set yourself clear and realistic goals for perceiving your partner or another person more realistically, then develop and implement a plan to achieve your goals.

4.   Assess the costs and consequences to you of choosing to work on discarding your unrealistic perceptions either of your partner or of another person.

---

## CHAPTER HIGHLIGHTS

You have a choice regarding how you perceive yourself and others.

How you perceive influences how you feel and act.

Facts are the true data of experience; inferences are deductions and conclusions drawn from that data.

You can learn to regulate your feelings by becoming more aware of your unrealistic perceptions and perceptual errors; and also by altering them through using the skills of logical analysis and conducting personal experiments.

By labelling yourself negatively you oppress rather than support yourself.

You can learn to become more aware of your unrealistic negative perceptions both of your specific characteristics and of yourself as a person.

Skills of reducing negative self-labelling include thought stopping, mental vacuuming and thought switching.

Skills of increasing positive self-perceptions include searching for and affirming your resources.

Defensive processes and perceptions are ways of maintaining your self-picture by changing and distorting discrepant feedback.

You may choose to let go of the childish ways of thinking involved in defensive processes, but this requires awareness and much work and practice.

Three ways in which you may misperceive others are: personifying them inaccurately; misperceiving their power to control how you think, feel and act; and misperceiving their behaviour and intentions.

Relevant skills for perceiving others more realistically include: collecting more information; understanding the origins of their behaviour; correcting specific perceptual errors; owning more responsibility for controlling your behaviour; using logical analysis; conducting personal experiments; altering oppressing personal rules; and improving specific relationship skills.

# 7 Attributing Cause

It is the act of an ill-instructed man to blame others for his own bad condition; it is the act of one who has begun to be instructed to lay the blame on himself; and of one whose instruction has been completed, neither to blame another, nor himself.

*Epictetus*

In Chapter 3 I introduced the notion of attributing responsibility accurately both for authorship of your life and also for your everyday problems and decisions. Here I elaborate on the relationship between your motivation and how you attribute cause for what happens in your life. Attributions are the explanations, interpretations or reasons you give yourself for what happens. They influence how you think about the future as well as how you feel and act. The theory is that you always seek explanations of what happens to you so that you can accurately understand and predict your world. This then enables you to act more effectively. The practice is somewhat different. You may make numerous explanatory errors that interfere with your motivation and effectiveness. Three areas of potential attributional error are focused on here. They are attributing cause for your problems, for positive and negative events and for academic success and failure.

## ATTRIBUTING CAUSE FOR YOUR PROBLEMS

### Failure to acknowledge problems

When you are attributing cause for your problems it is important to be able to separate fact from inference and to use your skills of making realistic inferences where there are limited facts. However, before you can attribute causes for your problems you must acknowledge their existence. Denial is one way of dealing with problems. For instance, in the immediate aftermath, people may deny the deaths of their loved ones. With more everyday problems they may say 'I'm not anxious' or 'I'm not depressed' rather than accept the challenge to their existing self-perceptions posed by these feelings. Also, in your relationships, it may be psychologically more comfortable to deny anger and conflict rather than to acknowledge their existence. However, the risk here is that these negative emotions fester and worsen. Then they may either 'come out sideways' in activities like gossip or directly in aggressive outbursts.

Not locating problems in yourself is another way of distancing yourself from their existence. For instance, in the case of a misbehaving child, neither the child nor his or her parents may own that they have a problem. The child thinks the parents' reaction to the misbehaviour is their problem and the parents consider the misbehaviour is a problem located in the child. The parents may fail to acknowledge that they too have a problem of how to deal with the child's misbehaviour if it bothers them. The child may thoroughly enjoy misbehaving, but be worried about parental reactions to it. Consequently, the child may need to own the problem of how to cope with negative parental reactions.

Another way of not locating problems in yourself is to project them defensively on to others. Thus, if you are unconsciously concerned about your own homosexual tendencies, you become very aware of homosexuality in others. This may even go as far as active oppression of homosexuals.

## Misattributing causes of problems

Once you have acknowledged the existence of a problem, there are many misattributions that can help you to stay unnecessarily stuck with it. These explanations are often partial truths that, because they are incorrectly treated as whole truths, weaken your motivation for change. They lead to predictions either that you will be unsuccessful in changing or that you will be unable to change unless others do first. Below is a list of possible misattributions about the causes of your problems.

- *It's my genes.* Undoubtedly your genetic endowment has limited your physical characteristics, for instance height, and abilities, for instance intellectual and musical ability. However, many people's work and study problems are compounded if not caused by lack of effort rather than lack of ability. Saying that you are naturally an angry person or that it is natural to feel angry obscures the role of your choices in generating and sustaining your anger.

- *It's my mental illness.* The concept of mental illness is a huge disservice perpetrated by the medical profession on an unsuspecting public. It overemphasizes the roles of heredity and physical factors in human problems and underemphasizes the roles of learning and choice. Fortunately, many physicians and most psychologists recognize that the concept of mental illness is largely a myth, except that there are a few, albeit important, biologically influenced conditions, such as schizophrenia.

● *It's my unfortunate past.* Your unfortunate past, or 'what others did to you', may have contributed to your acquiring skills weaknesses that make you prone to problems. However, you sustain your skills weaknesses mainly by 'what you do to yourself'. Some people with unfortunate pasts require counselling help to give them the nurturing and healing they never received from their natural parents. Many people, with or without professional help, have learned to overcome the skills deficiencies caused by their unfortunate pasts.

● *It's my bad luck.* Undoubtedly luck does play a part in life. However, you either wait for your luck to change, which may be for ever, or make your own luck. As one very successful golfer put it: 'The more and more I practise, the luckier and luckier I get'.

● *It's my poor environment.* As mentioned in Chapter 3, adverse social and economic conditions may make it more difficult for you to fulfil yourself. However, as in the example of Viktor Frankl and the Nazi concentration camps, you still have a choice in regard to how you cope with these deprivations.

● *It's all their fault.* Here at least you acknowledge that you have a problem, but attribute its cause entirely to another or others. Instead of looking from inside to outside, you look from outside to inside. Since you do not like what you see, this provides a convenient excuse for not looking at your own behaviour. Since it is all their fault, others must change before you can. Thus you allow others' behaviour to control your life.

● *It's all my fault.* This can be a misattribution of very depressed people. All negative events in their lives are their fault. Consequently, by overgeneralizing they weaken their confidence and motivation for dealing with the realistic difficulties in their lives.

● *The future is hopeless.* You may feel overwhelmed and not know where to start. The future may seem hopeless and you feel helpless to influence events. The fact that you have many problems does not mean that you have to work on them all right away. Instead, you may choose to work on one or a few and then move on to others when you are ready. Also, your perception of the amount and difficulty of your problems may alter as you start having your first and then subsequent successes.

● *I've tried before.* You may have tried to overcome your problems before and been unsuccessful. However, this need not be your guide to the future. For instance, this time you may try harder, possess more skills at coping with your problems and with setbacks, and be better at enlisting the support of others. The fact that you have tried before does not mean that you cannot now learn new and better skills to help you succeed.

● *I can't stand setbacks.* Setbacks are a part of learning any new skill. Problems are a part of living. Your unrealistic expectations about the learning process and smoothness of life make you vulnerable to setbacks. You can develop the skills of learning to handle stressful situations better and of being able to support rather than to oppress yourself when faced with setbacks.

### Changing misattributions about the causes of problems

Changing any misattributions you may have about the causes of your problems involves awareness, choice and action.

#### Awareness

You need to be aware in two ways. First, you need to acknowledge that *you* have a problem. Second, you need to become aware of what your specific misattributions are. Whenever you find yourself either unable to or not wishing to work on a problem, ask yourself whether you are eroding your motivation and confidence through unproductive misattributions. Then try to identify which ones you use.

#### Choice

If you think your misattributions may be helping you to stay stuck rather than to work on your problems, you can challenge them by logical analysis, gathering additional information and conducting personal experiments. Some ways of challenging your misattributions through logical analysis are provided in the descriptions for the previous list of misattributions. For instance, the misattribution 'it's my unfortunate past' might be disputed with examples of how people have overcome unfortunate pasts by learning new and better skills, possibly in more benign environments.

Misattributions like 'it's my genes' and 'it's my mental illness' can be challenged by collecting additional information. For instance, a maths aptitude test might provide more realistic information for someone attributing his problems in maths to biologically based inability. He may discover that his aptitude is higher than he realized. This in turn raises the issue of whether he is underachieving for other reasons, such as lack of effort, poor teaching, high anxiety or other stresses. People who think they are mentally ill can check with a competent helping professional. This is a matter of being screened for any biologically influenced mental disorders; if none are present, people receive information that helps them conceptualize their problems in learning terms.

Misattributions like 'the future is hopeless' and 'I can't stand setbacks' can be tested by personal experiments. You approach working on your problems by seeking to collect new information.

Whenever you successfully challenge a misattribution, make sure that you reformulate it in appropriate self-talk. For instance, the misattribution 'the future is hopeless' might be reformulated as 'I've started to work on my problems and, though I have still got to develop a lot more skills, I have made progress in doing so. I now think I can cope with the future.' In brief, 'the future is hopeless' becomes 'I can cope with the future'.

## Action

When you carry out personal experiments to challenge misattributions, you are already engaged in action. However, when you have convinced yourself through logical analysis or the collection of additional information that you misattribute the cause or causes of your problem, you still need to act on this insight. The only way to do this is to start working hard to change your behaviour in the problem area in question. It is hoped that you will now be free from misattributions that interfere with your motivation to change in your own best interests.

---

**Thinksheet 27    Changing misattributions about the causes of your problems**

*Instructions*
1.  Either for a particular problem you want to work on or in regard to your approach to your personal problems in general, note the extent to which you make or have made each of the attributional errors listed below on the following scale:

| | |
|---|---|
| Never | 0 |
| Sometimes | 1 |
| Frequently | 2 |

| *Misattribution* | *Your rating* |
|---|---|
| It's my genes. | _____ |
| It's my mental illness. | _____ |
| It's my unfortunate past. | _____ |
| It's my bad luck. | _____ |
| It's my poor environment. | _____ |
| It's all their fault. | _____ |
| It's all my fault. | _____ |
| The future is hopeless. | _____ |
| I've tried before. | _____ |
| I can't stand setbacks. | _____ |

2.  Challenge any misattributions with a rating of 1 or 2:
    **either** by logical analysis
    **or** by indicating what additional information you require
    **or** by formulating an appropriate personal experiment
    **or** by a mixture of one or more of the above.
3.  Reformulate each misattribution into appropriate self-talk that accurately attributes the cause or causes for your problem or problems.

4.   Assess the extent and manner in which altering self-oppressing misattributions into self-supporting attributions will free you to work more effectively on your problem or problems.

---

## ATTRIBUTING CAUSE FOR POSITIVE AND NEGATIVE EVENTS

The way you attribute cause for positive and negative events in your life may be either accurate or inaccurate. As such, it can affect both your motivation and your self-esteem. The importance of making accurate attributions about positive and negative events is illustrated here in relation to depression.

### Becoming aware of depressive attributions

There are many different reasons why people feel depressed. Some of these relate to areas covered in previous chapters, such as self-oppressing personal rules and perceptions. Another contributing factor may be that people who are depressed feel powerless or helpless to influence their environments to achieve desired outcomes. This is a position advocated by psychologists Lyn Abramson, Martin Seligman and John Teasdale (1978). The reason why people feel helpless is that they have learned a depressive attributional style when faced with negative events, for instance an unsuccessful job search.

Three main components are proposed for a depressive attributional style:

- *Internal attributions*. Negative events are seen as something caused by you as a person as opposed to something about the situation. For example, at the two extremes, an unsuccessful job search might be 'totally because of other people or circumstances' (external) or 'totally because of me' (internal). In varying degrees, it may be a mixture of the two.

- *Stable attributions*. Negative events are viewed as caused by non-transient factors in contrast to transient ones. Thus their effects are permanent. For instance, at the two extremes, the causes of an unsuccessful job search 'will never again be present' (unstable) or 'will always be present' (stable). Again, a mixture of the two is possible.

- *Global attributions*. Negative events are viewed as being the result of causes present in a variety of situations in contrast to causes specific to the situation in question. For instance, at the two extremes, the cause for an unsuccessful job search might be something that 'influences just this particular situation' (specific) or that 'influences all situations in my life' (global). Yet again, a mixture of the two is possible.

There is little doubt that you can undermine your effectiveness and mood by misattributing the causes both of negative and of positive events in your life. However, research findings on the relationship between depression and internal, stable and global attributions have been inconsistent. In a survey of the research literature by Peterson *et al.* (1985), roughly half the studies supported the links between internal and stable attributions and depression. Approximately three-quarters of the studies supported the links between global attributions and depression. There are problems in measuring attributional style, especially inter-nality, that may contribute to these inconsistent findings.

Below is a vignette of how an inaccurate internal attribution can adversely affect mood and leave you feeling more vulnerable.

Nancy and Gary experienced a lot of conflict in their marriage, not least because Gary was having an affair with Linda, an executive in the company that he managed. Recently, Nancy and Gary had made progress in their relationship and Gary said that he was trying to disengage from Linda. However, Gary later went on a business trip with Linda and shared a hotel room with her, although they did not have intercourse. Nancy found out and was depressed and also furious with Gary. This was partly because underneath she blamed herself for Gary's behaviour.

Thinksheet 28 encourages you to explore your attributional style for negative and positive events. It seeks to raise your awareness concerning how you may be lowering your motivation and mood by making attributional errors. Unlike Peterson and his colleagues' Attributional Style Questionnaire (Peterson *et al.*, 1982), the thinksheet asks you to focus on real as contrasted with hypothetical events.

---

**Thinksheet 28** Assessing how you make attributions about the causes of negative and positive events.

*Instructions*
1. Identify one recent or current event in your life in each of the following categories.

    (a) A negative event in one of your relationships, e.g. a row with someone.

    (b) A negative event in your work/study life, e.g. not getting a promotion, getting a low mark.

    (c) A positive event in one of your relationships, e.g. receiving appreciation from someone.

(d)   A positive event in your work/study life, e.g. receiving a salary increase, getting a high mark.

2.   For each of the above negative and positive events:

(a)   Write down the **one** major cause.

(b)   Rate the major cause on each of the following scales.

(i)   External–internal attribution.

Totally due to other
people or circumstances       1  2  3  4  5   Totally due to me

(ii)   Unstable–stable attribution.

Will never again be present   1  2  3  4  5   Will always be present

(iii)   Specific–global attribution.

Influences just this                                    Influences all situations
particular situation              1  2  3  4  5   in my life

3.   Assess what doing this thinksheet has suggested to you.

(a)   About the way in which you attribute cause for negative and positive events in your life.

(b)   What influence this has on your motivation and mood.

(c)   Whether and in what ways you need to change the ways in which you attribute cause for negative and positive events.

---

## Altering depressive attributions

Once you become aware that you may have a depressive attributional style concerning the causes of negative and positive events in your life, you can choose to alter it. The main way to do this is to monitor and question your attributions and then search for alternative explanations. Following this you select the attribution or attributions that best fit the facts in a particular situation. You should regard internal–external, stable–unstable and specific–global as potentially useful dimensions for thinking about your attributions. However, make sure that you avoid the trap of black-and-white thinking. What you seek is accurate or realistic attribution and frequently this entails attributing cause somewhere between the extremes on each dimension. When you have decided on a 'best fit' attribution, put it into simple and clear English so that you can remember and use it when necessary.

## ATTRIBUTING CAUSE FOR ACADEMIC SUCCESS AND FAILURE

### Becoming aware of your attributions

If you are a student, your motivation to achieve, and hence your achievements, can be influenced by how you attribute cause for your academic successes and failures. Suppose you have a test coming up. The following are four categories of attribution suggested by Weiner & Kukla (1970) that you may use before the test and also when evaluating how you did.

• *Ability*. This is an internal and stable attribution. Ability is something with which you were born. You have varying degrees of ability in different areas. Your levels of ability are basically outside of your control.

• *Effort*. This is an internal and variable attribution. Effort is more a matter of choice than of genetic endowment. It is largely within your control.

• *Task difficulty*. This is generally viewed as an external attribution. It is comprised of the realistic difficulty of the task and any of your perceptual distortions that magnify or minimize this. While the realistic difficulty of the task may be outside your control, the message of this book is that your perceptual distortions are potentially within your control. Thus, where perceptual distortions occur, what may first appear as an external category of attribution might also be viewed as an internal category.

• *Luck*. Good luck and its opposite bad luck are external attributions. Your academic successes and failures are due to chance. As such, they are outside of your control.

You can attribute a specific academic success or failure to all four of the above (ability, effort, task difficulty and luck) in varying degrees. You might also make attributions that are different from the above; for instance, poor teaching and incompetent marking. Additionally, there are numerous socioeconomic considerations that are relevant to how motivated people are to achieve academically and to how much effort they can put in. For instance, if you live in a noisy home, with few books, with no one who has achieved academically and with no one who is interested in your academic success, it may be much harder to make the required effort than if you live in the opposite circumstances. If as a student you have to support yourself with part-time jobs, you have less time and energy for academic pursuits. Additionally, your gender may have either contributed to or worked against your academic motivation and achievement. Females in particular may have been discouraged from attaining their full academic potential. However, higher education participation rates indicate that this situation is changing in Western countries.

There is considerable research evidence suggesting 'self-serving bias', in that people are more likely to take responsibility for their successes than for their failures. The results of a series of studies conducted in Australia by Herbert Marsh (1986) indicate that this self-serving bias is likely to be larger for the more able than for the less able students. A possible reason for this is that failure may be harder for more able than for less able students to accept, since it is more discrepant with their academic self-perceptions. In the short-term the self-serving bias may give students some artificial motivation in that they have cushioned themselves against discouragement. In the long-term they may find that they have been living in a 'fool's paradise' in which they have failed to make realistic connections between their failures and inadequate effort.

Below are some vignettes that highlight the importance of being able to make accurate attributions for your academic successes and failures.

> Rachel is a second-year psychology student at university. She is thinking of giving up psychology because she thinks she does not have the ability to do statistics. The reality is that Rachel's numerical ability is above average, but so is her numerical anxiety!

> Khalid is a 13-year-old Pakistani secondary school student who is 'under-achieving'. His use of English is still poor because his family migrated from Pakistan 18 months ago and English is a second and new language for him. He despairs at his inability to keep up with his classmates. At times he thinks he is stupid.

> Ching is an Asian student in mechanical engineering whose parents have made sacrifices to send him overseas. Ching is repeating the first year of his course. Even though he works all the time, the staff doubt if he has the ability to complete the course. Ching refuses to accept this feedback since he is terrified of going home as a failure.

> Sarah is a 15-year-old school student who cannot believe her luck. She has received A grades for her two most recent history assignments. She tells her friends: 'I just cannot believe that this is happening to me'. Her parents tell her that this is no fluke since she has finally started to take her homework seriously. They say her A grades are the reward for effort.

In each of the above vignettes, attributions are related to unfounded predictions and to possible self-defeating actions. Rachel might unnecessarily give up her psychology major. Khalid is at risk of stopping trying to catch up. Ching may keep 'bashing his head against a brick wall' rather than accept his limited ability for mechanical engineering. Although her parents are doing their best to make the connection between effort and outcome, if Sarah persists in thinking her success on her history assignments is due solely to luck she may stop working so hard.

## Altering unrealistic attributions

There are many thinking skills weaknesses that contribute to erroneous attributions concerning academic success and failure. Your personal rules may be such that you set yourself unrealistically high standards and so unnecessarily have to seek explanations for your failures. Your manner of perceiving maybe such that it is easier for you to notice either your failures or successes. Additionally, you may talk yourself into failing rather than succeeding.

As in all instances when your attributions may be faulty, you first try to become aware that this is the case and to identify specific questionable attributions. Then you question and dispute these seemingly shaky attributions to see the extent to which they are supported by facts. Where necessary, you then generate alternative attributions and consider which have the best fit. If necessary, you collect additional information. For instance, if Rachel's previous maths record did not give her sufficient information she could take a numerical aptitude test. She could also talk to someone in her university counselling service about her anxiety over statistics.

You can also conduct personal experiments to test the accuracy of your attributions about academic success and failure. For instance, Khalid might keep making an effort to see if he could catch up with his peers. Furthermore, he and his parents might look into the possibility of extra individual or group tutoring in remedial English. When you finally choose an attribution that best fits the facts, try to verbalize it simply and clearly so that you can use it in future. Just as you can do much to damage yourself by making inaccurate attributions concerning the causes of your academic success and failure, so you may do much to support yourself by verbalizing accurate attributions.

Thinksheet 29 encourages you to look at the attributions you make concerning success and failure. Although it is primarily aimed at students it is also relevant, with some adaptation, to those of you in other forms of work.

---

**Thinksheet 29**   Accurately attributing cause for your academic successes and failures

*Instructions*

1.   For this thinksheet academic successes are defined as results that pleased you and academic failures as results that displeased you. Get a piece of paper and draw a line down the centre. At the top of the left hand column write ACADEMIC SUCCESSES and at the top of the right hand column write ACADEMIC FAILURES.

2.   For your current or most recent academic experience, write down in the relevant column the extent to which each of the following causes accounts for or accounted for any academic successes and failures that you may be having or have had.

   ability
   effort
   anxiety

      task difficulty
      staff competence
      luck
      socioeconomic considerations
      gender-related considerations

3. Do you detect a self-serving bias in which you accept more responsibility for your academic successes than for your academic failures? If so, how big is it and what do you think about it?

4. Question and dispute any seemingly inaccurate attributions you possess concerning the causes of your academic successes and failures. Search for alternative attributions that best fit the facts. Put your best fit attributions into clear and simple English.

5. Think through what actions you need to take to support yourself in line with any changed attributions you have chosen concerning the causes of your academic successes and failures.

---

## CHAPTER HIGHLIGHTS

Attributions of cause are your explanations of what happens.

Failure to attribute cause accurately for your problems interferes with your motivation for change.

Misattribution about the cause of positive and negative events in your life can adversely influence your feelings and actions.

There is some evidence that depressive attributions are unnecessarily internal, stable and global.

Misattributions about the causes of academic success and failure can weaken both your motivation and your achievement.

Thinking skills for changing misattribution of cause include logical analysis and designing personal experiments.

# 8 Predicting and Creating Your Future

Like the prototype of the scientist that he is man seeks prediction.

*George Kelly*

*The future*. Anxiety about living in the context of anxiety about dying.

Humans lead their lives into the future. The future is the focus of most of their desires, hopes and fears. Sometimes their view of the future is bleak. George Orwell had a character in *1984* say: 'If you want a picture of the future, imagine a boot stamping on the human face—for ever'. Sometimes their view is rosy, perhaps unjustifiably so. The eighteenth-century wit Samuel Johnson said of a man who remarried immediately after the death of a wife with whom he had been very unhappy that it was 'the triumph of hope over experience'.

What is your future? One way of looking at your future is that it is what actually happens, or the objective reality of future events when they happen. This includes future events that you can influence and also those that are beyond your influence. Another way of looking at your future is that it is a mental construction based on your subjective as contrasted with objective reality. It is the words and pictures in your head about what is to come. You have no facts about the future since it has not happened. However, it is a fertile breeding ground for inferences of varying degrees of accuracy. You can also formulate goals and make plans to shape what is to come.

The way you view your future incorporates your attitude to time. Time is objective in terms of seconds, minutes and hours. However, it is also subjective. You may either contemplatively savour time or feel under constant pressure to use time to achieve. The latter attitude has been termed 'hurry sickness' by Friedman & Rosenman (1974) in their book analysing predictors of heart disease,

*Type A Behavior and Your Heart.* This constant time urgency affects people's attitudes to their present and future and also their life expectancy. Expressions like 'wasting time' put a subjective value, that of wasting, on to an objective concept, time as expressed in seconds, minutes and hours. Another way of viewing both time and the future is in terms of quantity and quality. Neither presupposes the other. For instance, you may either have a long and miserable life or be dying and still experience high-quality living.

This chapter examines two ways in which you may influence your future: making predictions of risk and reward, and setting goals.

## PREDICTING RISK AND REWARD

Let me assert my firm belief that the only thing we have to fear is fear itself.
*Franklin D. Roosevelt*

Fortis fortuna adiuvat (Fortune aids the brave).
*Terence (c. 190–159* B.C.)

As you lead your life into the future you constantly assess the probable outcomes of your actions. You also make predictions concerning others' actions and environmental events. George Kelly (1955b) took a rational approach to prediction when he wrote: 'The two factors from which predictions are made are the number of replications already observed and the amount of similarity which can be abstracted among the replications' (p. 53). However, predictions can also contain perceptual distortions. For instance, a pessimist might predict that it is always going to rain, an optimist that it is always going to be sunny, and a realist something in between. Since your predictions can either help you, by being accurate inferences, or oppress you, by being perceptual distortions, they are very important. Although you make predictions about others' actions and the environment, here I focus on making predictions about the risks and rewards of your own actions. In this context, risks may be defined as the chances of bad consequences and rewards as the chances of good consequences. You may overestimate or underestimate the probability of bad consequences or good consequences.

### Predicting risk inaccurately

Predicting risk and reward are interrelated. Here, I will first treat them separately before treating them together in the section on choosing to predict more accurately.

*Underestimating bad consequences*

You may deny or minimize the chances of bad consequences arising from your actions. Such perceptual distortions are highly relevant to preventive health measures. The research in this area suggests that people demonstrate a pervasive tendency to underestimate their own, relative to other people's, risk for various illnesses and negative life events (Weinstein, 1980, 1984). Thus, 'it is less likely to happen to me' may extend to total denial, 'it will not happen to me', for some people. The outcome of these unrealistic predictions is that people may fail to take proper care of their health and so become more rather than less at risk. Some of the underestimation of risk in health matters may be attributed to ignorance, some to negligence and possibly some also represents anxiety and denial about the prospect of death. Money is another area where many people underestimate the chances of bad consequences. In fact, many money problems are the direct result of distorted prediction, be it on the stockmarket, the racetrack or in grandiose business ventures. Getting married is a further area where a realistic assessment of negative consequences may fail to take place before rather than after the event!

*Overestimating bad consequences*

Fears about change, about failure and about success are three aspects of overestimating the negative consequences of your actions.

• *Fear of change.* You may have built up a way of dealing with the world that is based on the assumption 'the known ways are safest and best'. Change involves taking the risk of moving beyond the safety of the known. As such you may see it as a bad consequence in its own right. Here is a vignette illustrating this point.

Sean is a 30-year-old single man who still lives with his parents. He struggles with a number of decisions: moving out of home, changing his job and starting to go out with women. Over the years Sean has chosen consistently to make the safety rather than the growth choice. He is now terrified of change.

• *Fear of failure.* Failure can be defined in many ways depending on the area under consideration and your subjective standards. It often consists of two elements: fear of the occurrence of negative consequences and fear about your ability to cope with them if they occur. Additionally negative consequences can be magnified to the point both where they turn into catastrophes (Argyle, 1988). Also, you can unrealistically take them as reflections on your whole personhood. Fears of failure and of rejection are part of all relationships. In fact, for many they are present every time you open your mouth. For instance, most people are extremely sensitive about how their revelations of what they dislike and like about themselves will be received. In varying degrees they lead unnecessarily secret lives and may have a double standard by which they judge themselves more harshly than others. Of course, sometimes your prediction that you will be rejected for your disclosures is entirely accurate. Highly anxious people commonly both overestimate bad consequences and underestimate their ability to cope with them (for example, Lucock & Salkovskis, 1988). One way of viewing high anxiety is that it is a disorder of prediction that involves unrealistically negative estimates of risk and failure.

• *Fear of success*. Success can be a two-edged sword. As one psychiatrist used to joke: 'There is only one thing worse than not getting what you want and that's getting it'. If you succeed in getting the desirable partner, the promotion or the high marks, you are forced to handle the consequences. You may also have to handle the inconsistency with your previous negative self-perceptions. Success has negative as well as positive consequences. There are task demands inherent in the role of being a 'successful person'. The higher you rise the further the fall. Additionally you may not feel ready for your success.

> Robin was a 23-year-old clerk in a municipal office. He was extremely sensitive over a blushing problem and preferred to work on his own. However, he was proficient at his job and received a promotion in which he had to supervise three other people. While delighted to be offered the promotion Robin now became very worried that his supervisees would notice him blushing when he gave them instructions.

How others may react to your success can be another element of fear of success. Your success may challenge their perceptions of their own adequacy and cause hostility and envy. For some, *Schadenfreude*, the German word for malicious joy at another's discomfort, may be a more congenial feeling than genuine joy at another's success. Additionally, you may fear social ostracism; for example, academically successful females may be worried that this interferes with their social attractiveness to males.

Fears of change, failure and success often have some basis in reality. However, where they involve distortions that overemphasize risk they can lead to passivity, inhibition and a failure to take realistic opportunities to improve and enjoy your life.

## Predicting reward inaccurately

*Overestimating good consequences*

Overestimating good consequences frequently accompanies underestimating bad consequences. Your predictions go askew in a rosy glow of money, success, love, domestic bliss or other benefits. There may be disastrous consequences for your health, happiness, independence and financial security if you engage in rash actions based on these false predictions. Overestimating good consequences differs from underestimating bad consequences. For instance, you may underestimate the negative effects on your health of smoking, without thinking that smoking will positively benefit your health. Overgeneralization, involving drawing a broad conclusion from a specific observation, can lead to overestimations of reward. For instance, if the first horse you back wins a race this does not mean that all other horses you back will win too. Another thinking deficit that contributes to overestimating reward is that of selectively perceiving the positive events in a situation or relationships at the expense of a more balanced appraisal.

*Underestimating good consequences*

Probably far more people who see counsellors and psychotherapists underestimate good than overestimate bad consequences. They have a predictive style that focuses on risk far more than on reward. They often oppress themselves with the double negative of overemphasizing risk and underemphasizing reward.

There are two issues in regard to underestimating reward. First, some of you may be poor at generating perceptions of the potential rewards from your proposed courses of action. You may be much better at thinking up risks than rewards. Second, even when rewards are identified you may not give them the weighting that they deserve.

## Thinking errors and prediction

Some thinking errors already mentioned influence the accuracy of your predictions. These include the following:

- *Overgeneralizing*. Drawing a broad conclusion from a specific observation. For instance: 'I am alone and unhappy now, so therefore I will always be alone and unhappy'.

- *Black-and-white thinking*. Thinking in either/or terms. For example: 'If I go for the interview, they are either going to love me or hate me'.

- *Catastrophizing*. Making out that the negative consequences of not achieving your desired outcomes will be much worse than is justified.

● *Personalizing*. Predicting that you will be more the centre of attention than is warranted.

● *Self-rating*. Predicting that the outcomes of events are not only positive or negative in themselves, but have global indications for your worth as a person.

● *Misattributing*. By not owning your responsibility for what happens in your life, you increase the chances of self-fulfilling prophesies. For example, you may predict: 'Things aren't going to go well in our relationship'. Then you wait for the other person to make the first move and 'things do not go well'.

Thinksheet 30 encourages you to explore how you make predictions of risk and reward. Are you making realistic inferences about the future so that your actions are soundly grounded? If you are not, then are you viewing the future more bleakly or more through rose-tinted glasses than is justified?

---

**Thinksheet 30    Exploring how accurately you make predictions of risk and reward**

*Instructions*
1.  When you predict the consequences of your actions you can:
    ● underestimate the bad consequences (risks)
    ● overestimate the bad consequences (risks)
    ● overestimate the good consequences (rewards)
    ● underestimate the good consequences (rewards)

    Write down the extent to which you consider each of the above ways of predicting risk and reward describe how you make predictions. Where possible, give specific illustrations.

2.  Select a particular area of your life where you consider you may have been making self-oppressing rather than self-supporting predictions. Areas that you might choose include: looking after your health; meeting new people; being a more open person; looking after your money; relating to a partner or family member; an area of your work or study; taking examinations or completing reports.

    (a)    Using the above four-fold classification for overestimating or underestimating risk and reward, write down how you think you have been making inaccurate predictions in the area you selected.

    (b)    To what extent have your inaccurate predictions contained the following thinking errors?
    ● overgeneralizing
    ● black and white thinking
    ● catastrophizing
    ● personalizing
    ● self-rating
    ● misattributing

(c)    What have been the consequences of your inaccurate predictions for yourself and for others?

---

### Choosing to predict risk and reward more accurately

Changing the way you predict risk and reward depends on being aware of and pinpointing your weaknesses. Four approaches to improving your predictions are: assessing probability; assessing your coping capacity; generating and evaluating additional potential risks or rewards; and carrying out experiments to test the reality of your predictions.

*Assessing probability*

Assessing probability involves reviewing your assumptions concerning the likelihood of risks or rewards occurring. You may erroneously assign high probability to low probability events and low probability to high probability events. For instance, you maybe very afraid of dying in a scheduled airline crash. However, Dr John Marquis of Palo Alto Veteran's Administration Hospital has worked out the chance of this as 1 in 1 000 000 years of life expectancy (Emery, 1982). Actuarial tables are not available for most events about which you make predictions. Nevertheless, you can use your skills of distinguishing fact from inference and ensure that your predictive inferences have as much factual basis as possible.

Questions that you might ask yourself in assessing probability fall into two categories. First, what *rational* basis do I have for making a particular prediction? In mathematics, probability is the likelihood of an event as measured by the ratio of the number of favourable cases to the whole number of cases possible. You rarely have sufficient information for such predictive precision. Nevertheless, you can assess the number and similarity of previous events as a basis for predicting future events. You can collect additional information which may help this process. The second category of question is: what *irrational* considerations might interfere with the accuracy of my predictions? The thinking errors mentioned earlier, your state of emotional arousal and your physical condition might all interfere with your ability to predict.

*Assessing your coping capacity*

Your predictions may be based on an inaccurate assessment of your skills at coping with a particular situation. You may have been engaging in negative self-labelling and need to counteract this with a search for your resources. Additionally you may have many support factors that you have inadequately taken into account. For example, you may have someone who can help you prepare for an upcoming task, you may have friends and relatives who can support you emotionally, and you may be allowed to repeat a task that you failed at the first time. Acknowledge your support factors. One approach to seeing both your present situation and your coping capacities more in perspective entails visualizing the worst possibility occurring. If you can see yourself managing to cope in such dire circumstances, this may give you courage to cope with your current less dire circumstances.

*Generating and evaluating additional risks or rewards*

If your errors in prediction have more to do with overestimating the potential for reward and underestimating the potential for risk, you may need to develop the skill of generating what other risks there might be. However, many of you are likely to be overestimating the risks and, hence, may need to develop the skill of generating and evaluating rewards. I illustrate this in relation to Sean, the 30-year-old single man mentioned earlier in the chapter.

> Despite his age and his heterosexuality, Sean had little experience of going out with women, his longest experience lasting for three dates. In his church group Sean was on a committee with Suzanne, who had been friendly to him and whom he wondered if he should ask out. Sean asked: 'Why bother to take the risk of seeking the reward?' With his counsellor, Sean generated both the potential risks and rewards of taking this initiative. He was already expert at acknowledging risks and needed to learn that 'it is in my interests to look at rewards as well as risks in my decisions'. His list of potential rewards for asking Suzanne out included the following:
> 'I might have a chance of a strong relationship.'
> 'I might gain more experience in developing relationships.'
> 'This might contribute to helping me become happier.'
> 'I might gain confidence and a more positive self-image.'
> 'I might develop my ability to express my feelings more.'
> 'I might give myself the opportunity of Suzanne taking some of the initiative too.'
> Sean evaluated the rewards of asking Suzanne out as outweighing the risks. She later became his first steady girl-friend.

*Reality testing through personal experiments*

The most conclusive way of ensuring the accuracy of your predictions is to reality test them. This is similar to carrying out personal experiments to test the accuracy of your perceptions, as mentioned in Chapter 6. Below are some people who may need to reality test their predictions.

Debbie, aged 19, wants to move out of home. She predicts: 'I'll never find a flat that I like.'

Maureen, aged 27, is afraid to tell her husband how she would like him to make love. She predicts: 'If I tell him, he will get furious.'

Amy, aged 33, did not learn to swim as a child. She predicts: 'I will never overcome my fear of the water.'

In each of the above instances, the individual needs to set herself a specific goal. For example, Debbie's goal might be to find a flat within three months, Maureen's goal to tell and show her husband what she likes in lovemaking within the next month, and Amy's goal to be able to swim by the end of the year. Then each of them needs to think through how best to attain her goal. If necessary, they should write out plans that specifically outline how they intend changing their behaviour. Their experiments involve testing their predictions by changing their behaviour and seeing what happens. The information gained from the experiments requires accurate assessment, with inference separated from fact where necessary. The original predictions are then confirmed, disconfirmed or modified. Any more realistic reformulations should be stated clearly and simply. For instance, Debbie might tell herself: 'Though I had to spend a lot of time on it, I did succeed in finding a nice flat and can probably do it again if I have to'.

Reality testing your negative predictions may become easier if you carefully break tasks down, take small steps before larger steps, rehearse what you are going to do and, where appropriate, enlist the support of other people. Those of you whose unrealistic predictions are deeply embedded in your style of relating to the world might consider seeking professional help.

---

Thinksheet 31    Challenging your inaccurate predictions of risk and reward

*Instructions*
1. Think of a situation in which your negative predictions may block you from achieving a goal that is important to you.

2. Review the accuracy of your predictions in the following ways:
   assessing probability
   assessing your coping capacity
   generating and evaluating additional rewards.

3. Design a personal experiment that tests the accuracy of your previous negative predictions. If possible, carry out and evaluate your experiment and then change your predictions in the light of this additional information.

4. Repeat the above steps for other situations in which your possibly inaccurate negative predictions may block you from attaining your goals.

---

## SETTING YOURSELF GOALS

> People often say that this or that person has not yet found himself. But the self is not something one finds; it is something one creates.
>
> *Thomas Szasz*

As well as making accurate attributions and predictions, you can beneficially influence your future in a third way by setting yourself realistic goals. Although the grave is your ultimate destination, the quality of your living will be enhanced through improving your skills at setting goals. Some of the *rewards* to be gained from setting yourself realistic goals include the following:

• *Authorship of your life.* Setting your own goals enables you to create your future rather than either to drift aimlessly or to attempt others' goals under the guise of attempting your own.

• *Clarity of focus.* Well-stated goals clearly identify the directions in which you want to go. What may previously have been ignored or only partially sensed now becomes articulated in your full awareness.

• *Increased meaning.* Well-thought-through goals give meaning to your existence. They can give you hope and a sense of purpose. They help you avoid feelings of emptiness, boredom and existential despair.

• *Increased motivation.* Since goals provide you with something tangible to work for they can increase your motivation and persistence. Goals require implementation. This creates a pressure to plan the appropriate steps to attain your goals.

There are also risks to setting yourself goals. Such risks are often more that the goals have been set in the wrong way or at the wrong time than that they should not be set at all. Some *risks* of setting yourself goals include the following.

• *Self-alienation.* Your goals represent other people's ideas and values rather than your own. They are based on self-oppressing rather than on self-supporting personal rules.

● *Doing rather than being*. Your goals may involve you in constant activity. You may fail to find time to become attuned to the flow of your own being and of nature. Your goals may be overly focused on achieving rather than on more contemplative and responsive values.

● *Too much pressure*. Your goals may be unrealistically high and place you under constant pressure. Friedman & Rosenman's (1974) Type A Behaviour Pattern illustrates the danger of overstriving. They state: 'Type A Behavior Pattern is an action–emotion complex that can be observed in any person who is *aggressively* involved in a *chronic*, *incessant* struggle to achieve more and more in less and less time, and if required to do so, against the opposing efforts of other things or other persons' (p. 67). This kind of achievement striving has negative psychological consequences for yourself and others, not least because you are less likely to achieve your personal goals.

● *Health risks*. Unrealistic goals can contribute to your having stress-related physical problems, such as heart disease and hypertension. They can also contribute to unhealthy attempts to cope with stress; for instance, by eating, smoking and drinking too much.

## Values and goals

A man who knows the price of everything and the value of nothing.
                                        *Oscar Wilde's definition of a cynic*

What are the values by which you choose to live your life? What ultimately is of worth to you? While your goals are your objectives, your values are the underlying principles and priorities on which they are based. Another way of viewing your values is as representing your philosophy of life. This should not be something static, but rather is a process reflecting your development and increased experience of life. Oscar Wilde's cynic appeared to have had a materialistic philosophy of life centred on economic values.

Below are a list of some possible values relevant to choosing your philosophy of life.

● *Survival*. Survival is the primary instinctual value, although other values may sometimes override it, such as patriotism or religious belief.

● *Love*. Loving and being loved. Appreciating others for what they are and not just what they do.

● *Friendship*. Being joined to others outside your family by mutual intimacy and interests.

● *Family life*. Having and being part of a family. Valuing parenthood.

● *Religious*. Acknowledging the need for connectedness to some ultimate and superhuman controlling power.

● *Economic*. Materialistic values centred on the accumulation and control of money.

● *Aesthetic*. Appreciating beauty and good taste, with special reference to the arts, such as music, literature and painting.

● *Intellectual*. Valuing analytical and rational pursuits.

● *Social*. Helping others. Showing social concern.

● *Hedonistic*. Valuing fun, pleasure and having a good time.

● *Career*. Valuing having a career.

● *Practical*. Valuing practical pursuits and, where practical matters are concerned, self-reliance.

● *Outdoors*. Appreciating and valuing being out of doors. Liking being in communion with nature.

● *Autonomous*. Valuing independence and thinking for yourself. Valuing enterprise.

● *Conventional*. Appreciating tradition. Valuing obedience and conformity to the *status quo*.

● *Self-actualizing*. Being committed to personal growth and development.


This list of values is not exhaustive. At any time, you have a profile of values. This profile is comprised of what you value and the weightings attached to what you value. Sometimes your values will conflict. For instance, women especially may experience a conflict between family life and career values.


**Your philosophy of life**

One approach to creating your future is to start by clarifying your values or philosophy of life. Thinksheet 32 asks you to write out a statement of your philosophy of life. Below are two philosophy of life statements; one for an older and one for a younger person. The younger person's statement is more tentative since, with limited life experience, she is still in the earlier stages of defining her philosophy. Each statement is expressed in the first person singular.

My name is John. I am a 46-year-old married man with three children. My Catholic faith is my most fundamental value. I attend church regularly with my family and strive to be an honest and caring person, both within and outside the family. Family life has a very high priority for me, though at times I find this value comes into conflict with my work as a social worker focusing on the needs of the senile elderly and their relatives. Other values and activities that give meaning to my life are friendship, being able to spend time with nature, listening to music and playing my guitar. I'm not particularly materialistic, though as a family we seem to manage all right. I'm deeply committed to a more equal distribution of wealth and of educational and health resources.

My name is Susan. I'm aged 18 and in the first year of an accountancy course at college. Right now as a young person I want to have fun and live my life to the full. I enjoy going out to parties, meeting people and having friends. I want to be successful in my career. Money is very important to me, though it is not everything. I'm uncertain whether I want to be my own boss or work for a large firm. I would like to get married, but not until my late twenties. Part of me would like to have a family, but I'm concerned about the effect that this will have on my career and independence. I was brought up in a religious home. Frankly, I'm not that interested in helping others, but wish them no harm. I don't go to church and can't make up my mind whether there is a god. Apart from my boyfriend, the main things that I enjoy at the moment are my car, going sailing and partying. I'm not academically inclined, but am clever in a practical way.

---

**Thinksheet 32**   Choosing your philosophy of life

*Instructions*

1. Below is a list of values. Rate each value, in terms of its importance for you, on the following scale:

    | | |
    |---|---|
    | Very important | 3 |
    | Important | 2 |
    | Slightly important | 1 |
    | Of no importance | 0 |

| List of values | Your rating |
|---|---|
| Survival | _____ |
| Love | _____ |
| Friendship | _____ |
| Family life | _____ |
| Religion | _____ |
| Economic | _____ |
| Aesthetic | _____ |
| Intellectual | _____ |
| Social | _____ |
| Hedonistic | _____ |
| Career | _____ |
| Practical | _____ |
| Outdoors | _____ |
| Autonomous | _____ |
| Conventional | _____ |
| Self-actualizing | _____ |

Are there any values not included in the above list that are important for you? If so, what are they?

2.  At the top of a piece of paper write MY PHILOSOPHY OF LIFE. Then write out a statement, using the first person singular, of your philosophy. This statement should incorporate the values you choose as being the most important for you.

---

## Stating your goals

If your goals are going to help you, they need to be stated clearly and cogently. Below are some considerations for when you set and state goals for yourself.

● *Reflection of your values*. Your goals should reflect what you consider worthwhile in life. This is not necessarily a straightforward process. You may have to think, listen to your inner valuing process and discuss with others both long and hard to discover what goals truly reflect your values. Sometimes this information can come from trial and error.

● *Realism*. Your goals are realistic to the extent that they adequately acknowledge the constraints of your own emotional resources and personal skills. These should be neither overestimated nor underestimated. Your goals should reflect realistic and potentially attainable standards.

● *Specificness*. State your goals as specifically as you can. Ideally your goals should be stated in such a way that you can easily measure the success of your attempts to attain them. For instance, 'I want to be happier' is too vague. You need to state specific goals for making yourself a happier person.

● *A time frame*. Goals can be short-term, medium-term or long-term. State whether you wish to attain each goal within a week, a month, a year or some other time frame. Good intentions are insufficient.

Thinksheet 33 asks you to state your goals in five broad areas: relationships, work/study, recreation, health and finances. I provide an example before the thinksheet.

> Joe is a 21-year-old college student. All Joe's goals are stated within the time frame of one month.
>
> *Relationships*
> I will ask Laura for a date.
> I will tell my father how much I appreciate his support.
> I will stand up to my flat-mate and not agree with him all the time.
>
> *Study*
> I will study for a minimum of two extra hours every weekday (Monday to Friday).
> I will ask my biology lecturer how I can get extra tuition in the subject.
> I will participate at least once in every seminar that I attend.
>
> *Recreation*
> I will join the college swimming club.
>
> *Health*
> I will cut down my smoking to five cigarettes a day.
>
> *Finances*
> I will pay off the short-term loan I have from the bank.

Some of you are already reasonably good at setting realistic goals for yourselves. Others of you may assume much more control over your future by developing this skill.

---

Thinksheet 33   Choosing and stating goals for yourself

*Instructions*
1.   State at least one goal for yourself in each of the areas listed below. Your statement of each goal should reflect your values, be realistic, be specific and give a time frame.

     Relationships

Study/work
Recreation
Health
Finances

2.   Think of other areas of your life in which you would like to assume more control for creating your future. Articulate your goals in each of these areas.

3.   Take a piece of paper and write at the top, MY FIVE-YEAR GOALS. List the most important goals you want to attain during this period.

---

## CHAPTER HIGHLIGHTS

The future is both what is to come and what you tell yourself about this.

Predictions are estimations about the probability of future events and can contain perceptual distortions.

In predicting risk and reward you may err in the directions of either overestimating or underestimating good or bad consequences.

Thinking skills for improving your predictions include: assessing probability more systematically; assessing your coping capacity; generating and evaluating potential risks and rewards; and reality testing your predictions through personal experiments.

Setting realistic goals for yourself can help you to become the author of your life.

Your values are your choices about what is worthwhile and these principles and priorities constitute your philosophy of life.

Helpful statements of goals reflect your values, are realistic and specific, and give a time frame for their attainment.

# 9 Visualizing with Your Mind's Eye

Imagine all the people, living life in peace.

*John Lennon*

I have a dream that one day this nation will rise up, live out the true meaning of its creed: we hold these truths to be self-evident, that all men are created equal.

*Martin Luther King*

In the above quotations John Lennon and Martin Luther King use words to present a vision or mental picture of how they would like people to behave. This chapter focuses on visual, as contrasted with verbal, thinking. There are a number of colourful metaphors for visual thinking, such as 'the pictures in your head', 'the movies in your mind' and the 'videos in your brain'. All of these are oversimplifications. Visual thinking, or visualizing, is often accompanied by verbal thinking; for instance, Lennon and King used words to conjure up images. Additionally, visual images interact with feelings; for instance, in one research study some 90 per cent of anxious patients reported visual images before and during their anxiety (Beck *et al.*, 1974).

You think in pictures before you think in words. Babies' visual capacities are not fully developed at birth. However, from the first days of life they create internal visual representations of experience called *schemata*. By their first birthday, infants are entering the world of verbal thinking and beginning to apply language labels to familiar phenomena. I stress the visual foundations of your thinking because even with adults much thinking remains visual. In fact, William Glasser (1984) asserts that 80 per cent of the perceptions people store in their memory albums are visual. Consequently, the ABC framework used earlier requires elaboration to make it:

> A   The activating event
> B   Your thoughts and *visual images*
> C   Your feelings and actions

At B you have a choice of what you see as well as what you say to yourself.


## The language of visualizing

There are a number of terms that are used to describe aspects of visualizing. Some of these are listed below.

- *Daydreams*. These are pleasant, dreamy visual images and thoughts.

- *Dreams*. These are sequences of images and thoughts that pass through your mind while you are asleep. Additionally, dreams can be your conscious hopes for the future.

- *Fantasies*. These mental images represent your fanciful speculations and reveries.

- *Illusions*. Illusions represent false rather than real images and thoughts. Hallucinations, such as seeing and hearing imaginary sights and voices, are an extreme example.

- *Images*. Images are visual and verbal representations of people or things.

- *Imagining*. Creating mental images of what is not present. Creating new visual and verbal ideas.

- *Memories*. Your recollections are visual as well as verbal.

- *Symbols*. Visual objects used to represent something else, for instance the eagle, the lion, the bear or the cross.

- *Vision*. Something seen in a dream or in the imagination.

- *Visualizing*. Forming mental pictures and visual representations of people, things and ideas.

The cornerstone of Sigmund Freud's psychoanalytic approach was the interpretation of dreams. However, in this chapter, unlike Freud, my emphasis is on the conscious use of visualizing as a self-help skill.


## AWARENESS OF VISUALIZING

Some of you may be unaware of the extent to which visualizing forms a part of your daily thinking. Sex provides an excellent example of this. You may conjure up past pleasures and anticipate future ones with your mind's eye. You may experience in your imagination what is currently unattainable. The following limerick about a virgin, either male or female, illustrates this.

> There once was a virgin from Wye,
> Who wanted to have a good try
> To find out about love
> From below and above,
> Not just visualizing it in the mind's eye.

Sharing your sexual fantasies with your partner can be a good way of improving your sex life. However, partners should feel under no pressure to participate in them if they do not wish to. Additionally, fantasies greatly enhance masturbation. In fact, masturbation might be viewed as a one word definition of goal-directed visualization!

Visualizing enables you to go on mental journeys. These journeys may be into your past or into your future, into reality or into fantasy, into scenes which make you feel either good or bad, and into scenes that involve other senses, such as touch and smell. Thinksheet 34 is designed to increase your awareness of different aspects of how you visualize.

---

**Thinksheet 34   Visualization awareness exercises**

*Instructions*
Below is a series of exercises that highlight aspects of visualizing. When doing each of them you should be in a quiet room, with soft lighting and no interruptions. Relax and sit in a comfortable chair. After reading the instructions for each exercise or segment of an exercise, put the book down and close your eyes. Take your time. It may help those of you finding difficulty visualizing to say out loud what you try to see.

1.  *Photographic visualization*
    Visualize someone with whom you are in a close relationship. Focus on their face and try to visualize every detail you can as though you are recreating a good photograph of them.

2.  *Visualizing your past, present and future*
    (a)   *Your past.* Picture the childhood home that holds most meaning for you. Visit its various rooms and conjure up its atmosphere.

    (b)   *Your present.* Visualize your current home. Pay special attention to visualizing the room you feel most at home in. What are its sights? What are its textures? What are its smells?

    (c)   *Your future.* Visit a home that you would like to live in five years from now. Picture this and the lifestyle that would go with it.

3.  *Visualizing images associated with other senses*
    (a)   *Taste.* Visualize eating a favourite food, such as chocolate ice cream.

(b)    *Touch.* Visualize taking a hot shower or bath, including the sensations of the water on your skin.

(c)    *Smell.* Visualize looking at and smelling a rose.

(d)    *Sound.* Visualize a thunderstorm.

4.    *Visualizing images associated with feelings*
(a)    Visualize something or someone that 'makes' you feel **happy**. Stay with the image and reflect on what it is that produces this happy feeling.

(b)    Visualize something or someone that 'makes' you feel **angry**. Stay with the image and reflect on what it is that produces this angry feeling.

(c)    Visualize something or someone that 'makes' you feel **afraid**. Stay with the image and reflect on what it is that produces this feeling of fear.

(d)    Visualize some place where you feel **calm** and **relaxed**. Stay with the image and reflect on what it is that produces these feelings of calmness and relaxation.

5.    *Using your imagination*
Think of as many visual symbols for yourself as you can in five minutes. At the end decide which symbol best suits you.

---

People differ in how vividly they can visualize. Some of you have well developed powers of imagery. Others of you may experience much difficulty in visualizing and need to emphasize other ways of controlling your thinking. In general, the more you can experience the senses and feelings attached to your images, the better you can use visualizing as a self-help skill.

The remainder of this chapter looks at how you can use visualizing skills in five different, though somewhat overlapping, areas: managing your feelings; performing better; clarifying your goals and roles; enhancing your relationships; and avoiding negative consequences.

## MANAGING YOUR FEELINGS

Visualizing skills may help you manage a variety of feelings better. They may be helpful in their own right or as adjuncts to other thinking and action skills.

### Becoming more relaxed

I deal with relaxation first because when you visualize it is best that you feel relaxed. Additionally, relaxation can be a useful skill for those of you with problems such as tension headaches, hypertension and feelings of excessive stress. The most common approach to relaxation in counselling is probably the

Jacobson progressive muscular relaxation technique (Jacobson, 1938). Clients are encouraged sequentially to tense and then relax various muscle groupings throughout their body. For instance, an abbreviated version of progressive muscular relaxation might involve tensing and relaxing in turn: the muscles in your face, your arms, the trunk of your body, and your legs and feet. Progressive muscular relaxation requires regular practice for the maximum benefit to be gained from it. It is best done in a quiet environment, without distractions, with you either sitting in a comfortable chair or lying down with your eyes closed. Your clothing should be loosened to increase your sense of freedom.

Visual imagery can be used to enhance the process of progressive muscular relaxation. For instance, as you tense and relax your various muscle groupings you can use the metaphor of switching lights off in the rooms of a house until the whole house is completely dark. You can also make mental pictures of tight muscles and of the tension flowing from them. Additionally, when you complete your muscular relaxation you may visualize a restful, calming scene.

Visual relaxation may be used independently of as well as in conjunction with muscular relaxation. Each of you probably has one or more favourite scenes where you feel relaxed. Some of you can think of one of these right away, whereas others of you may require more time. The following is an example of a visual relaxation scene.

> I'm lying on an uncrowded beach on a pleasant, sunny day enjoying the sensations of warmth on my body. There is a gentle breeze. I can hear the peaceful noise of the sea lapping against the shore nearby. I haven't a care in the world and enjoy my feelings of peace, calm, relaxation and well-being.

There are many other scenes that people find conducive to relaxation. These include looking at a valley with lush green meadows and sitting in a favourite comfortable chair at home. Thinksheet 35 focuses on using visualizing to relax. Some of you may wish to insert progressive muscular relaxation in the exercise.

---

**Thinksheet 35   Using visualizing to relax**

*Instructions*
Allow plenty of time to complete the following steps. The first time you do the exercise you may need to open your eyes to check on the next step. Later you should complete the exercise with your eyes closed.

1.   Go to a quiet room with soft lighting and no distractions. Sit in a comfortable chair and loosen any clothing that feels tight.

2.  Become aware of your breathing. Take a few deep breaths and as you let out each breath say the word 'relax'.

3.  Focus on your face. Visualize the tension leaving your face and your face feeling more and more relaxed.
    Focus on your arms. Visualize the tension leaving your arms and your arms feeling more and more relaxed.
    Focus on the trunk of your body. Visualize the tension leaving the trunk of your body and your trunk feeling more and more relaxed.
    Focus on the lower part of your body and legs. Visualize the tension leaving the lower part of your body and legs and the lower part of your body and legs feeling more and more relaxed.
    Focus on the whole of your body. Visualize the tension leaving the whole of your body as the whole of your body feels more and more relaxed.

4.  As you sit there feeling relaxed, visualize a restful and relaxing scene. Evoke not only the sights, but also the sounds, smells and other sensations that make this such a calm and peaceful scene for you. Stay in the scene for two to five minutes as you enjoy your feelings of relaxation and well-being.

5.  Let the muscles in your eyelids lighten up as you get ready to open your eyes and become aware of your surroundings. Open your eyes and carry on with your activities feeling refreshed.

6.  Practise the above exercise daily for a week as you build up your skills of visualizing and relaxing.

---

Many of the other thinking skills in this book are relevant to becoming more relaxed. For example, if you overcome perfectionist personal rules you will place yourself under less stress; if you perceive yourself, people and situations accurately you are more likely to avoid unnecessary troubles; and if you talk to yourself with coping as contrasted with negative self-talk you will feel more like a human being.

The exercise in Thinksheet 35 can be used as a prelude to other visualization activities. The quality of your visualizing is likely to be better if you are relaxed rather than tense. Remember that all visualizing skills require practice if they are to be properly learned and maintained.

## Self-desensitization

In self-desensitization you imagine yourself coping with anxiety-evoking situations when relaxed (Lazarus, 1977; Wolpe, 1982). There are three main steps. First, learn to relax yourself. The previous section provided an introduction to this. Include muscular relaxation along with visual relaxation. Second, draw up a hierarchy of anxiety-evoking scenes that you can visualize. These scenes should be based on a theme that you find difficult; for instance, taking tests, public speaking or dating. Third, when you are relaxed, visualize coping with each scene, from the least to most anxiety-evoking.


*Constructing hierarchies*

A hierarchy is a list of scenes on a theme marked according to the amount of anxiety they evoke.


> Barb, 26, is a PhD student in biology. Her moment of truth comes when her departmental head wants her to give a seminar to the staff and other doctoral students on her research. Barb is so terrified at this prospect that she seriously thinks of abandoning her dissertation. Her hierarchy is comprised of progressively more difficult scenes on the theme of her fear of public speaking.


A common way of assessing the anxiety-evoking potential of a scene is to say that zero is a feeling of no anxiety at all and 100 is the maximum anxiety you can feel in relation to a particular theme. You then rate individual scenes according to their positions in your subjective anxiety scale. One way to generate scenes for your hierarchy is to make a list of all those situations on a theme that evokes anxiety. Another way is to keep a journal for a week or more in which you log anxiety-evoking situations.

When you consider that you have sufficient scenes, you form them into a hierarchy. Each scene should include sufficient detail to trigger your imagination. So that you take a gradual approach, try not to have gaps of more than 10 to 15 units of anxiety in your hierarchy. For instance, Nate, aged 19, constructed the following hierarchy concerning an important economics test.

1. (Rated 10) Thinking about the test while revising at my desk one month before.
2. (Rated 20) Thinking about the test while revising at my desk one week before.
3. (Rated 30) Thinking about the test while revising at my desk the night before.
4. (Rated 40) Travelling by train on the way to the test.
5. (Rated 50) Waiting outside the test room.
6. (Rated 60) Going into the test room.
7. (Rated 70) Sitting down and waiting to see the test.
8. (Rated 80) Looking at the test paper for the first time.
9. (Rated 90) Feeling that I have insufficient time near the start of the test.

10.   (Rated 95) Feeling that I have made a mess of an answer.
11.   (Rated 100) Struggling to complete the test 10 minutes before it ends.

*Visualizing scenes from your hierarchy*

The following are some points to remember when visualizing scenes from your hierarchy.

● Get yourself relaxed.

● Emphasize coping rather than mastery. Your aim is to manage your anxiety rather than to have no anxiety at all.

● Strive for a clear image. Verbalize the contents of the image if you have difficulty visualizing it.

● Take a step-by-step approach. Visualize the less anxiety-evoking scenes before moving on to the more anxiety-evoking scenes.

● Use coping self-talk. Using coping self-talk, with its coaching and calming dimensions, will help you manage any anxiety evoked by your visualizations.

● Use repetition. When you experience anxiety, these reactions may become considerably less with repeated visualizations of the scene.

● Intersperse relaxation. When you find yourself getting tense, be prepared to relax yourself again.

● Move on when you feel comfortable. When you feel that you have coped adequately with a scene and can comfortably manage any anxiety attached to it, move on to the next scene.

● Be flexible. If you get stuck with a scene after repeated visualizations, consider placing one or more less anxiety-evoking scenes before it.

● Do not do too much in a single session. Only continue with a session as long as you consider your relaxation, visualization and concentration are good. If necessary, you can return to the task later.

Self-desensitization is not the only way to deal with fears such as test anxiety. Many test-anxious people have to work on personal rules involving unrealistic standards of achievement. Some require better revision and test-taking skills. Still others are anxious because tests confront them with the fact that they have not done much work throughout the term. They need to prepare better.

---

**Thinksheet 36    Self-desensitization**

*Instructions*

1.  Construct a hierarchy in an area where your fears interfere with your effectiveness. Rate the anxiety-evoking potential of each scene in your hierarchy. Your hierarchy should contain a minimum of five scenes.

2.  Relax yourself.

3.  Taking your time, visualize the scenes in your hierarchy when you are relaxed. Follow the guidelines mentioned earlier for visualizing hierarchy scenes.

4.  Try out the behaviours you feared in real life using your self-desensitization skills to help you cope with anticipatory anxiety.

    An alternative when visualizing hierarchy scenes is to put them on to a cassette and then play them back, switching off the cassette recorder after each presentation of a scene.

---

## Visualizing the worst possibility

Self-desensitization involves taking gradual steps. Another approach to overcoming your fears involves visualizing the worst-case scenario. Ask yourself '*so what if the worst were to happen*' and then visualize it happening. Spell out the worst in detail.

> Tania, aged 16, had great difficulty saying no when she was asked out for a date. On one level she feared hurting the boy's feelings if she said no. Underneath she was terrified that if she said 'no' she would be subject to a torrent of abuse in which she was angrily told how hard, ugly, selfish and insensitive she was and asked why anyone would want to ask out such a wimpish, unattractive, unintelligent and inferior slob.

When Tania visualized her worst fears being realized she first experienced some anxiety. However, as she stayed with the scene she began to realize that, although she might not like being ridiculed, it was not the end of the world for her. Even better, she realized that she had the inner resources to cope with her worst predictions. She also acknowledged that this kind of feedback was highly unlikely. Visualizing the worst helped her to acknowledge her faulty perception of her own vulnerability and her inaccurate prediction of a highly hostile response to her saying 'no'. Tania still felt her nervousness might cause her to say 'no' more sharply than she wanted. Consequently, she decided also to work on the skill of saying 'no' in a calm and supportive way.

There are numerous situations where visualizing the worst possibility may help you to get feared situations more in perspective. However, you need to stay with the visualization long enough to work through the initial increase in anxiety that you may experience. By actually spelling out your catastrophic fears you may decatastrophize them. For instance, if you are afraid of losing your job, it may help you to visualize the consequences of this happening. Confronting your worst fears can rid them of much of their power. Also, you may identify the sources of support available to you; for instance, your family, your friends and others.

Some therapists, such as Albert Ellis (1980), actively encourage their clients to engage in shame-attacking exercises. Here clients go beyond visualization to carrying out personal experiments in which they reality test their dire predictions about social disapproval. For instance, try either shouting out the names of the tube stations or going to a chemist's shop and discussing in a loud voice the merits and demerits of different condoms!

---

**Thinksheet 37    Visualizing the worst possibility**

*Instructions*

1.   Think of a situation in your life that causes you anxiety.

2.   Spell out in some detail what you consider is the worst that could happen.

3.   Visualize the worst happening and stay in the visualization.

4.   If the worst were to happen could you cope with it? What strategies would you adopt and what sources of support would you have?

5.   Review the original situation causing you anxiety. Has visualizing the worst helped you to get it more in perspective and also freed you to think of more effective ways of coping with it?

---

## Visualizing positive images

The happiness habit is developed simply by practising happy thinking.
                                                            *Norman Vincent Peale*

I do not advocate happy thinking when the circumstances do not warrant it. Nevertheless, as mentioned in Chapter 6, many people choose to oppress themselves through negative self-labelling. Below are some ways that you can use positive visualizing to counteract tendencies to self-downing and also to acknowledge realistic sources of happiness and strength.

### *Listing positive images*

Make a list of positive images that you can pass through your mind. The giving and receiving of love and friendship is a rich source of positive images. List visual images of people you love and of your friends. List images of your making others happy as well as of receiving affection. Other sources of positive images include: achievements by you or others of which you are proud; favourite leisure pastimes; scenes from nature; and, if you are religious, religious images. You can actively choose to focus on these positive images at various times during the day. It may help if you write out each image on a 3 × 5 inch card.

You can also list positive images as ways of anticipating and of counting your blessings. For instance, before you get up in the morning, you can visualize positive things that may happen that day. Before you go to sleep, you can visualize the positive things that have happened. Visualizing your blessings either in advance or retrospectively can cover any time period you wish.

### *Stopping and switching*

In Chapter 6 I mentioned thought stopping, mental vacuuming and thought switching. The thoughts from which and to which you switch can be visual as well as verbal. When you become aware of oppressing yourself with negative thoughts and images you can: (1) instruct yourself to 'stop!', and mentally vacuum the negative thoughts and images away; and (2) switch to more positive thoughts and images.

### *Visualizing rewards*

In predicting the future some people have a tendency to overemphasize risk and to underemphasize reward. If this is a problem of yours, you can develop the skill of visualizing the rewards or benefits that might flow from taking specific actions. You still realistically evaluate your positive visualizations. However, now you have given yourself a vision of what good might come from your actions instead of, at worst, only dwelling on catastrophic thoughts and images.

> Ken and Frances were a couple in their mid-twenties who had reservations about having a baby because of the negative effects that this might have on their time and on their emotional and financial independence. They found it easy to list the negative aspects of parent-

hood. However, when they visualized what it would actually be like living with their first child, they were able to get in touch with the love, joy and feelings of fulfilment that also might come from parenthood.

### Visualizing mastery

You may be able to counteract feelings that you are no good at anything by visualizing yourself accomplishing something that you can manage. Depressed people often have feelings of helplessness in which they feel unable to influence their environment positively. If you are feeling low, identify some activity, however mundane, that you accomplish to your satisfaction. This may be cooking a meal, driving a car, playing a game, gardening, going for a walk, writing a letter, talking to a friend and so on. If you relax and visualize yourself carrying out your accomplishment, you achieve at least two important things. First, you have successfully challenged your perception of being no good at anything. Second, by acknowledging that mastery of a task is possible for you, you are in a better position to try this and other tasks.

Arnold Lazarus (1977) gives the example of a 54-year-old woman who had excelled at golf and skiing, but became depressed when she was forced to give these activities up after a stroke. He looked for other sources of mastery in her life. Finally, she came up with making a fancy cake using a special recipe. Then she identified other things that she was good at, including canasta and poker, and amateur photography. Lazarus had her visualizing and getting in touch with her subjective feelings of mastery in each of these areas in turn. As a consequence, her gloomy and depressed feelings started to lift.

---

**Thinksheet 38    Visualizing positive images**

*Instructions*

1. Search for and write out a list of positive images that may help you to feel happier and more fulfilled. Try to get at least ten images on your list.

2. At least once a day for a week, relax, sit in a comfortable chair, close your eyes (when not looking at your list) and visualize the positive images on your list. Each time when you finish doing this assess whether you feel any different.

3. During the day, when you get unwanted negative thoughts and images instruct yourself to 'stop!' and switch to visualizing positive images.

4. Practise, practise and practise to build up your skills of using positive visual as well as verbal thinking.

---

**Time projection**

Time projection or 'time tripping' is a useful skill for helping you cope with negative feelings related to transient difficulties. These difficulties may seem big, even overwhelming, at the time they occur. The ways in which you can use time tripping to get matters more in perspective are as follows.

● *Visualizing looking back on the present.* If you visualize many difficulties from a vantage point three, six or twelve months 'down the track', it may be easier for you to see their true significance. This may help you to manage negative feelings like depression as well as to act more constructively. For instance, you may be reeling from the fact that someone has broken off a relationship with you. However, if you take a trip six months into the future and look back on this break-up you will probably realize that it is one with which you have the resources to cope. You may also get more in touch with the realization that there are many other fish in the sea to whom you can relate.

● *Visualizing looking into the future.* The ability to visualize how your life might be different at some point in the future is also a useful skill for managing difficult periods. For example, rejected lovers might imagine what their lives could be like a year from now. They may need to fight against catastrophic predictions to visualize the reality of how their lives might be different. Other examples where visualizing yourself, say, six months into the future might help include when you: are bedridden for some weeks; have an awkward colleague who will leave within six months; receive a letter or rejection from a job application; go through messy divorce proceedings; are renovating a house; or many other possibilities.

## PERFORMING BETTER

Some of the visualization skills already described, for example self-desensitization, may help you perform better. Here I focus on visualizing the processes and outcomes of skilled performance. Sports people are increasingly using visualization to improve their performance, for example Chris Evert, Jack Nicklaus and the USA National Olympic Ski Team. However, you do not have to be a top sports person to use these skills.

### Visualized rehearsal and practice

Suppose you are anxious about an upcoming public speaking task. Many of you will have limited opportunities to rehearse and practise your skills, other than performing in front of the bathroom mirror. However, you have virtually unlimited opportunity for visualized rehearsal and practice. I do not propose that you substitute it for the real thing. Nevertheless, visualized rehearsal and practice can help you in the following ways.

- Providing a method of rehearsal and practice when there is no easy opportunity for real-life practice; for example, visualizing an important interview.

- Providing a method of rehearsal and practice in addition to existing ones; for instance, as well as working on your actual assertion skills with a friend you can visually rehearse them on your own.

- Helping you to break tasks down and to focus on the processes of skilled performance.

- Helping you to identify potential setbacks and to develop ways of coping with them; for example, before a match, Chris Evert visualizes herself countering her opponent's tactics.

- Providing you with an opportunity to rehearse and practise your coping self-talk along with your visualizing skills.

- Allowing you the chance of sufficient practice so that those aspects of your performance that you want to be virtually automatic have a higher probability of becoming so.

Here is an example of using visualized rehearsal and practice to help attain a personal goal.

> Tony, aged 27, had worked for a consultant engineering company for 15 months. When he was taken on he was promised a salary review after a year. This review had still not taken place. Tony decided to take the initiative and ask his supervisor for the salary review. He thought about the best ways to do this, focusing on his vocal and body messages as well as his words. He also thought of approaches to handling the different ways his supervisor might respond. Tony acknowledged his anxiety over what he was about to do. However, he engaged in repeated visualized rehearsal and practice until he felt confident that he could handle himself well. He asked for the review, then during it he calmly stated the contribution he thought he was making to the company. Tony received his hoped for salary increase. Even if he had not got what he wanted, Tony had visualized how to handle this.

## Visualizing attaining goals

Visualized rehearsal and practice focuses on the *processes* of skilled performance. However, you may also enhance your performance if you visualize yourself being successful in attaining your goals. For example, if you have rehearsed hard and then visualize that you are going to perform like a great actress, you may be more likely to do so than if you visualize lack of success. Again, if you have practised hard, you may be more likely to play a better game of tennis if you think of yourself as a champion like Steffi Graf or Ivan Lendl than if you think of yourself as a tennis incompetent.

I present some research evidence that suggests the power that positive visualizing immediately before a performance has to enhance that performance. Robert Woolfolk and Shane Murphy of Rutgers University in conjunction with Mark Parish of Princeton University studied the effect of different visualizing instructions on subjects' ability to putt a golf ball (Woolfolk *et al.*, 1985). Thirty college students were randomly assigned to one of three experimental conditions: (a) positive visualizing, (b) negative visualizing and (c) a control group. Subjects in the positive visualizing group imagined the ball 'rolling, rolling, right into the cup'; subjects using negative visualizing imagined the ball 'rolling, rolling, towards the cup, but at the last second narrowly missing'; subjects in the control group received no visualizing instructions. Each subject made 10 putts on each of six consecutive days. Over this period the positive visualizing group improved by 30 per cent over their initial score per 10 putts; the negative visualizing group showed a decline in accuracy of 21 per cent; and the control group showed an increase in accuracy of 10 per cent. No wonder Jack Nicklaus believes in positive visualizing! Unlike some of us much lesser golfers, Nicklaus also practises hard.

---

**Thinksheet 39    Using visualizing to perform better**

*Instructions*

1. Think of a specific situation that is not too difficult and that you would like to handle better; for example, Tony's request for a salary review.

2. Think through how you would like to behave in the situation by breaking the task down into its component parts. Also think through how you might cope with setbacks.

3. Every day for the next week spend some time relaxing and then visually rehearsing and practising managing the situation. Adjust your performance if you get better ideas for how to handle it. As appropriate, use coping self-talk along with your visualizing. During this period you may also engage in live rehearsal and practice.

4. Perform your changed behaviour in the real-life situation after visualizing yourself attaining your realistic goals immediately before your performance.

5.   Assess whether and how using visualizing helped you to perform better.

---

## VISUALIZING GOALS AND ROLES

> Where there is no vision, the people perish.
> *Proverbs*, 29:18

### Clarifying your goals

Although the thinking skills involved in making decisions are covered more fully in the next chapter, I will mention here some ways in which you can use visualizing to clarify your goals and make better decisions.

• *Tapping into your daydreams.* Your daydreams concerning your future can be a rich source of data for planning your life. The question 'what have been your occupational daydreams and what do you feel about them now?' is relevant to such varied groups as school and college students thinking about their first job, women returning to the workforce after raising a family and people who contemplate mid-life career moves. You may also gather useful information from your daydreams and fantasies in numerous other areas: what sort of lifestyle you want; whether or not you want marriage and a family; possible leisure interests; educational aspirations; retirement activities; and sexual behaviour.

• *Visualizing what you want in life.* Visualizing can help you to achieve a clear picture of what sort of person you want to be and what sort of life you want to have at various stages in the future. For instance, 'how would I like to see myself develop as a person over the next five years?', 'what sort of work and leisure interest would I like to have five years from now?', 'what sort of financial position?', 'what sort of home would I like to live in?', 'what sort of relationships would I like to have?' Visualizing your answers to these and other questions is a process in which you are likely to clarify and refine your goals. Clarifying your goals does not mean that they have to be rigid. You can still change them in the light of new information and fantasies. Like those of John Lennon and Martin Luther King, some of your visions may go beyond self-interest to social interest. Here you may visualize answers to the questions: 'what sort of district, region, country or world would I like to see?' and 'what actions am I prepared to take to bring this about?'

• *Visualizing what it would be like.* Another use of visualizing is to try to imagine the detail of what some sort of contemplated activity would actually be like. Here you attempt to 'flesh out' and visually reality test your daydreams and visions of the future. Thomas Skovolt and Ronald Hoenninger (1974) developed a script in which people in a career exploration group were asked to imagine events throughout a typical workday in their lives six years later. The script covered: being at home before going to work; travelling to work; what sort of workplace and what sort of work; what you do for lunch; what your fellow workers are like; what it is like when you get home; what sort of home you have; and what you do in the evening. Visualizing what it *would be* like is not a substitute for collecting on-the-spot information about what it *is* like. For instance, someone contemplating a career as a dentist may profitably spend a day in a dentist's practice (though not in the chair!). However, sometimes collecting on-the-spot information is difficult or impossible and visualizing can be the next best thing.

In sum, your daydreams and visual images are a precious part of your existence. The poet W.B. Yeats wrote: 'Tread softly because you tread on my dreams'. If you can develop your skills of freeing yourself to dream and then of fashioning your dreams into realistic goals, your life will be the richer for this.

### Changing your role

Earlier I mentioned visualized rehearsal and practice as an approach to changing your behaviour. Another approach to changing your behaviour is based on the late George Kelly's (1955a) idea of fixed-role therapy. Here I adopt the term *changed-role visualization* for a modification of Kelly's approach. Changed-role visualization consists of the following steps.

1.  *Write out a self-characterization.* You write out a description of yourself as though it were written by an imaginary friend who knows you intimately. You write this description in the third person; for example, 'John/Jane Doe is . . .'.

2.  *Develop a changed-role sketch.* You use your self-characterization as the basis for a sketch of a different role that you will portray as an experiment for the next one, two or three weeks. Visualize yourself as you would like to be and incorporate some realistic changes so that your role sketch depicts a different, yet plausible, person. You deliberately use your sketch to try out new behaviours to see whether they suit you. After the trial period, you have no commitment to adopt any aspect of your changed role that does not suit you.

3.  *Visually rehearse and practise your role sketch.* Visual rehearsal and practice develops your confidence and skills to enact your changed-role sketch. In your mind's eye work out how you are going to implement it, including handling others' reactions to your changed behaviours.

4.  *Enact your changed role*. Enact your changed role for the period of time you decide is appropriate. Throughout this trial period keep your vision of your role in mind to guide your actions.

5.  *Evaluate your experience*. Inevitably you will evaluate your experience during your role enactment. However, at the end be sure to evaluate which parts of your changed role you wish to incorporate in your future self-perceptions and behaviour. You should also have gained more insight into your freedom to choose what sort of person you want to become. George Kelly (1955b) was an advocate of a philosophical position he termed 'constructive alternativism'. He wrote: 'We assume that all of our present interpretations of the universe are subject to revision or replacement' (p. 15).

---

**Thinksheet 40    Visualizing goals and roles**

*Instructions*

1.  *Visualizing goals*
    Picture the kind of life you would like to be living five years from now. When doing this be prepared to tap into your daydreams. However, keep your goals within the bounds of reality. Cover the following areas, plus any others you consider relevant.

    How would I like to see myself develop as a person?

    What sort of work?

    What sort of leisure interests?

    What sort of intimate and family relationships?

    What sort of friendships?

    What sort of home?

    What sort of financial position?

    What sort of health and physical condition?

2.  *Visualizing a role*
    *Either* carry out the five-stage changed-role visualization procedure described in the text. *Or* develop a one-page changed-role sketch for yourself that includes new behaviours that you are prepared to try out for a week. Visually rehearse your sketch, then enact and evaluate it.

---

## ENHANCING YOUR RELATIONSHIPS

Developing your visualizing skills may improve your relationships. I illustrate this by suggesting some ways in which you can use visualizing skills in four areas: understanding others; managing anger and resentment; positive assertion; and sharing sexual fantasies.

### Understanding others

Visualizing can be an important skill in understanding others. Visual words and phrases are often used to describe this process; for example, understanding their *viewpoint* or how they *see* things. Ways in which visualizing can help you to understand others include the following.

- *Keeping in touch.* Probably many of you already use visualizing to help you understand and keep in touch with others. For instance, if you are parted from loved ones you evoke a picture of them. Additionally, if you phone or write you may visualize them as you do this. Each of you may try to visualize what the others' lives are like so that you can understand more what they are experiencing.

- *Listening.* Good listening requires you to be empathic. Empathy involves you in understanding another person on his or her terms. It means overcoming egocentric thinking to get into another frame of reference. People vary in the degree to which they use graphic images in their speech. Nevertheless, you may relate to people better if you try to understand the pictures in their heads as well as the words that they say.

- *Comprehending another's world.* In caring relationships partners develop a good understanding of what it is like to be the other person, with his or her hopes, fears and activities. They collect information that enables them to create pictures of what the other's life is like from his or her viewpoint. They create a three-dimensional model of each other's lives. If these models are reasonably accurate, they provide a good information base for each partner to feel loved and understood.

- *Role-taking.* You can visualize to improve your understanding of different experiences that people go through; for instance, unemployment and dying. Additionally, you can visualize to deepen your understanding of differences between you and others; for instance, being of a different gender, sexual preference, age or ethnic grouping. Visual role-taking is a skill that may help you develop and show social interest. You may visually project yourself into the plights of those less fortunate; for instance, the homeless and starving in third world countries.

## Managing anger and resentment

Ways in which you can use visualizing skills to prevent and manage destructive anger include the following.

● *Visualizing another's position*. When in conflict, it usually helps to understand the other person's position as well as your own. Another's position may be easier to grasp if you visualize how your behaviour is perceived by the other person. Having a visual picture of how you behave can also give you insight into whether your behaviour matches your intentions.

● *Taking a balanced view of another*. Just as you may perceive yourself too negatively, so you may perceive others in the same way. You may help to manage your anger better if, instead of dwelling on negative thoughts and images about another person, you balance this out by visualizing positive incidents in your relationship and things that you like.

● *Overcoming resentment*. Resentments tend to be hurts held over from the past. The Simontons, who run a cancer counselling and research centre in Dallas, Texas, consider that holding on to resentment is a stressing experience that contributes to cancer. They have developed a visualization procedure which they claim has helped many patients to let go of their resentments (Simonton *et al.*, 1978). Briefly it consists of: relaxing; getting a clear image of the person you resent; visualizing good things happening to that person and his or her reactions to this; being aware of your own reactions to this visualization; reviewing the original situation in terms of your own role and how it looked from the other person's point of view; acknowledging that you now feel more relaxed and less resentful; and resuming your normal activities. This visualization procedure may need to be repeated a number of times. Often as people get greater insight into their own behaviour, they feel a need to forgive themselves as well as the other person.

## Positive assertion

In this context, positive assertion means being able to state positive thoughts and feelings and take positive actions towards others.

> Dorothy and Clifford, both in their late teens, had been going steady for a year. Their relationship was getting increasingly negative and 'heading towards the rocks'. Each felt the other was no longer appreciative and was continually finding fault. They were replacing their positive 'pictures in the head' of each other and their relationship with negative ones.

As the section in Chapter 6 on perceiving others realistically showed, it is very easy for relationships to enter downward spirals when partners engage in matching negative comments about each other. Often people are blocked in their capacity to express affection and appreciation for each other. They often find it difficult to do the 'little things that mean a lot' for others, let alone the large things.

Visualizing can be a useful tool for overcoming blocks to positive assertion. First, you can visualize either some or all the people to whom you would like to be more positive. Second, you can think of all the different ways in which you could be more positive towards them. These include smiling, stating appreciations, paying compliments, touch, a phone call, a letter, an invitation, a gift, a visit or any one of a number of other possibilities. Third, you can visualize yourself being positive to one or more people in ways that they appreciate. Picture how it makes them feel and acknowledge your reactions to this. Fourth, you may wish to take the next step of implementing your positive assertions and seeing what happens. A simple, if not invariable, rule of thumb is that the more positive you are to others the more positive they will be to you in return.

## Sharing sexual fantasies

Sex can be a matter of routine coupling or it can involve tenderness, fun, variety, imagination and play. You may have difficulty owning and acknowledging your sexual fantasies. You may expect your partner to read your mind and know instinctively what you desire. You may make it difficult for your partner to share his or her sexual fantasies. All these characteristics interfere with your sex life. Most if not all partners have ideas of how they would like their lover to act; what variations they would like introduced into their lovemaking; what they would like their lover to do to or for them, when and where. Take the time to get in touch with and visualize your own fantasies. Do not feel you have to edit them. There is a difference between the image and the deed. Imagine what it would be like to play more the opposite gender role in your lovemaking. Visualize different ways of telling your partner about fantasies that you have not already shared. Visualize his or her reactions. Visualize asking your partner to share more of his or her sexual fantasies with you. How might you go about this? Think about and visualize the risk and rewards of having a more open sex life with your partner. If you think the rewards outweigh the risks, you may wish to take the risk of obtaining the reward.

---

**Thinksheet 41**   Using visualizing to enhance relationships

*Instructions*
Complete those parts of this thinksheet that you consider to be relevant for you.

1. Understanding others. Visualize what it would be like to be someone of the opposite sex of about your own age from the time you wake up in the morning to the time you go to sleep at night.

2. Managing anger and resentment.
   (a)  Use visualizing skills in relation to someone with whom you either are or have recently been angry to:
   - understand their position, including how they see your behaviour,
   - take a balanced view of them in which you acknowledge their positive and not just their negative qualities.

   (b)  Use visualizing skills in relation to someone with whom you have a long-standing resentment to imagine good things happening to them and also to explore your own role in the situations causing resentment.

3. Positive assertion. Using visualizing, draw up a plan for increasing the amount of your positive assertion with at least one person. Visually rehearse and then implement your changed behaviour.

4. Sharing sexual fantasies. Acknowledge and own your sexual fantasies in relation to your partner. Visualize ways of sharing them more with your partner and of encouraging him or her to do likewise. Visualize the likely outcomes of increasing mutual sharing of your sexual fantasies.

---

## AVOIDING NEGATIVE CONSEQUENCES

I couldn't help it. I can resist everything except temptation.

*Oscar Wilde*

Ah, the sweet delights of giving way to temptation! However, sometimes you may not want to face the negative consequences of giving way. You may wish to strengthen your willpower in relation to such matters as chocolate fudge sundaes, high-speed driving, sniffing cocaine, heavy alcohol consumption, chain smoking or various pleasures of the flesh. Although virtue may have its rewards, they may be insufficient to curb your cravings. This section focuses on visualizing the negative consequences of unwanted behaviours. The objective is to decrease significantly your motivation for engaging in them.

### Visualizing realistic negative consequences

When discussing prediction, I mentioned that, although some people had difficulty perceiving potential rewards, others failed to predict and give sufficient weight to potential risks. Preventive health care is an area in which many people inadequately assess the risk factors. If you wish to give up bad habits it may pay you to collect visual images of their potential negative consequences. These can be used in two ways. First, by being able to visualize clearly these negative consequences you may predispose yourself to be less inclined to experience the temptation. Second, when you do experience temptation, you have a self-help strategy at your disposal. You can instruct yourself to 'stop!' and then visualize hard the negative consequences of giving in to the temptation. You may also choose to engage in some substitute rewarding activity that involves little or no risk.

> Bernie, aged 33, enjoyed having casual sex with other males. He had read much in the papers about AIDS, but still found it difficult to change his behaviour. However, as time went by, he developed a number of negative images about promiscuous and unsafe sex. He saw a video of a San Francisco Shanti Project counselling group in which AIDS sufferers openly shared their psychological and physical pain. He collected a number of graphic coloured medical photographs that depicted AIDS-related symptoms like Kaposi's sarcoma and malignant lymphomas. Additionally, he spent a few hours a week in volunteer work with AIDS sufferers, including attending one of their funerals. With his store of negative images he found it much easier to resist the temptation to cruise.

Lazarus (1977) equates the difference in people's willpower to the extent to which they are able to have well-defined images of negative consequences. He observes that weak-willed people, instead of dwelling on negative consequences, often switch to dwelling on the short-term rewards. If you sincerely wish to break a bad habit, the time to reward yourself is when you have resisted temptation and *not* when you have given in to it.

## Visualizing exaggerated negative consequences

Joseph Cautela (1967) of Boston College developed what he termed a 'covert sensitization' approach to undermining and resisting temptations. You visualize exaggerated negative consequences whenever an unwanted temptation is experienced. For instance, if the habit you wish to break is overeating and you have chosen rich cakes as a food to avoid, you might visualize the following sequence when relaxed.

> You are at home sitting at the table for dinner and a rich cake is being served. As you see it you start getting a nauseous feeling in your

stomach. You accept a piece. As you take your first bite, you vomit all over the table and your clothes. You keep puking as the food you have previously eaten comes out in a disgusting smelly mess. Seeing and smelling your vomit makes you retch even more violently. You feel very weak and faint. Everybody looks at you in disgust. As you get up from the table having made up your mind to eat no more you feel much better. You wash, change and feel great.

Visualizing exaggerated negative consequences is not for the squeamish. You need to rehearse and practise the negative imagery until it becomes a virtually automatic response to the real-life temptation. My preference is for visualizing realistic rather than exaggerated negative consequences. The realistic consequences can be horrific enough in their own right. However, some of you may find that the exaggeration increases the power of your negative imagery with a beneficial effect on your willpower.

---

**Thinksheet 42    Visualizing negative consequences**

*Instructions*
1.  Think of a bad habit you wish to break.

2.  What graphic images of the realistic negative consequences of your bad habit might serve as a 'turn-off' for you?

3.  Make a systematic effort to collect graphic negative images of the consequences of your bad habit, like Bernie's medical photographs of AIDS-related symptoms.

4.  Play the negative images through your mind for 10 to 15 minutes each day for at least a week whether or not you feel tempted that day. Additionally, at any other time you experience temptation, instruct yourself to 'stop!' and switch to visualizing your negative images. If you find it helps to exaggerate visually the negative consequences of your bad habit, then do so too.

5.  Practise, practise and practise visualizing the negative consequences of your bad habit until you become able to resist the temptation involved in it.

---

Visualizing skills are often most helpful when used in conjunction with other thinking and action skills. However, it is probable that most people, including most professional helpers, underestimate rather than overestimate the power of visual thinking.

## CHAPTER HIGHLIGHTS

Much of your thinking is visual.

Visual imagery can help you become more relaxed both independently of and in conjunction with progressive muscular relaxation.

Self-desensitization involves three steps: (1) relaxing yourself; (2) compiling a hierarchy of anxiety-evoking scenes around a theme; and (3) presenting the scenes to yourself when relaxed.

Visualizing your reactions to the worst possibility may help you obtain a better perspective on your ability to cope with an existing problem.

Visualizing positive images can counteract tendencies to self-downing, help you see realistic rewards and put you in touch with feelings of mastery.

Time projection can help you get present difficulties more in perspective by visualizing both the present from a vantage point in the future and also the future from the vantage point of the present.

Visualized rehearsal and practice and also visualizing attaining your goals may help you to perform better.

Visualizing can help you clarify your goals by tapping into your daydreams, visualizing what you want and visualizing what it would actually be like.

Visualizing can help you formulate, try out and evaluate a new role for yourself.

Visualizing skills may help you understand others better, manage anger and resentment, assert yourself positively, and own and share your sexual fantasies.

Visualizing may help you break bad habits by imagining both their realistic negative consequences and their exaggerated negative consequences.

# 10　Making Decisions

Life is the art of drawing sufficient conclusions from insufficient premises.

*Samuel Butler*

How could I have been so stupid?

*John F. Kennedy, in retrospect, on the Bay of Pigs invasion*

There is a famous cartoon caption by Virginia Simon that goes as follows: 'Lou makes all the *big* decisions . . . like should we have a trade agreement with China, should we set up a space station on the moon. He leaves all the *little* decisions to me . . . like where we should live, where we should send the kids to school.' This chapter is about making the 'little' decisions that may have major implications for your happiness and fulfilment. Such decisions include choice of job and career, major areas of study, college and graduate school, getting married, getting divorced, having a family, your recreational activities, where you live, what you do with your money and how you look after your health, to mention but some. It has been said that 'life is just one darned decision after another'. Each decision defines your existence and is an act of renunciation. Every 'yes' involves a 'no'.

Decisions involve varying degrees of conflict and anxiety. Sometimes the most appropriate way for you to act is unclear. Furthermore, you may fear the consequences of making the wrong decision. You may be under stress at the time of the decision; for instance, if you contemplate divorce. Decisions also involve commitment. For example, if you have decided 'yes' and act 'no', you have not made your decision at a very fundamental level. Commitment entails being prepared to carry through your decision, although you can still take realistic feedback into account.

This chapter is divided into three sections. First, you are encouraged to explore your decision-making style. Second, a framework for and some skills of rational decision-making are presented. Third, based on the thinking skills described in this book, some ways are suggested for improving your decision-making.

## YOUR DECISION-MAKING STYLE

> He who hesitates is sometimes saved.
>
> *James Thurber*

Your style of decision-making is the way you approach and make decisions. It is the pattern of your information processing and deciding behaviour. The notion of decision-making style should not be viewed rigidly since you may make different decisions in different ways. Additionally, you may possess more a profile of different decision-making styles rather than a single strongly predominant style. Your style may also alter if you make decisions in conjunction with other people.

### Styles of individual decision-making

When you are faced with a decision, are there any characteristic patterns in your behaviour? Below are seven styles, albeit overlapping, of how you may make decisions.

- *Rational*. In a rational style of decision-making you dispassionately and logically appraise all the important information pertinent to your decision. You then select the best option in the light of your objectives. Where you experience decisional conflict, your aim is to resolve the conflict by obtaining the best solution under the circumstances.

- *Feelings-based*. Here the basis for your choice is what intuitively feels right. This style does not mean that you are in a state of heightened emotionality in which your decision-making is impaired. Rather the emphasis is on getting in touch with what you truly feel, with your subjective preferences and with your inner valuing process. In the feelings-based style you may generate and appraise different options. However, the final criterion for choice is how you feel rather than what you think.

- *Hypervigilant*. Here you try too hard. You become so anxious and aroused by the conflict and stress involved in the decision that the efficiency of your decision-making decreases. For instance, you may engage in a lengthy and frantic search and appraisal process for the 'right' decision. In this process you may fail either to take into account or to weigh adequately relevant information. You may get bogged down in so much detail that, losing perspective, you fail to see 'the wood for the trees'.

- *Avoidant.* Here you cope with decisions by not acknowledging them or hoping they will go away, and/or engaging in delaying tactics like procrastination. You may also defensively avoid information pertinent to the decision. Your objective is to maintain your short-term psychological comfort whatever the long-term costs.

- *Impulsive.* Here you make decisions rapidly and based on sudden impulses rather than on a cool and rational appraisal of the facts. The impulsive style differs from the feelings-based style in that you act on initial or early feelings rather than explore and evaluate options by getting in touch with your deeper feelings.

- *Compliant.* Here you conform to what others expect of you. You depend on them for signs on how you should decide. The outstanding feature of this style is passivity. You allow your decisions to be influenced, if not made, by others rather than actively make them yourself.

- *Ethical.* Here the basis for your choice is a code of ethics. For instance, if you are a devout Catholic you make your decisions with reference to Catholic teachings and papal infallibility. If you are not religious you may still make your decisions on what you consider to be moral principles of right and wrong. Your decisions take into account the 'good' of humanity and reflect social interest as well as self-interest.

## Styles of joint decision-making

In your relationships there are decisions that are best made jointly. Much of the above section on styles of individual decision-making still applies; for instance, joint decisions can be of varying degrees of rationality and also be avoided by both parties. Joint decisions may subject you to the stresses and inner conflicts of individual decisions. Additionally, you may experience further conflict if you have different interests, wishes and needs from the other person.

> Larry and Nora are an engaged couple in their final year of university. Nora wants to go on to do a Master's degree but, if they then wish to live together, this has implications for where Larry gets a job. Larry has already been offered an excellent job where there are no Master's degree programmes in Nora's field.

In situations such as this you are confronted with a potential conflict of interest with your partner. Assuming you confront the need for a decision, there are three main decision-making styles you can adopt: the competitive, the compliant and the collaborative.

- *Competitive.* Here you view the decision as one in which there are scarce resources and, consequently, there has to be a winner and a loser. The loser is not going to be you. You adopt an 'I win–you lose' approach to the decision and do all in your power to get your way. The risks of such an approach include that you do not necessarily arrive at the best solution and that your partner feels violated.

- *Compliant.* Here you are unassertive and go along with or give in to your partner. You may deceive yourself as to your motivation for complying, but basically this is an 'I lose–you win' decision-making style. The risks include not finding the best solution and you feeling violated.

- *Collaborative.* Here you both search for a solution that best meets each partner's needs. You work together to find an 'I win–you win' solution that is freely entered into by each of you. Neither of you attempts to impose your wishes on the other. As well as acknowledging and stating your individual wishes, you both have a sincere commitment to the welfare of each other and of the relationship.

Thinksheet 43 is designed to help you explore your decision-making style. Do you always make decisions rationally or do you use another or other styles?

---

**Thinksheet 43  Exploring your decision-making style**

*Instructions*
A   *Personal decisions*

1.  Write out the extent to which, when you have personal decisions to make, you adopt each of the following decision-making styles:
    - rational
    - feelings-based
    - hypervigilant
    - avoidant
    - impulsive
    - compliant
    - ethical

2.  Assess the extent to which your current profile of decision-making styles either supports or oppresses you.

B   *Joint decisions*

1.  Write out the extent to which you and your partner, when you make decisions that affect both your interests, use each of the following decision-making styles:
    - competitive
    - compliant
    - collaborative.

2.  Assess the extent to which you and your partner's current style(s) of making joint decisions supports or oppresses your relationship.

---

## RATIONAL DECISION-MAKING

Rational decision-making can be viewed as taking place in two main stages: first, confronting and making the decision; and second, implementing and evaluating it. Below a seven-step framework for rational decision-making is presented within the context of these two main stages.

Stage 1: confronting and making the decision
Step 1: *confront* the decision.
Step 2: *generate* options and *gather information* about them.
Step 3: *assess* the predicted consequences of options.
Step 4: *commit* yourself to a decision.

Stage 2: implementing and evaluating the decision
Step 5: *plan* how to implement the decision.
Step 6: *implement* the decision.
Step 7: *assess* the actual consequences of implementation.

The above is a simplified version of the decision-making process. Sometimes the steps overlap. Sometimes you need to backtrack from a later step to an earlier one. Nevertheless, if you are to make major decisions effectively—and even some minor ones too—you need to consider each of these steps. They are now discussed in turn.

### Step 1: confront the decision

Rational decision-makers do not avoid decisions. Confronting decisions comprises a number of different elements.

- *Being open to external information*. Many of your decisions are stimulated by your environment. For example, you see an interesting job advertised and then have to decide whether or not to apply. Another example is that you learn more about the hazards of smoking and are then faced with the decision of whether or not to give up smoking. If you are a rational person you are open to information from external sources.

- *Being open to internal information*. Here the stimulus for a decision is more proactive than reactive. You become attuned to changes in your wants and wishes, such as the desire for an intimate relationship or a more rewarding leisure life. These inner changes stimulate you to make decisions about how to attain what you want. If you are out of touch with your feelings, you may fail to confront the need for some decisions.

● *Clarity of focus*. Decisions need to be clearly identified and stated. For instance, Mandy is very unhappy in her job. She needs to go beyond a vague statement of feelings to a specific statement about the decision she faces. This decision is either to stay in and if possible improve her job or to seek a better one.

**Step 2: generate options and gather information about them**

*Generating options*

Decisions frequently do not involve black and white choices. You may need to generate and consider different options.

> Fred, aged 22, wondered what to do when he did not get into any of the clinical psychology courses he wanted. His immediate reaction was to think of joining his father's timber business. He saw a careers counsellor who encouraged him to explore other opportunities in the helping professions. Fred ended up enrolling in a social work course. He was thankful that he had been encouraged to explore further options rather than going into the timber business 'on the rebound'.

Coming up with different options is a creative process. The objective is to generate a range of options which may contain effective ones. Sometimes it can be helpful to brainstorm. Brainstorming originally developed as a procedure for 'idea finding' in groups. Nevertheless, you can apply some of its rules on your own. These rules include: criticism of ideas is ruled out; free-wheeling is welcomed; and quantity is wanted. The quantity rule is particularly important. Several research reports have supported brainstorming, indicating that it is more likely to generate effective ideas than any attempt to produce *only* good quality options (D'Zurilla & Goldfried, 1971).

*Gathering information*

Good decisions depend on good information. Sometimes further options emerge from your information gathering. Rational decision-makers aim to gather as much information as they need to make a successful decision. This requires a disciplined approach to finding out and surveying sources of information and also to knowing when to stop.

Frank, aged 28, worked as a computer operator for the telephone company. He decided to explore whether or not he could get a better job. His approach was to gather as much relevant information as he could. He divided his information search into two main areas: jobs within and jobs outside the telephone company. He set himself a deadline of two months to collect this information. His approach to finding out more about jobs within the telephone company included: finding out more about how his own section operated and the opportunities within it; looking at notice boards where inhouse jobs were advertised; and having a discussion with the personnel office. His approach to finding out more about jobs outside the telephone company included: discussions with contacts; looking at current job advertisements in the papers; going to the library and surveying newspaper ads for relevant jobs for the past three months; and registering with an employment agency specializing in his area. As Frank gathered this information he became clearer not only about possible jobs but about what his own occupational goals were.

Thinksheet 44 focuses on generating options and gathering information. Try doing it in relation to a current decision in your life and see if you think and feel differently about the decision as a result.

---

**Thinksheet 44    Generating options and gathering information**

*Instructions*

1. *Confronting a decision.* Think of a current decision in your life on which you want to work. State it as clearly as you can.

2. *Generating options.* Is your decision a simple black and white one or are there other possible options? Spend 10 minutes brainstorming and listing as many options for your decision as possible. Adopt the following rules of brainstorming: criticism of ideas is ruled out; free-wheeling is welcomed; and quantity is wanted. At the end of your brainstorming period put a star (*) by each option that you wish to consider further.

3. *Gathering information.* What, if any, further information do you need to collect to increase

the probability of your making the 'best' decision? Specify the information, develop a plan for gathering the information and implement your plan.

4. *Evaluation.* Do you see your decision differently in the light of completing this thinksheet? Has it helped you to take a more rational approach to the decision than you might otherwise have done?

---

### Step 3: assess the predicted consequences of options

Decision-making involves assessing options as the basis for choosing the best course of action. Your choices are likely to be guided by considerations of *probability* and *utility*. Considerations of probability relate to your estimations of the possibility of different options achieving desired outcomes. Considerations of utility are your subjective estimations of the value of various outcomes.

Psychologists Irving Janis and Leon Mann (1977) have advocated a balance-sheet procedure for assessing the consequences of decisions. They write: 'The more errors of omission and commission in the decision maker's balance sheet at the time of becoming committed to a new course of action, the greater will be his or her vulnerability to negative feedback when the decision subsequently is implemented' (p. 148). Janis & Mann's balance-sheet procedure entails taking into account a series of considerations in four areas: gains and losses for self; gains and losses for others; self-approval or self-disapproval; and approval or disapproval from others.

Table 10.1 presents a balance sheet for assessing the consequences of each of the major options in a decision. Thus, for any decision, you may need as many balance sheets as there are options under serious consideration. The balance sheet only helps you to list the possible consequences of an option. You then need to weigh the consequences. The consequences for yourself may include the following: consistency with your goals and values; amount of time and effort; amount of tangible reward; emotional cost or gain; approval or disapproval from others; and physical well-being.

The consequences you need to take into account vary with the decision. For example, if you are choosing a job relevant consequences may be location, travel time, income, amount of work, difficulty of work, interest, degree of autonomy, security, status, superannuation, chances of advancement, chances to develop skills, physical environment, social considerations, perceived competence of management and so on. The relevant consequences for others of a decision depend on the nature of the decision. For instance, Dave, a married man considering whether to accept promotion that means moving to the other end of the country, takes into account his family's thoughts and feelings about the disruption this would entail. Debbie, a separated woman seeking a divorce, takes into account the potential impact of this on her children. Frequently, the best way

Table 10.1    *A balance sheet for assessing the consequences of a decision option*

*Description of option:*

*Consequences of option*

For myself

|            | Positive | Negative |
|------------|----------|----------|
| Short-term |          |          |
| Long-term  |          |          |

For others

|            | Positive | Negative |
|------------|----------|----------|
| Short-term |          |          |
| Long-term  |          |          |

to assess the possible consequences of your decisions on others is to let those concerned speak for themselves rather than trying to read their minds.

Thinksheet 45    Assessing the consequences of decision options

*Instructions*

1.  Select a decision on which you wish to work. This could be either the decision you used for Thinksheet 44 or another decision.

2.   What are the major options from which you can make your decision?

3.   Make out balance sheets for assessing the consequence of each of the above options.

4.   Do you see your decisions differently in the light of completing this thinksheet? Has it helped you to take a more rational approach to the decision than you might otherwise have done?

---

### Step 4: commit yourself to a decision

> There is no more miserable human being than one in whom nothing is habitual but indecision.
>
> *William James*

Assuming that you have systematically been through the previous steps, you are now ready to make your decision. However, it is one thing to make a decision rationally and another to commit yourself to carrying it out and doing your best to make it work. Making major decisions confronts you with your existential isolation. Ultimately nobody else can make them for you. Especially if the decision has been finely balanced, you may have regrets about the possibilities that you have renounced as well as doubts about whether you have chosen the right course of action.

How can you strengthen your resolve to carry out a difficult decision? First, you can endeavour to see that the decision is in accord with your key values. Second, you can be thorough in generating, gathering information about and assessing options. Third, you can state your goal or goals clearly and list the specific rewards and pay-offs for you and others for attaining your goals. The balance sheet for your preferred option should provide this information. Fourth, you can carefully plan how best to implement your decision, including how to handle setbacks and negative reactions from others. Fifth, you can adopt a flexible attitude and adjust both the decision and how you implement it in response to feedback. Being flexible does not necessarily entail a weakening of resolve. You may choose to reaffirm your original decision at the same time as adopting different tactics to carry it out. However, if the evidence warrants it, you may choose to modify or even totally reject your original decision. Sixth, you can acknowledge and keep in mind the rewards of your decision as they occur. Your decisional balance sheet can be completed *during* the implementation of as well as *before* your decision. This may help you gain more perspective as you experience the efforts and frustrations of implementing it.

**Step 5: plan how to implement the decision**

Plans are outlines of how to proceed. You may need to engage in planning as part of your decision-making process and not just when you consider implementing your final decision. For example, Frank, the telephone computer operator, developed a plan to gather information about different job possibilities.

Once you have arrived at a decision—say to obtain a divorce, move to a new location, take up a new recreational activity, give up smoking, engage in some form of community service—you are still faced with planning how best to act. The skills of planning include the following.

- *State clearly your goals and subgoals.* In Chapter 8 it was suggested that adequate statements of goals should not only reflect your values, but also be realistic and specific and give a time frame. In planning you may require clear statements of your subgoals as well as of your overall goal. Subgoals are the steps you need to take to obtain your overall goal. For instance, Sally and Mike are a young couple who have decided to buy a house and start a family. One of their subgoals is to save a stipulated sum within 12 months for a deposit on a house. Peggy has just moved to a new city and has decided to join a physical fitness club for exercise and also to meet some new people. One of her subgoals is to gather information by the end of the month about all the physical fitness clubs within a stipulated distance from where she lives.

- *Break tasks down.* The notion of subgoals implies that you often need to break tasks down. You do not have to do everything at once. For instance, Edna decides to divorce Jack, from whom she has been separated for nearly two years. She breaks implementing this decision down into a number of different parts: how best to handle the legal aspects of divorce; how to relate to Jack; how to inform and relate to her children; what to say to her family, in-laws and friends; how to handle her own feelings about divorce; and how to build a more independent life for herself.

- *Generate and consider alternative courses of action.* For each of the subgoals, you ask yourself: 'How can I best achieve this subgoal?' You may need to use skills of brainstorming, for generating different courses of action, and of evaluating which courses of action are most likely to help you achieve your goals and subgoals.

- *Anticipate difficulties and setbacks.* Where possible take realistic difficulties and setbacks into account. For instance, Lynne knows that her decision to go abroad for a year is not going to please her boyfriend Sam. She thinks in advance about how she can break the news to him in an assertive, yet caring, way.

- *Identify sources of support.* Difficult decisions can often be adhered to in the context of an adequate support system. For example, Brad realizes that he is much more likely to adhere to his decision to give up drinking if he is part of a support group rather than trying to break the habit on his own. Consequently, he has joined Alcoholics Anonymous. Brad thinks it will also help him if he establishes better relationships with his wife and family as well as with those of his friends who do not encourage his drinking.

- *Write your plan out.* If your plan is at all complex, it may help you to write it out. You might be able to commit yourself better to implementing its steps if they are clearly set out. A written plan can act as a reminder if it is put in an easily visible place. In writing out a plan do not get lost in its detail. Your plan is an outline or map of how to get from A to B. You do not have to fill in every building, field and tree along the way. Write it out with a clear structure built around attaining your central goal and its related subgoals.

---

**Thinksheet 46    Planning to implement a decision**

*Instructions*

1. Select a decision that you wish to implement. This could be a decision that you worked on in Thinksheets 44 and 45 or another decision.

2. Write out a realistic plan to implement your decision adhering to the following guidelines:
   - state clearly your goals and subgoals
   - break tasks down
   - generate and consider alternative courses of action
   - anticipate difficulties and setbacks
   - identify sources of support

   As you write out your plan remember to avoid the twin pitfalls of giving insufficient detail and giving too much detail. Ensure that your plan is easy for you to understand and follow.

3. Assess your skills in your daily life of making and implementing plans that help you attain goals.

---

## Step 6: implement the decision

The time has come for you to implement your decision. This may be a straightforward matter in which you are clear on both your decision and how to proceed. Considerations in implementing decisions include the following.

- *Timing.* You can often choose the best time for you to implement a decision. Considerations here include your having worked out how to proceed and your feeling reasonably confident that you can carry out your plan. Sometimes, however, the timing of when you implement your decision will be heavily influenced by others' needs; for instance, if you are a parent, not wishing to move location during the last year at school of one of your children.

- *Post-decisional conflicts.* There are many reasons why you may have conflicting feelings about implementing a decision. You may be sad at some of the trade-offs and compromises you are making to get what you want. You may still feel you need the confidence to implement your decision. You may have realistic reservations about the wisdom of your original decision and wish to reconsider it. You may become highly anxious at having to act and then engage in avoidance behaviour. Post-decisional conflict may be especially intense as you start to implement a decision, but become less so as you carry on and gain confidence in the wisdom of your decision. However, if you experience persistent conflict in implementing a decision, you may choose to reconsider it.

- *No excuses.* The guideline of 'no excuses' is another way of indicating the importance of your assuming responsibility for implementing your decision. When you face setbacks you need to ask yourself questions like: 'Stop . . . think . . . what do I need to do to handle this situation?' or 'How is my behaviour helping me?', rather than indulge in an orgy of excuse-making.

- *Openness to feedback.* As you implement your decision you may get feedback from many sources: yourself, others and your environment. You require sensitivity and good judgement to sort out helpful from harmful feedback. If necessary, you may decide to modify your plan to help you better obtain your goals. Flexibility in the light of a realistic assessment of feedback is desirable. You can be strong and flexible at the same time.

- *Use of positive self-reward.* Implementing some decisions can be rewarding in its own right. On other occasions you can use rewards to strengthen your motivation. For instance, you may use positive self-talk, like 'that's great', 'well done' or 'I'm glad I made it', that clearly acknowledges your satisfaction at performing a desired behaviour. Another method of positive self-reward is to make a contract with yourself in which there is a clear connection between specific achievements and self-administered rewards. These rewards can fall into two categories: (1) rewards that are outside your everyday life, such as a new item of clothing or a special event; and (2) initial denial of some pleasant everyday experience and later administration of it contingent upon doing something.

- *Handling guilt.* Guilt may be one of the feelings you need to work on when you make your decision. However, here I refer to the guilt you may feel when you do not live up to your decision. You can handle your feelings of guilt in ways that weaken or strengthen your resolve. If you engage in much self-disparagement this may lower your self-esteem to the point where your self-talk might be something like: 'I'm worthless anyway, so why bother?' or 'I've made a mess of it once, so its obvious that I'm not going to succeed'. However, a more rational approach is to try to understand why you did not live up to your decision and make plans to stop this happening again. Furthermore, you may need to tell yourself that setbacks are often part of the process of implementing difficult decisions and giving up bad habits. You need to have the courage to persist and not think yourself into giving up.

### Step 7: assess the actual consequences of implementation

You need to assess both how you implement your plan and the consequences of either attaining or not attaining your goals. Do not stay stuck with decisions and plans that do not work for you. You may decide to review your original decision, in which case this seven-step model comes full circle and you start off with step 1 again. Rational decision-making involves accurate perception of feedback and a willingness to act on it. Efficient processing of information helps you to make and to assess decisions.

## IMPROVING THE QUALITY OF YOUR DECISION-MAKING

How can you increase the probability of making decisions that work for rather than against you? How can you increase the self-supporting and decrease the self-oppressing elements of your decision-making? In this section I review the ways that many of the skills discussed earlier in the book can improve the quality of your decisions. I start with the example of Grace, who is coming to terms with a poor decision.

Grace, aged 33, was a salesperson with a bedding company. She was becoming bored with the job, wanted more money, and had started not getting on well with Ed, her sales manager. For instance, she resented him asking her to make him coffee. However, Ed had been given a promotion and was not going to be around much longer. Within three weeks of seriously thinking she should move, Grace had started a new job as a sales representative for an entrepreneur who was marketing a special kind of display plant to hotels, offices and retailers. This was the only job Grace looked at and she rushed into it. During her first week doing the new job she started getting anxious, depressed and 'worried sick that I have made the wrong decision'. Additionally, she suffered from insomnia. Her reservations about her new job included: the product has limitations; my new boss seems egotistical; I have a less good car than in my previous job; the new job involves much more work than the previous one; and I am on a poor percentage sales commission in addition to my base salary, so I may not make more money.

In this example Grace is paying for her impulsive decision-making style. She says that getting more self-esteem is one of her main goals in life. However, she has behaved in a way that it makes it harder for her to see herself as a successful person than if she had adopted a more systematic decision-making approach. She not only suffers physical symptoms and an unsatisfactory work environment, but this poor decision has also probably cost her a lot of money. Had she taken a more rational approach she might well have found a higher paying job or, failing that, been able to negotiate a more competitive commission rate in the job she took.

Many of the skills discussed earlier might have helped Grace. For instance, if she had used coping self-talk in relation to Ed she might not have been in such a desperate hurry to change jobs. Additionally, if she had more realistic personal rules concerning being bored and not wanting her own way immediately, she might have looked around more. Her self-perception was also negative. Instead of thinking 'I'm a good salesperson with valuable skills to offer and I need to find a place where I can use my skills to best effect', she jumped at the first opportunity. Additionally, in her emotional state, Grace failed to perceive her position in the bedding company accurately since she did not sufficiently take into account that Ed was about to leave anyway. If Grace had collected more information, she would have made more accurate predictions about her job; for instance, since it was an important criterion for her, she could have found out in advance what sort of car she would get. Grace did not use visualization skills. She could have developed a clear picture of what sort of life she wanted. She could have imagined what it would actually be like doing the job she chose *before* she accepted it.

Table 10.2 is a decision-making checklist that might help you to improve the quality of your decision-making if, like Grace, this is a problem for you. It starts with checking whether you are engaging in the steps of rational decision-making. It then asks a series of questions about whether you are using the thinking skills discussed earlier in this book to support your decision-making. The steps of rational decision-making have already been presented. Consequently, the remainder of this chapter reviews the other nine questions on the checklist. I do not suggest that you use the checklist for every decision, however small. Life is too short. However, if you have an important decision and are afraid you might make a mistake, that is a good time to use the checklist.

### Am I owning responsibility for the authorship of my life?

There are many ways in which you may fail to own responsibility for the authorship of your life. You may not be fully aware of your capacity to make your life through your choices. You may lack a full existential awareness in which you have not adequately grasped the transitory nature of life. You may expect others to be responsible for what happens to you.

Decisions are often fraught with anxiety. You may bring your ongoing anxieties to your decision-making. Additionally, some decisions themselves involve more anxiety and inner conflict than others. This can be because the stakes are

Table 10.2    *A decision-making checklist*

When making a decision you may help yourself by asking the following questions.

1.  Am I engaging in the steps of rational decision-making?
2.  Am I owning responsibility for the authorship of my life?
3.  Am I in touch with my underlying feelings?
4.  Am I using self-talk constructively?
5.  Are my personal rules and directives helping rather than harming me?
6.  Are my perceptions accurate regarding myself and others?
7.  Are my attributions of cause accurate?
8.  Are my predictions realistic?
9.  Am I articulating my goals clearly and do they reflect my values?
10. Am I using visualizing to best effect?

high, the decision is complex, it involves a value conflict and there is no clear 'best' option. You may handle your anxiety about decisions through some of the styles mentioned earlier, such as avoidance, impulsiveness and hypervigilance.

Decision-making can involve courage. Some of you may be passive rather than active in your decision-making. You may have become used to depending on others, such as your parents, for advice as to how you should act. You may be hypersensitive to the rules of your peer group and afraid to lose their esteem. You may feel the need to obey authority figures and cede responsibility for your decision-making to them. Thus you may gain external approval at the expense of losing integrity.

Some simple questions that you can ask yourself that are relevant to assuming authorship of your life include: 'am I too passive in my approach to life and wait for things to happen?; do I take the easy way out by avoiding decisions?; do I get so anxious that I am afraid to make up my mind?; and do I lack the courage of my convictions and become too dependent on others for my decisions?'

**Am I in touch with my underlying feelings?**

As you make decisions, you define and create yourself. In general, good decisions involve skills not only of reasoning but also of getting in touch with your underlying feelings. In the example of Grace, she was almost too aware of her short-term feelings of boredom, annoyance with Ed and wanting to leave. However, she lacked the capacity to get more deeply centred in listening to her own valuing process. Consequently, because she listened to her superficial rather than to her deeper feelings, she made a poor decision. Put another way, Grace was a woman with severe problems of self-esteem and identity. She was receiving counselling to be healed after a very emotionally deprived upbringing and also to acquire self-help skills. Grace's being out of touch with her feelings contributed to her making decisions too quickly. Others of you may be out of touch with your wants and wishes and be in a state of *indecision*, as contrasted with too ready decision.

There are a number of approaches to getting more in touch with your feelings. These include the following.

- *Taking more time*. Sleeping on it is a common approach to making important decisions. This should not involve sleepless nights. The idea is that a night's sleep helps you get matters more in perspective, lessens the risk of making hasty decisions and allows you to decide when refreshed. There are issues of timing and pacing that are very important in decision-making. Sometimes, given more time, you may find yourself confident enough to make a previously difficult decision.

- *Gathering external information*. Again this relates to your readiness to make a decision. Making decisions is a process. You may find that as you collect more relevant information you are able to understand what you really want. Attention to the process has produced a decision with which you are comfortable.

- *Inner listening*. A vital source of information comes from within. You may need to develop your skills of inner focusing and of giving yourself more chance to listen to your feelings (Gendlin, 1981). If you always rush around you may not allow yourself time for creative contemplation. Part of Thinksheet 7 (Chapter 3) focused on inner listening when you had a decision that was bothering you. The skills of inner listening include: physically and psychologically clearing a space; spending periods of 'quiet time', possibly after relaxing yourself; when you have your eyes shut, not trying to analyse or think through the decision, but just experiencing your flow of feelings in relation to it; and at the end of the periods of 'quiet time' seeing if you feel any differently about the problem.

- *Asserting yourself*. You may need to assert yourself more since the noise from outside can be so great that it blocks your inner listening. I deal with assertion more thoroughly in the final chapter. Suffice it for now to mention that numerous other people may have vested interests in the outcomes of your decisions. Even if they do not, they may still be very ready to offer advice rather than to help you to your own conclusions.

- *Anxiety-management skills*. Anxiety can be a devastating anaesthetic for feelings. Many of the thinking skills covered later in the checklist, such as coping self-talk and possessing realistic personal rules, may help you to lower debilitating anxiety. Thus you may become more in touch with your wants, wishes and feelings.

**Am I using self-talk constructively?**

There are a number of ways in which you can use self-talk to help with your decision-making.

- *Using 'I' self-talk.* You can use 'I' self-talk constructively. For example, it is much more self-supporting to say 'I can't make up my mind', rather than 'You fool, why can't you make up your mind?'

- *Using calming self-talk.* Earlier it was mentioned that coping self-talk consisted of two elements: *calming* self-talk and *coaching* self-talk. When you experience anxiety over a decision you can use calming self-talk, such as 'keep calm, relax and I can cope'.

- *Using coaching self-talk.* You can consciously instruct yourself through the steps of a rational decision-making process. For example, you can ask yourself questions about each of the steps, such as 'am I adequately confronting the decision?; the next thing I need to do is to generate options and gather information, how do I go about this?; what do I predict as the consequences of my options and what are my criteria for assessing them?; and what seems to be the best option and am I prepared to commit myself to implementing it?'

- *Engaging in a self-talk dialogue.* One approach to resolving a decision-making conflict is to conduct a dialogue. For instance, the part of you that is in favour of an option can hold a dialogue with the part of you that is against it. You tend to weigh the pros and cons when you make any decision. Some of you may find it helpful to become more aware of these existing self-talk processes, even to the extent of moving from one chair to another as you alternate roles. Given privacy, you can hold your self-talk dialogue aloud.

**Are my personal rules and directives helping rather than harming me?**

You may have mustabatory personal rules in regard to the way you make decisions and the content of your decisions. Self-oppressing personal rules in regard to the decision-making *process* include: I *must* always make the right decision; I *must* always make decisions quickly and easily; the information I need to make a decision *must* always be available immediately; in decisions involving other people I *must* always get what I want.

Mustabatory rules concerning the *content* of your decisions alter with the areas under consideration. For instance, if you make a career decision, possible self-oppressing personal rules include: I *must* get into the most prestigious career possible; I *must* make more money than my contemporaries; I *must* choose a career that will please my parents; I *must* be accepted by every company and agency to which I apply; when I go for interviews I *must* be liked by everyone.

Related to your mustabatory personal rules you may have pressurizer and inhibitive directives that impair your decision-making. Possible pressurizer directives include 'hurry up' and 'be in control'. Possible inhibitor directives include 'don't think', 'don't feel' and 'don't take risks'.

If you become aware of your self-opposing rules you can dispute them and reformulate them into language that is more self-supporting. If you become aware of pressurizer and inhibitor directives you can dispute them, understand their origins and grant yourself permission to think and act differently. You may have to struggle hard to counteract your self-defeating 'voices in the head', internalized from others, with your own rational rules and directives.

### Are my perceptions accurate regarding myself and others?

You may need to check whether you are making the distinction between facts and inferences and, where facts are limited, whether you are making your inferences as realistic as possible.

- *Self-perceptions*. Are you evaluating yourself realistically or do you attach false negative or positive labels to yourself? For instance, when Grace came to make her decision about leaving the bedding company, she insufficiently valued not only her specific characteristics as a salesperson but also her worth as a human being. She would have done much better to have taken a more balanced approach, acknowledging and listing her resources and realistically perceiving her limitations. Focusing on your weaknesses and unnecessarily putting yourself down can cause you to be over-anxious and hence to miss good opportunities. Similarly, being defensive and not acknowledging realistic weaknesses distances you from having a sound information base for your decisions.

- *Perceptions of others*. Many decisions require you to perceive other people accurately. If you have tendencies to focus on other people's weaknesses rather than their strengths you may find yourself making decisions to end relationships and jobs when it might have been in your interests to stay in them. Other perceptual errors that may contribute to your perceiving others unrealistically include black and white thinking (he/she is either all for me or all against me) and overgeneralizing 'because he/she ignored me once, he/she will always do so'.

As mentioned earlier, good decisions require good information. The more you misperceive, the more likely you are to make poor decisions. Remember that the first perception is not necessarily the best perception. Rational decision-making involves you taking the time and trouble to check out the accuracy of your perceptions of yourself and others. These are important building blocks for your decisions.

**Are my attributions of cause accurate?**

Below are three examples of people who are making decisions on the basis of their attributions.

> Shirley, aged 26, has decided to get a divorce. She attributes the cause of this decision to her own growth as an assertive and independent woman while her husband remains the same spoiled little boy that he has always been.

> Ron, aged 38, was fired a year ago. He has decided to leave the town where he has lived all his life. He attributes the reason for this decision to there being no opportunities available in his home town for electronics engineers like himself.

> Norman, aged 21, has decided not to go on to postgraduate study. His marks at college this year have not been as good as he wanted. He attributes this to lack of ability.

In the above examples Shirley, Ron and Norman are all making important decisions on the basis of their explanations of the situations in which they find themselves. These explanations may or may not be accurate. When making decisions, especially important ones, you need to consider carefully the explanations you give yourself for what is happening to you. Useful skills for doing this include separating facts from inferences and logically analysing the factual underpinning of any causal inferences that you make.

**Are my predictions realistic?**

When you make decisions do you collect sufficient information to increase the probability of your predictions being realistic? You may have a general decision-making style that is either too optimistic or too pessimistic. Although you make many decisions well, you may rush into others on the basis of rosy expectations and then live to regret it. Alternatively, you may fail to create and take good opportunities by being too pessimistic.

Poor decisions are often founded on faulty predictive reasoning. You jump to erroneous and simplistic conclusions. Statements in the careers area that may involve faulty predictive reasoning include the following.

I could never work under a woman.

I can't stand the sight of blood and therefore I can never become a doctor.

The fact that they did not employ my friend means that they will not employ me.

A few people in the company are getting fired so I am likely to be the next.

A woman like me will never be able to compete in a man's world.

Because I have received one letter of rejection, this means that I am unemployable.

They are not going to pay much attention to the fact that I've had ten jobs in eight years when I next apply for a job.

As with other thinking skills, you need to discipline your thinking so that you sort out facts from inferences in making predictions. You may have some basis for some of your perceptions. However, the conclusions you draw from them may be inaccurate. For example, you may have realistic evidence that as a woman it is harder than if you were a man to succeed in your chosen career, but it is probably a leap of logic to say that you will never be able to compete. There is increasing evidence of women succeeding in areas, such as medicine and the law, that have traditionally been dominated by males. You may also have strengths that you do not fully acknowledge.

**Am I articulating my goals clearly and do they reflect my values?**

When you engage in the decision-making process your goals may not be altogether clear. Part of the process can entail making decisions about what goals you choose as well as about how to obtain them. I illustrate this by reverting to the earlier examples of Frank and Grace.

Frank, aged 28, the computer operator for a telephone company, had the overall goal of getting a better job. He had thought of some criteria for the job he wanted. This included: a 15 per cent increase over his present salary; the chance to do mmore programming and less administration; continuing to work in the city centre rather than in the outer suburbs; and being part of a team rather than working on his own. He had articulated these goals at the start of his job search. He intended to use the job search process not only for finding out what was available, but also for refining and adding to his goals about the position he was looking for.

Grace, aged 33, the bedding company sales person, had goals at the start of her job search that were as much negative as positive. She wished both to be less bored and to get away from Ed. Although she realized that she wanted to make more money, she never thought out

specific criteria for choosing a new position. It was only when she
started the job selling display plants that she articulated what should
have been some of her original goals; for example, having a company
car at least as good as her previous one, which she had not got, and a
total salary plus commission that exceeded her previous salary by 20
per cent, which she now thought was highly unlikely. These were her
two main goals. However, since Grace contemplated another job
move, together with her counsellor she articulated eight more goals.
In descending order of importance to her, these goals were: having a
good quality product to sell; working for a reputable company; having
a boss who possessed professional management and relationship
skills; getting good secretarial and delivery of goods support; having
her own desk and phone in a modern office; availability of inservice
training; opportunity for advancement; and being offered a clear
contract, the terms of which she could negotiate. Grace openly admitted that she had made a poor decision in rushing into the job selling
display plants. She very much wanted to learn how to go about
making better decisions.

Ideally your goals reflect your values. However, on occasions your values may
conflict, thus making it hard for you to articulate your goals. For example, you
may have materialistic values at the same time as wanting to help others in your
work. You then need to spend time clarifying your values and goals before
making a more specific decision concerning what jobs you apply for. The trade-
offs and compromises involved in articulating your goals are more likely to help
than to harm you if you approach your values decisions in a rational way. This
should also take into account your deeper feelings and ethical commitments.

**Am I using visualizing to best effect?**

Ways that you can use visualizing to improve your decision-making include
clarifying your goals, reviewing options, using positive imagery and considering
the worst possibility.

- *Clarifying your goals*. It helps to have a vision of what you want to make of your
  life. Your daydreams are one source of ideas for your goals. When you
  articulate your goals it may help you to visualize what it would be like attaining
  them. As you visualize your goals you may choose to modify them.

- *Reviewing options*. As you review and weigh options in a decision it may help
  you to picture implementing the main options and experiencing their consequences. For instance, you might visualize: a day in the life of different career
  options; what it might be like being married to someone; what it might be like

being divorced; and what it might be like living with your first child. You probably do this already, but may not be sufficiently systematic about it.

- *Using positive imagery*. If you use positive imagery concerning your strengths and coping capacities you may feel more confident about making certain decisions. For example, if you are afraid about the consequences of accepting a promotion, visualizing yourself coping in the more demanding job might assist you in deciding to accept rather than reject the offer.

- *Considering the worst possibility*. If you avoid making a decision, one approach is to visualize the 'worst-case scenario' of carrying out one or more options. You should try to picture how you would cope with such difficulties and what support you would be able to call upon. Visualizing yourself coping in adversity may help you to overcome blocks both to making and to implementing the decision.

---

**Thinksheet 47    Reviewing how you make important decisions**

*Instructions*
Think how you make important decisions and write out your answers to the following questions.

1.   Do I make important decisions in a systematic and rational way?

2.   Do I own responsibility for the authorship of my life?

3.   Do I get in touch with my underlying feelings?

4.   Do I use self-talk constructively?

5.   Do my personal rules and directives help rather than harm me?

6.   Do I perceive myself and others accurately?

7.   Do I attribute cause accurately?

8.   Do I make realistic predictions?

9.   Do I articulate my goals clearly and do they reflect my values?

10.   Do I use visualizing to best effect?

When you have completed the above review, list the main points you need to remember for improving your decision-making in future.

---

## CHAPTER HIGHLIGHTS

Poor decisions can cost you dearly in time, effort, emotional upset and money.

Decision-making styles are characteristic patterns of making decisions. Styles of individual decision-making include rational, feelings-based, hypervigilant, avoidant, impulsive, compliant and ethical. Styles of joint decision-making include competitive, compliant and collaborative.

Rational decision-making involves: confronting the decision; generating options and gathering information about them; assessing the predicted consequences of options; committing yourself to a decision; planning its implementation; implementing it; and assessing the actual consequences of implementation.

You may improve the quality of your decision-making if you: engage in the steps of rational decision-making; own responsibility for authorship of your life; use self-talk constructively; possess helpful personal rules and directives; perceive yourself and others accurately; attribute cause accurately; make realistic predictions; articulate your goals clearly; and use visualizing to best effect.

# 11 Preventing and Managing Problems

No problem is so big or so complicated that it can't be run away from.

*Schultz*, Peanuts *caption*

Definition of having a problem: loving yourself more than your analyst.
Definition of overcoming a problem: loving your analyst more than yourself.

Like death and taxes, problems are a big equalizer. Everybody has them. However, some people have more problems than others. Also, some are better at making the choices that prevent avoidable problems and that help to manage unavoidable ones. A chess problem is an arrangement of pieces on the board to which a player is challenged to find an answer. Similarly, in your life there are likely to be many times when you are challenged to find answers to personal problems. Adapting one of Rodgers and Hammerstein's most famous songs:

> Some enchanted evening,
> I may lose my hang-ups,
> And face reality.
> And no one will believe,
> Believe even then,
> That I will be different,
> Again and again.

In Chapter 1 I mentioned two ways of viewing personal problems. One viewpoint is preventive. The challenge is how to prevent problems. The second viewpoint involves managing problems. The challenge is how best to cope with problems once they occur. These problems have often been around for a long time. You may have tried to solve them unsuccessfully and your attempted solutions have now become part of your problems. Many of you may feel stuck in your problems. You both want to and have tried to cope better, but your problems still persist. I do not wish to imply that all personal problems can be solved. However, if you choose to use the thinking skills described in this book they may help you to prevent some problems, overcome others and live more comfortably with those that are unavoidable and relatively permanent features of your life.

Decision-making and problem management overlap. The focus in Chapter 10 was on making decisions at major and minor turning points where you needed to decide between different options. Here the focus is more on using thinking skills to prevent and manage feelings and behaviours that are problematic for you. This does not mean that you have caused all your problems. External events often contribute heavily to them; for instance, other people's behaviour, accidents, socioeconomic conditions and so on. You have been heavily influenced by your learning environment. Nevertheless, you have a choice about how to cope with your problems, whatever their origins.

**Styles of managing problems**

Although you may manage different problems in different ways, you may have a characteristic pattern or style of managing problems. As shown later, the skills involved in managing problems differ somewhat from those for making decisions. Nevertheless, the decision-making styles discussed in the previous chapter have some relevance for how you manage problems. You may be rational in your approach. You may get in touch with your deeper feelings. Alternatively, you may avoid problems, impulsively find solutions, be hypervigilant and get too bogged down in sifting through the details of problems, or try to manage your problems by complying with others' wishes. Some of you will also approach your problems within ethical frameworks that may either harm or help you.

The remainder of the chapter is divided into three main sections. First, I discuss the application of thinking skills to preventing problems. Second, I present CASIE, a five-step framework for managing problems. Third, I illustrate how thinking skills provide some useful 'handles' for working on common problems.

**PREVENTING PROBLEMS**

Proverbs such as 'an ounce of prevention is worth a pound of cure' and 'a stitch in time saves nine' tell the home truths that you are often better off preventing problems than having to deal with them later. In Chapter 1 I used the analogy of the golfer who tries to stay on the fairway to prevent the problems of having to play out of the rough. Similarly, you too should try to keep on the fairway.

One way of viewing thinking skills as prevention is to see yourself as being less predisposed to problems the more you use good thinking skills in your everyday life. You are a more confident person who is less prone to be threatened by imaginary rather than real difficulties. Your commitment to effective thinking helps you to lead your life in ways that minimize the occurrence of unnecessary problems.

Another way of using thinking skills as prevention is where you anticipate a specific problem may occur. Here your early warning system detects that you are at risk of making a self-oppressing contribution that will either create or worsen a problem on the horizon. Table 11.1 provides a checklist that you can use to review how you might prevent a problem. The negative consequences of many problems are immense, for instance the break-up of families or heart attacks, so time spent trying to prevent these consequences is often time well spent. Table 11.1 is also a checklist that you can use for *managing* as contrasted with *preventing* problems.

Table 11.1   *A checklist for preventing and managing problems*

---

When you wish either to prevent or to manage a problem you can help yourself by asking some or all of the following questions.

1.   Am I engaging in the steps of effective problem management?
2.   Am I owning responsibility for the authorship of my life?
3.   Am I in touch with my underlying feelings?
4.   Am I using self-talk constructively?
5.   Are my personal rules and directives helping rather than harming me?
6.   Are my perceptions accurate regarding myself and others?
7.   Are my attributions of cause accurate?
8.   Are my predictions realistic?
9.   Am I articulating my goals clearly and do they reflect my values?
10.  Am I using visualizing to best effect?

---

## Preventing excessive stress

Let me illustrate what I mean by using thinking skills in a preventive way in relation to a specific problem, excessive stress. Let us assume that your goal is to have an optimal level of stress, where you feel sufficiently challenged but not overwhelmed by demands made by yourself, others and your environment. No one has total control over his or her stress level. Consequently, you wish to choose the level of stress and activity that works best for you and also to cope effectively with stresses originating outside you. You may not feel excessively stressed now. Nevertheless, you see excessive stress as a potential problem that you wish to avoid or contain. For instance, you may have had a relative who suffered from stress-related ailments like hypertension and heart attacks. You decide therefore that for you prevention is better than a cure.

How can you use your thinking skills to prevent excessive stress? Below are some suggestions with reference to items 2 to 10 of the checklist.

- *Am I owning responsibility for the authorship of my life?* You may need to review whether you are at risk of making faulty choices that lead you not to look after your health and achieve a balanced level of activity. You may need to become more aware of your mortality and physical limitations. The more you can assume responsibility for *making* your life, the less likely you are to allow yourself to be stressed beyond reasonable limits.

- *Am I in touch with my underlying feelings?* If you operate as a healthy animal you use your feelings as a guide for your behaviour. For example, if you feel you are a worthwhile person in your own right, you are less likely to want to overstrive to meet others' unrealistic expectations. You possess the capacity to listen to your body. When you start feeling tired and stressed you acknowledge this and then act, if possible, to protect your overall effectiveness.

- *Am I using self-talk constructively?* Part of preventing excessive stress involves dealing with the stresses you face daily in self-supporting rather than in self-oppressing ways. One of the main uses of coping self-talk is to be able to manage stressful events more effectively. By being able to talk yourself through stressful events in calming and coaching ways, you diminish your frustration and increase your effectiveness.

- *Are my personal rules and directives helpful?* If you make perfectionistic mustabatory demands on yourself, others and the environment, these can contribute to feelings of excessive stress and burn-out. The more you can work towards having functional, realistic and flexible personal rules that are based on preferences rather than demands, the less likely you are to choose to be a candidate for stress-related misery and illness. For instance, you may have mustabatory personal rules about study and work achievement and about needing others' approval. If so, you need to challenge and reformulate these rules. If you possess a potentially dangerous pressurizer directive like 'hurry up', dispute this and give yourself permission to live at a pace that better suits your animal nature.

- *Are my perceptions accurate regarding myself and others?* What you perceive as stressful involves a transaction between you and the stressor. For instance, if you can avoid negative self-labelling and acknowledge realistic positive attributes you should feel more adequate to cope with stress. Additionally, if you avoid distortions of others, you can prevent causing stress for yourself. For example, Graham experiences his boss as much more threatening than his behaviour to date has justified. In reality, Graham has transferred his perception of a previous boss, who was difficult, to his current boss, who has not been difficult so far. If Graham overreacts negatively towards his new boss he may further create his stress.

- *Are my attributions of cause accurate?* If you realistically acknowledge your own contribution to your problems, you are in a position to work on them successfully. This relieves stress in the long run. Additionally, if you are realistic about the causes of your successes and failures, you are in a better position to improve your performances than if your attributions of causes are inaccurate. An example of an inaccurate attribution of cause leading to stress is that of Sophie. She gets uptight because she refuses to acknowledge that her not getting a job was due to another candidate being stronger rather than to the bias of the interviewing panel.

- *Are my predictions realistic?* You might prevent excessive stress if you adopt an 'it can happen to me' instead of an 'it can't happen to me' attitude to the negative consequences of overstressing your body. Accurately predicting the consequences of your actions can help you avoid costly mistakes and the stresses that accompany them.

- *Am I articulating my goals clearly and do they reflect my values?* Clear goals help prevent the stresses of confusion. Realistic goals are a protection against overstriving. Goals that reflect your values as much as possible can help to prevent stress-inducing inner conflicts arising from discrepancies between your goals and your values. If you are able to create your future on the basis of well thought through goals and values, you should enjoy the beneficial as contrasted with the harmful effects of stress.

- *Am I using visualizing to best effect?* You can prevent distress by: visualizing realistic goals for yourself; visualizing the consequences of decisions before you make them; and using visualizing to improve your relationships. You can also prevent excessive stress through visualized relaxation, in which you take time out to visualize a calm and peaceful scene.

These are only some of the ways that you can use your thinking skills to prevent the psychological and physical miseries of self-inflicted excessive stress. The more you can think effectively when actually faced with problems and decisions the more you support yourself in avoiding and containing excessive stress.

### Preventing problems and superior functioning

Much of psychology focuses on remedying psychological pain rather than on how to live effectively. Living effectively involves not just managing problems but preventing them. Humans have the capacity to transcend the unhappiness that blights so many lives and often gets handed on from parents to children. If you can develop and use the thinking skills described in this book you should be able to prevent many of the problems that represent and sustain psychological distress. Superior human functioning entails making 'smart' rather than 'dumb' thinking choices. Effective people are good information processors. They realize that if they discipline themselves to think effectively, not only will they create much happiness but they will also avoid much misery for both themselves and others.

---

**Thinksheet 48    Using thinking skills to prevent problems**

*Instructions*

1.  Think of a possible future problem, such as excessive stress or a deterioration in your relationship with your partner, that you wish to prevent.

2.  Review the following broad areas of thinking skills with a view to identifying ways of preventing your potential problem.

    - owning responsibility for authorship of my life
    - being in touch with my underlying feelings
    - using self-talk constructively
    - having helpful personal rules and directives
    - having accurate perceptions about myself and others
    - having accurate attributions of cause
    - making realistic predictions
    - having goals that I articulate clearly and that reflect my values
    - using visualizing to best effect

3.  Summarize what you have learned from the above analysis about how to prevent the problem. Start putting your insights into practice now.

---

## CASIE: A FIVE-STEP FRAMEWORK FOR MANAGING PROBLEMS

Managing your problems effectively involves you in using many of the same skills you use in making decisions. Nevertheless, there are some important differences, perhaps especially in the areas of assessing and defining problems. Below I present a five-step framework for managing problems. I have given it the acronym CASIE to make it easier for you to remember. The five steps of CASIE are as follows.

C    *Confront* your problem.
A    *Assess* and *define* your problem.
S    *Set goals* and *plan.*
I    *Implement* your plan.
E    *Evaluate* the consequences of implementation.

CASIE is intended to provide a framework for the processes of managing your problems. It is not intended to be a straitjacket, but to be used flexibly. It can be used with varying degrees of formality and rigour depending on how difficult and important your problem is. For many minor problems you may rightly think it is not worth the bother of systematically going through its five steps. Each step is now discussed in turn.

**Step 1: confront your problem**

Confronting your problems involves a number of different elements.

- *Orientation.* Orientation refers to your attitude to problems. Considerations relevant to your orientation towards problems include the degree to which you think that: problems are a normal part of life; the best approach to problems is to try to cope with them; it is important to identify problems either before or as they arise rather than when they are full-blown; and a 'stop . . . think . . . what are my choices?' approach is better than impulsiveness.

- *Ownership.* Ownership involves acknowledging that you have a problem. There are numerous reasons why it may be convenient to deny your problems or to dilute their significance. Acknowledging problems may mean, among other things; admitting to yourself that you were wrong; confronting the need for change; and having to develop new and better skills. It may also involve assuming responsibility for how you think, feel and act rather than choosing to perceive others as responsible.

- *Clearing a space.* Confronting a problem goes beyond awareness of its existence to acknowledging that you need to work on it. This involves clearing a space. You may need to find a physical environment free from distractions. You need the psychological space to give the problem the time and emotional energy it deserves.

**Step 2: assess and define your problem**

You may make the following statements of problems.

I'm bored.

I'm unhappy.

I'm lonely.

I'm shy.

I can't control my anger.

My marriage is heading for the rocks.

I get tense and nervous about tests.

I'm disorganized and good at procrastinating.

I suffer from hypertension.

I'm afraid of having another heart attack.

I feel dominated by my parents.

All these statements are descriptive. None of them offers any 'handles' on how you might work for change. In Chapter 2 I stressed the distinction between how you *acquired* your thinking skills weaknesses and how you *sustain* them. The former is often 'what others have done to me', whereas the latter is more 'what I do to myself'. Assessing your problem entails the detective work of searching for what you do, or fail to do, that sustains your problem. The purpose of your assessment is to move from a descriptive statement to a working definition of your problem. A working definition specifies the *thinking* and *action* skills weaknesses whereby you sustain your problem or your share of it.

*Describing problems*

When you have decided to clear a space and focus on a problem, you then need to develop a fuller understanding of it. One way to get such an understanding is to ask yourself questions that elicit specific information about your problem. At this stage you are *describing* your problem. Although the two stages overlap, the next stage involves your *explaining* how you sustain your problem.

You can elaborate your initial description of your problem by asking yourself a series of *how* questions. These include the following.

How would I like to be?

How long has the problem been going on?

How severe is it?

How important is it?

How do I feel in relation to it?

How do I think in relation to it?

How do I act in relation to it?

How have I attempted to cope with it so far?

How is my behaviour helping or harming me?

To answer some of these how questions you may need systematically to focus on your thoughts and actions. Below are three methods that can help you to become more aware of your thoughts in relation to a problem.

- *Thought listing.* Make a list of all the thoughts you have about your problem. If necessary, add to this list daily until you consider that you have identified most of your more important thoughts in relation to it.

- *ABC analysis.* Think of a recent problem situation. Use the ABC framework to identify your thoughts, feelings and actions in relation to this situation. The ABC framework is:

    A   The problem situation (or activating event).
    B   Your thoughts and visual images about A.
    C   How you felt and acted in relation to A.

You should try to be as specific as possible when describing your thoughts.

- *Double-column technique.* The double-column technique is a method of monitoring, for a specific period, your thoughts relating to your problem. For example, if your problem is 'I can't control my anger', you keep a log of times when you were angry. At the top of the left-hand column write 'What happened' and at the top of the right-hand column write 'My thoughts'. In the left-hand column fill in the dates, approximate times, descriptions of what happened to trigger your anger and how you behaved. In the right-hand column fill in your thoughts before, during and after each anger incident.

---

**Thinksheet 49   Describing your problems more fully**

*Instructions*
1.   Think of a problem on which you wish to work.

2.   Write out your answers to the following questions.

- How would I like to be?
- How long has the problem been going on?
- How severe is it?
- How important is it?
- How frequent is it?

- How do I feel in relation to it?
- How do I act in relation to it?
- How have I attempted to cope with it so far?
- How is my behaviour helping or harming me?

3. Review your thinking in relation to the problem by at least one of the following methods.

- Thought listing
- ABC analysis
- Double-column technique

---

*Explaining how you sustain your problems*

Defining problems involves generating and weighing different explanations of how you sustain your problems. The final product is a list of specific skills weaknesses that you can work to change. Elements in *explaining* your role in your problems include the following.

- *Gathering information.* In the section above, you gathered information to describe your problem more fully. You can also seek out information from others, such as what they think about the problem and how supportive they are likely to be.

- *Knowing what to look for.* When you are thinking of explanations for how you sustain your problems, how do you know what to look for? This is an issue for professional helpers as well as those wishing to help themselves. Professional helpers tend to rely on a mixture of theory, research findings and professional experience. They then pragmatically adapt this to the needs of individual clients. This book has described many of the thinking skills weaknesses that a professional cognitive psychotherapist might use to explain your problems. Table 11.1 provides a checklist that can act as a reminder of the various thinking skill weaknesses that you can take into account. Additionally, you can look for action skills weaknesses that sustain your problems. These vary from problem to problem; for instance, you focus on specific relationship skills weaknesses for improving how you related and on specific study skills weaknesses for improving how you study.

- *Generating explanations.* You may need to be creative about generating alternative explanations for how you sustain your problems. As with decision-making, the first option frequently is not the best option. You may need to brainstorm for different options. If so, remember the rules: criticism of ideas is ruled out; free-wheeling is welcomed; and quantity is wanted, the more suggestions the better.

- *Weighing explanations.* You need to decide on the explanations that best suit your particular problem. Which do you think are the most accurate and important? There are various considerations you may use in weighing explanations. For instance, your past history in relation to other similar problems may have sensitized you to look for characteristic skills weaknesses. Some explanations appear to fit the facts better than others. You anticipate that the predicted consequences of certain explanations are more likely to get you what you want than those of other explanations. You think that certain explanations lead to changing your thoughts and actions in ways that are more within your abilities than others.

### Stating working definitions

A working definition reflects your decisions about how you sustain all or part of your problem. It identifies specific thinking and action skills weaknesses that you can work on. You have now moved beyond description to provide yourself with specific 'handles' to guide your attempts to change. Working definitions are made on the best information you have available at the time. They are open to modification and updating in the light of new information.

Below are two examples of working definitions.

> Angry Al was a middle-aged man with two teenaged daughters. He had great difficulty in controlling his temper and had recently struck one of his daughters. He was afraid that his inability to control his anger would lead to the break-up of his family. A working definition of Al's anger problem included the following *thinking* skills weaknesses: (1) inadequately acknowledging his responsibility for his thoughts, feelings and actions; (2) not using coping self-talk when faced with provocations; (3) having rigid and unrealistic personal rules concerning standards of behaviour in the family; and (4) misperceiving and insufficiently acknowledging the connection between how he behaved towards his family and how they behaved towards him. *Action* skills weaknesses that Al needed to work on included poor listening, assertion and conflict communication skills.

> Neil was a shy 22-year-old college student. A working definition of his shyness included the following *thinking* skills weaknesses: (1) using self-talk in social situations in ways that heightened his anxieties; (2) having a self-oppressing personal rule about the need for universal approval and the catastrophe of any sign of rejection; (3) being quick to perceive situations, such as someone not talking to him, as 'put downs' without checking if there were other explanations; and (4) a tendency to think passively rather than actively about how he might assume responsibility for making things happen in his life. Neil's

*action* skills weaknesses included: (1) revealing very little of his thoughts and feelings to others; (2) speaking in a very quiet voice; and (3) not using 'I' statements.

---

**Thinksheet 50    Formulating a working definition of your problem**

*Instructions*

1.   Select a problem on which you wish to work, preferably the problem you used for Thinksheet 49.

2.   Generate and weigh different explanations of how you sustain your problem. In particular, focus on what may be the thinking skills weaknesses that sustain your problem.

3.   State a working definition of your problem that includes at least two thinking skills weaknesses and one action skills weakness.

---

## Step 3: set goals and plan

In step 2 you attempted to answer the question: 'how do I sustain the problem?' Given your working definition arrived at in step 2, step 3 focuses on the question: 'how can I best manage the problem?' It consists of two phases: setting working goals and developing a plan.

### Setting working goals

Goals can be stated broadly, such as 'I want to become less angry' or 'I want to become less shy'. Although these descriptive statements of goals may provide an overall vision, if you are to work for change you need to state your goals more specifically. Statements of working goals are the reverse or 'flip side' of your working definitions of your problems. Below I change Al's and Neil's working definitions of their problems into statements of working goals.

> Working goals for angry Al include the following *thinking* skills strengths: (1) adequately acknowledging his responsibility for his thoughts, feelings and actions; (2) using coping self-talk when faced with provocations; (3) having realistic personal rules concerning standards of behaviour in the family; and (4) realistically perceiving how his behaviour affects his family's behaviour towards him. Al also

needed to acquire the *action* skills strengths of good listening, assertion and conflict communication skills.

Working goals for shy Neil included the following *thinking* skills strengths: (1) using coping self-talk in social situations; (2) possessing a realistic personal rule concerning approval and acknowledging that, when others seem to reject him, he does not have to reject himself; (3) realistically perceiving others' behaviour in social situations; and (4) assuming more responsibility for making things happen in his life. Neil also needed to acquire the *action* skills strengths of: (1) greater self-disclosure; (2) speaking in a louder voice; and (3) using 'I' statements.

In Chapter 8 I mentioned four characteristics in stating goals. Your goals should reflect your values, be realistic, be specific and give a time frame. In the above examples both Al and Neil need a time frame for working on their problems. Both wished to start immediately. Since Al feared the negative consequences of a divorce and family break-up, his goal was to make significant progress in attaining his managing anger goals by the end of a month. Neil gave himself three months to make significant progress in attaining his managing shyness goals. As they grappled with their problems both Al and Neil still needed to spell out their working goals further; for instance, what kind of coping self-talk to use in which anger-evoking or shyness-evoking situations. However, they had sufficient information in their initial statements of working goals to give them a sense of direction. The details could be filled in later.

*Developing a plan*

In the previous chapter I listed six considerations in planning how to implement a decision. These six characteristics are also relevant to developing a plan to manage a problem.

- *State clearly your goals and subgoals.* For instance, Al's overall goal was to become less angry. Each of his working goals might be viewed as subgoals.

- *Break tasks down.* You may need to break the skills you need to acquire down. A simple example is that of breaking coping self-talk down into coaching self-instructions and calming self-instructions.

- *Generate and consider alternative courses of action.* Generating and considering alternatives applies to how best to attain both your thinking and your action working goals. You can generate alternative ways of thinking as well as of acting.

- *Anticipate difficulties and setbacks.* You need to acknowledge that difficulties may occur when you implement your plan and also how best to cope with them.

- *Identify sources of support.* Sometimes 'a problem shared is a problem doubled, if not tripled or quadrupled'. For instance, someone diagnosed as having AIDS may face all sorts of unwanted reactions if this information is disclosed indiscriminately. Nevertheless, discriminating identification of sources of support can greatly help you to manage a difficult problem better.

- *Write your plan out.* If a problem is important to you, it is very likely to merit the time and attention to write your plan out. Written plans can give you clarity of focus and strengthen your commitment.

A further consideration when developing your plan is that you may not be ready to act out certain parts of it right away. Consequently a seventh consideration is:

- *Build in homework, rehearsal and practice.* You may acquire a better understanding of the thinking skills weaknesses contributing to your problem, if you work through relevant thinksheets. Additionally, you can use visualized rehearsal in which you rehearse the thinking and action components required for successfully performing a task. Furthermore, you may be able to practise your thinking and action skills on easier problems before moving on to more difficult ones.

When you develop plans, you outline ways of approaching specific problems. Your plans need to take into account the particular circumstances of the problem under consideration. Plans need to be both firm and flexible: firm so that you discipline yourself to take appropriate steps to implementing them and flexible so that you are open to realistic feedback. Thinksheet 51 is designed to give you practice at stating working goals and developing a plan to manage a problem.

---

Thinksheet 51    Stating working goals and developing a plan

*Instructions*

1. Select a problem on which you wish to work, preferably the problem you used for Thinksheet 50.

2. Translate your working definition of your problem into a statement of working goals.

3. List the negative consequences to yourself and others of not managing your problem effectively.

4. Develop and write out a plan to manage your problem. Focus especially on how to improve specific thinking skills, but also focus on improving at least one action skill. In developing your plan remember the following considerations.

- State clearly your goals and subgoals.
- Break tasks down.
- Generate and consider alternative ways of thinking and courses of action.
- Anticipate difficulties and setbacks.
- Identify sources of support.
- Build in homework, rehearsal and practice.

As you write out your plan remember to avoid the twin pitfalls of giving insufficient detail and giving too much detail. Ensure that your plan is easy for you to understand and follow.

---

### Step 4: implement your plan

Many of the considerations relevant to implementing decisions are also relevant to implementing plans. These include: paying attention to timing; working through reservations about aspects of your plan; no excuses; openness to feedback; using positive self-reward; and working through the guilt you may feel when you do not adhere to your plan. Altering long established habits of thinking and behaving can be difficult. Setbacks are to be expected. Your learning may take place in fits and starts. However, if you persist, you might start reaping the rewards of your changed thinking and behaviour. Success can do wonders for commitment.

### Step 5: evaluate the consequences of implementation

By stating your working goals clearly, you have given yourself guidelines for monitoring and evaluating changes in how you think and act. Three important questions to ask yourself are: 'how well am I using my thinking and action skills?; what are the consequences for myself and others of changes in my thinking and action skills?; and do I need to modify my plan in the light of feedback and new information? Below is the example of Al who, when he thought through the consequences of his changed thinking and actions, was encouraged to persist in them.

When Al started being more rational and less aggressive in approaching family problems he thought that he had lost some of his power. He did not like this. However, Al evaluated the gains and losses from his changed thinking and acting. He then realized that: (1) Sara, the daughter he had struck, was now more understanding and supportive of him; (2) both his daughters were behaving more considerately at home; (3) his daughters' boyfriends were more friendly to him; (4) the family bonds had definitely been strengthened; and (5) the break-up of his family had been averted. This confirmed Al in continuing to make different and better choices in his family life.

## MANAGING SPECIFIC PROBLEMS

So far in this chapter I have provided illustrations of how to use thinking skills for preventing excessive stress and for managing anger and shyness. The remainder of this chapter tries to give you some 'handles' for using thinking skills for managing three other common problems: test anxiety, feeling depressed, and relationship conflict. I mainly focus on thinking skills weaknesses by which people sustain these problems. Where both the problem and the thinking skills weaknesses seem relevant to you, you may have a 'handle' to open the door of change. For each problem I first present a case example. Then I broaden the discussion of the problem by looking at it in relation to the Table 11.1 checklist for preventing and managing problems.

### Managing test anxiety

> Angie, aged 18, was coming to the end of her first year at university. Throughout the year she had been depressed and anxious each time she was required to take a test. Her marks were near the top of her year but she still did not think that was good enough. Angie had very little social life. She worked and worked to prove that she was worthy of her parents' sacrifices in supporting her at university. She found that as the year went on her concentration seemed poorer when she was revising. She was increasingly tense during tests. For instance, at the start of a test, she had to struggle to hold her pen since her hand shook so much. Additionally, her mouth went dry, her stomach felt knotted, her mind felt empty and she was afraid of fainting.

Most people experience some anxiety when they take a test that is of some importance to them. A certain amount of anxiety tones you up and facilitates your performance. However, as in the case of Angie, too much anxiety can be debilitating in terms of both discomfort and performance. Let us look for some 'handles' for people like Angie to work on their test anxiety problems.

- *Am I owning responsibility for the authorship of my life?* Angie may not possess a full awareness of herself as a chooser. In particular, she may inadequately realize that all the time she is making thinking choices and that these choices influence how she feels. Angie may have the illusion of assuming responsibility for the authorship of her life and yet not possess the knowledge and skill to be able to do this effectively.

- *Am I in touch with my underlying feelings?* There is a good chance that Angie is out of touch with her own valuing process without realizing this. She does not appear to be listening to her needs for recreation and social companionship. Instead she treats herself like a machine. If she continues to do this, she risks converting her feelings of burnout into a full-blown breakdown.

- *Am I using self-talk constructively?* Angie could use the calming and coaching elements of coping self-talk to help her take tests. Coping self-talk might help her revise more efficiently. If when revising or taking tests, she uses 'you' messages like 'you fool', she needs to replace these with coping 'I' messages.

- *Are my personal rules and directives helping me?* Angie may be making mustabatory demands on herself. She may have the personal rules: 'I must do extremely well every time I take a test' and 'I must always obtain my parents' approval'. She may engage in unnecessary self-rating, 'if I do not do well then I am a worthless person', and catastrophizing, 'if I do not do well, this is an awful catastrophe that I will be unable to handle'. Angie may also possess pressurizer directives, like 'achieve at all costs, be in control and hurry up'. She may also have some inhibitor directives, like 'don't feel, don't be sensual, don't enjoy yourself and don't take risks'.

- *Are my perceptions accurate regarding myself and others?* Angie needs to explore whether she has a realistic perception of her academic ability. On the one hand she may be trying to reach standards that, without making huge sacrifices, are too high for her. On the other hand, she may be an extremely able student whose anxieties and negative self-labelling interfere with her achievement. A logical analysis of the available evidence regarding her academic strengths and weaknesses should help her perceive herself more accurately. Additionally, Angie needs to test out her perceptions of her parents. They may be proud of her in her own right and not want her to feel under constant pressure to achieve for their sakes.

- *Are my attributions of cause accurate?* Angie may be overworking because she makes inaccurate attributions about why she may not do well. For instance, she may regard any 'failure' on her part as due to lack of effort. If so, she needs to review whether there are 'better fit' explanations for her not performing as well as she would like in some tests. Such explanations include insufficient ability, lack of interest in the subject, high anxiety, task difficulty, bad luck, poor teaching, emotional staleness, poor revision skills and poor test-taking skills. Possibly Angie may undermine her confidence by seeing the causes of her poor performances as internal and stable and the causes of her good performances as being external and transient. In sum, Angie needs to review carefully her explanations of the causes of her test anxiety problem.

- *Are my predictions realistic?* Angie may be making unrealistic predictions concerning the tests she takes. For example, she may be so afraid of doing poorly that this contributes to her predicting that she will not do well and thus getting even more anxious. If she were to acknowledge and assess the evidence, she might alter this prediction. Additionally, she may predict that she cannot cope with not doing well. Again, a realistic assessment of the evidence might indicate otherwise.

- *Am I articulating my goals clearly and do they reflect my values?* Clearly one of Angie's goals needs to be to manage her test anxiety better. If she has not articulated this as a goal, she needs to. Angie may have unrealistic goals concerning how well she expects to do. She needs to articulate specific and realistic goals for herself. Also, Angie seems to be leading an unbalanced life— she should articulate some social and recreational goals. Possibly, as Angie explores herself and her situation more deeply, she may find that much of her current behaviour reflects others' values rather than what she wants for herself.

- *Am I using visualizing to best effect?* The answer is probably no. Angie appears to imagine herself as behaving incompetently when she takes tests and as unable to cope with poor results. Angie might use visualizing to clarify her goals and to get more in touch with her strengths. Furthermore, she could use visualized rehearsal and practice, including coping self-talk, to prepare for upcoming tests. As part of this she might engage in goal-directed visualizing, in which she pictures herself taking tests calmly and competently.

This is an illustrative rather than an exhaustive analysis of how Angie's thinking skills weaknesses might contribute to sustaining her test anxiety problem. Angie may also have to look at specific action skills, like planning her revision time or allocation of time in tests better, to arrive at a full working definition of her problem. Once she has confronted her problem and adequately assessed and defined it, she has laid a sound foundation to work for change.

### Managing feelings of depression

Pete, aged 42, was fired from the foreman's job he had held for six years when the small electronics company he worked for was taken over. He was devastated. Secretly he blamed himself for his ill fortune. He felt anxious, worthless and depressed. He kept going over in his mind how, if he had acted differently, he might have held on to his job. Pete was eating and sleeping badly. He moped around the house a lot, watched too much television and had started drinking more than he used to. His interest in sex declined. He hated being dependent on his wife Ellie to be the main breadwinner in the family. He thought his teenaged children, Hugh and Jenny, did not understand how hurt he was and he blamed them for their insensitivity. Pete wallowed in self-pity. He tried for a few jobs unsuccessfully. However, after a couple of months, he came to the conclusion that he was too old at 42 to ever get a good job again. The future seemed hopeless.

Pete's vulnerability to getting depressed was exposed by his receiving a hard knock. His vulnerability comprised many thinking skills weaknesses which were activated by adverse circumstances. Pete was not psychiatrically ill. He was going through what numerous others have faced, namely the challenge of how to come to terms with an unpredictable economic world. Let us look for some possible 'handles' for Pete to work on his feelings of depression.

- *Am I owning responsibility for the authorship of my life?* Pete does not appear to have a clear sense of his responsibility for making the choices that support rather than oppress him. He does not appear to be sufficiently aware that if he works on his thinking choices he can alter how he feels. Some of Pete's behaviour indicates that, under high stress, he is becoming less rather than more responsible for his life, such as in his passive TV watching.

- *Am I in touch with my underlying feelings?* Unemployment can be a frightening experience that cuts to the core of people's anxieties about existential isolation and not being able to survive. Pete appears in touch with some of these feelings. However, he does not appear to be fully in touch with his underlying drive to actualize his potential. There are opportunities in his being fired as well as drawbacks. If he listens to himself carefully he may find that he wants to change the direction of his work. Other areas of feeling with which Pete does not seem fully in touch include his competences as a worker and his affection for his family.

- *Am I using self-talk constructively?* Possibly Pete puts himself down with 'you' messages, like 'you idiot' and 'you useless fool'. Additionally, Pete may be talking himself into rather than out of depression. He may oppress himself with statements like 'I'm not going to be able to put my life right'. He needs to use coping self-talk, like 'Calm down. Relax. Break down the tasks of getting re-employed and of handling unemployment. I can manage it if I hang in there.'

- *Are my personal rules and directives helping me?* Pete appears to make a number of mustabatory demands on himself, others and the environment. These include:

I *must* always be employed.
I *must* never make mistakes at work.
As a male I *must* always be the breadwinner.
My children *must* always understand my difficulties.
The environment *must* never do things to me which might cause me to feel uncomfortable.

Pete's feelings of depression may be partly caused by his negatively rating himself as a *person* when he, others and/or the environment do not live up to his personal rules.

- *Are my perceptions accurate regarding myself and others?* Possibly Pete engages in much negative self-labelling in which he dwells on his imagined weaknesses. He does not seem to be listing and affirming his resources. Pete may also be jumping to conclusions unfavourable to himself in his relationships with others. For instance, he may misperceive his children's behaviour as unsupportive when, in reality, they sympathize with his position but lack the skills of being able to show this. Pete may also exhibit perceptual errors, such as: overgeneralizing, 'the fact that I was turned down for some jobs means that I will always be turned down'; black and white thinking, 'either people are all for me or they are against me'; and tunnel vision.'I can only look for jobs that are very like my previous one'.

- *Are my attributions of cause accurate?* Pete may unrealistically blame himself for being fired. He may be taking responsibility more for his failures than for his successes. Additionally, he may misunderstand the causes of his not getting work immediately. For instance, Pete attributes his inability to find work to his age when there may be numerous other explanations: poor information-gathering skills; living in an economically depressed area; lack of effort; out-of-date skills; and so on. Pete appears to be waiting for his employment situation to change so that he can feel better at home. However, if he attributed the cause of some of his depression as his failure to use his extra spare time creatively, he might be in a better position to do something about it.

- *Are my predictions realistic?* Pete seems to predict that whatever he does it will not improve matters. He needs to review carefully the evidence for this counsel of despair. His belief that the future is hopeless ignores his own potential, despite adverse circumstances, to create much of his future.

- *Am I articulating my goals clearly and do they reflect my values?* Possibly Pete has not thought through a clear statement of his work, family and leisure goals. His seeming uncertainty about his underlying values and self-worth makes it harder for him both to articulate and to adhere to goals. At the moment he allows himself to be the victim of fate.

- *Am I using visualizing to best effect?* Pete could use visualizing to support himself in many areas. He could get a clearer picture of his goals and strengths. He could visually rehearse and practise upcoming stressful events like job interviews. He could use visualizing to deepen his understanding of how his family see his behaviour. Visualizing restful scenes might be a useful self-help skill to cope with his anxieties. Additionally, visualizing himself coping with 'worst case scenarios' and imagining himself living successfully at a date in the future, say in 12 months, might enhance his confidence and motivation.

As for Angie, this search for Pete's possible thinking skills weaknesses has not been exhaustive. Nevertheless, it may have located some thinking skill 'handles' that allow Pete to open the door of working for change. Pete also needs to review the adequacy of his action skills; for instance, in how to search for jobs, use leisure time effectively and relate better to his family.

### Managing a relationship conflict

After 21 years, Liz and Harry's marriage was heading for the rocks. They had two children Nick, aged 19, and Karen, aged 16. Harry thought that Liz was very critical of him as a husband, lover, father and businessman. Liz had previously suspected and recently found out that Harry was having an affair with Martha. Whereas Harry saw Liz as uptight and angry, he experienced Martha as much less inhibited. Harry thought that he loved two people. He was in much inner conflict about what he was doing. Liz intensely disliked Harry's affair. Although she contemplated divorce, she held off for three main reasons: her loving Harry, her insecurity about making it on her own, and her hope that he might honour his marriage commitment to her by giving up Martha. Although they were at each others throats much of the time, Liz and Harry still had good times together. They enjoyed going camping, spending time with their children and having sex. Liz had worked for the past 10 years as a secretary/book-keeper in their jointly owned company, which Harry managed. However, by mutual agreement, she recently left this job. She now worked as a receptionist in a law office. Liz and Harry went to a counsellor to discuss how to save their marriage.

I saw Liz and Harry in my private practice. Harry had been referred for counselling by a minister who was concerned at the potential break-up of his family. I started by having a few individual sessions with Harry and then some joint sessions with Liz and Harry. Harry was pleasant, but not heavily invested in this process. When Liz first came for counselling she was extremely nervous. However, she was prepared to work and thought she would gain from counselling whether or not she stayed married. Consequently Liz, with Harry's agreement, decided to come for individual sessions with the option of joint sessions when it seemed desirable to both. Liz was the more psychologically accessible of the two. In this instance, the most likely solution to the relationship conflict seemed to lie in Liz altering her thinking and behaviour. This might make it easier for Harry to change and to recommit himself to their relationship. Let us now search for some thinking skills 'handles' on how Liz could work for change.

• *Am I owning responsibility for authorship of my life?* Liz and Harry both thought that they related to each other in programmed ways that were frequently unhelpful. They had not fully acknowledged their capacity to be choosers in how they thought, felt and acted. Liz's behaviour indicates some flexibility in being prepared to make the choices that would work for her. First, when she found out about Harry's affair, she realized she had a *choice* as to whether to end the relationship. Second, despite her hating his affair, she was prepared to try the personal experiment of changing her thinking and behaviour in the hope that it would achieve her goal of bringing about change in Harry.

- *Am I in touch with my underlying feelings?* Liz had received a strict upbringing, especially from a martinet of a father; for instance, she was only allowed to touch the handle when she closed a door. To cut a long story short, she now insufficiently acknowledged her feelings of strength and competence and allowed herself to be overcome by feelings of powerlessness and inadequacy. Not feeling good about herself made her much more prone to not feeling good about Harry. Along with this, she had an insufficient sense of her own identity. She found it difficult to acknowledge her needs and to want to do things for herself. Liz felt as though she was primarily an appendage of others.

- *Am I using self-talk constructively?* Liz used self-talk in ways that heightened her feelings of anxiety and powerlessness. Instead of trying to calm herself down and make her points, she talked herself into feeling small and then overreacting by screaming and scratching. She later regretted this behaviour. One of the ways in which she talked herself into feeling vulnerable was to say to herself that she doubted if she could cope on her own without Harry.

- *Are my personal rules and directives helping me?* Liz possessed a number of mustabatory personal rules that left her exposed to self-downing. These included: 'I *must* be approved of all the time; I *must* be superwoman in the home and meet everybody else's needs; my husband *must* always know what my needs are without my telling him'; and, although not all the time: 'when Harry and I have a problem in our relationship we *must* compete with each other to find out who is right'. Liz also oppressed herself with a number of inhibitor directives, such as 'don't think, don't be different and don't take risks'.

- *Are my perceptions accurate regarding myself and others?* Both Liz and Harry admitted how quick they were to take offence at each other's behaviour. They did not give the benefit of the doubt, but instead looked out for slights and malevolent intentions. Liz was a mistress of negative self-labelling and putting herself down. Although sometimes she acknowledged her strengths and resources, she attached insufficient importance to them. Liz also tended to perceive Harry more negatively than was warranted. When they were working on improving their relationship, Harry asked Liz to make a list of the things she found positive about him. He did not expect much. Both Liz and Harry were amazed at how long the list was. Liz realized that she had previously not fully acknowledged many of these appreciations, let along communicated them. Harry was also blocked in his ability to give positive feedback.

- *Are my attributions of cause accurate?* On one level Liz blamed Harry for causing and sustaining their marital conflict through his relationship with Martha. On another level, she had great doubts about her adequacy as a wife and, without knowing what to do, blamed herself for his affair. As she worked on the problem she realized that, whatever the *past* causes of Harry's affair, she had some power to influence *future* events in her favour. Increasingly she changed her attribution of cause from 'poor me, I am the victim of my husband, this scheming woman Martha and my own inadequacies' to 'I can play to win and achieve my goals by altering some of the ways I think and behave. Even if Harry and I do not manage to repair our relationship, I can still make a success of my life.'

- *Are my predictions realistic?* Trusting a person entails confidence that they will behave in a trustworthy fashion. Harry's affair seriously undermined Liz's trust in his commitment to their relationship. He said he wanted their relationship to work, but was reluctant to give up seeing Martha. Liz now needed to assess not so much what Harry said but how he acted to predict if she could trust him more. Harry was starting to become much more attentive to her, including writing a first-ever poem on her birthday. Also, Liz had some inconclusive evidence, such as Harry's coming home earlier, that he might be withdrawing from the affair with Martha. As Liz began both to succeed in and to enjoy her employment move from Harry's business, she realized that her predictions of catastrophe if she were to be divorced were inaccurate. Her exaggerated fears of the consequences of abandonment had contributed to her high anxiety and tendencies to overreact.

- *Am I articulating my goals clearly and do they reflect my values?* Liz had a much clearer idea of where she wanted to be five years from now than Harry. She had a strong commitment to and liking for her family life. To achieve this was her first priority, but not at any cost. Liz was moving towards the decision that if, despite her own best efforts, Harry did not give up Martha, then she would re-evaluate her goals and might seek a divorce.

- *Am I using visualizing to best effect?* Liz was tense much of the time. Independently of her counselling she had started to use visualizing to relax herself. Liz had a reasonably clear vision of her goals. However, she might profit from using visualizing to rehearse and practise coping with situations she found difficult in a more goal-oriented fashion; for instance, when feeling criticized by Harry.

This is an abbreviated and simplified account of how Liz was able to identify some thinking choice 'handles' that enabled her to work for change. As Angie and Pete did, Liz needed to review certain action skills; for instance, how she communicated with Harry in their fights and how to give positive and not mainly negative feedback. Liz had the courage, even though she thought Harry was at fault, to try changing her thinking and behaviour in order to give him the opportunity to change his. Love has many faces.

Thinksheet 52 is designed to give you further practice at thinking through a problem.

---

**Thinksheet 52    Thinking through a problem**

*Instructions*
1. Select a problem that you have not used for previous thinksheets.
2. Describe the facts of your problem more fully.
3. Using the Table 11.1 checklist conduct a thorough search for thinking skill 'handles' that help to explain how you may sustain your problem.
4. Formulate a working definition of your problem mainly focused on thinking skill weaknesses but containing at least one action skill weakness.
5. Translate your working definition into working goals.
6. Write out a realistic plan for managing your problem better.

---

## CHAPTER HIGHLIGHTS

Prevention is better than a cure. Effective thinking skills may both make you less predisposed to problems and also help you prevent those that are avoidable.

Whatever their origins, you have choices as to how you manage your problems.

CASIE is a five-step framework for managing your problems: Confront; Assess and define; Set goals and plan; Implement; Evaluate.

In assessing and defining your problem your objective is to move from a description of it to a working definition that identifies specific 'handles' that enable you to work for change.

As well as identifying thinking skill weaknesses, your working definitions should identify action skill deficits that sustain your problem.

When searching for 'handles' for how you can either prevent or manage problems better, consider the following thinking skill areas; responsibility for authorship of your life; being in touch with feelings; using self-talk constructively; helpful personal rules and directives; accurate perceptions of self and others; accurate attributions of cause; realistic predictions; clear goals; and using visualizing effectively.

Translate your working definitions into statements of working goals.

Where problems are important to you, time spent thinking them through and planning how to manage them is likely to be time well spent.

# 12 The Courage to Think for Yourself

The buck stops here.

*Harry S. Truman*

I have nothing to offer but blood, toil, tears and sweat.

*Winston S. Churchill*

Having read about the many thinking skills relevant to preventing and managing problems you may feel like the centipede that came to grief because of too much thinking about which leg came after which. However, I encourage you to persist in working on your thinking skills. Like the skills you use when driving a car, in time you will be able to use them without great self-consciousness. The *price* of possessing effective thinking skills to prevent and manage your problems is eternal vigilence. Once acquired, these skills need to be maintained and developed. You are constantly challenged to renew and recreate them. The *prize* of using effective thinking skills is that you are likely to realize much more of your human potential. You should spend less time and energy on the hassles of life and more on activities and relationships that you find fulfilling.

## MONITORING YOUR THINKING SKILLS

Effective thinking about your problems and decisions requires you to keep monitoring your thinking choices. Some of this will be done as you are 'thinking on your feet'. On other occasions you may either pause for reflection or clear a longer space to think through a problem. There is a case for periodically reviewing your thinking skills. As with servicing your car, there may not be anything obviously wrong, but time on upkeep and prevention can be well spent.

Thinksheet 53 is a questionnaire designed to help you to review systematically your thinking skills. I suggest that you answer it now in the light of reading this book and completing many, if not all, of the thinksheets. Thinksheet 53 can also be used for monitoring your thinking skills at points in the future.

---

**Thinksheet 53   Monitoring your thinking skills**

*Instructions*
Using the scale below, rate how satisfied you are with your skills in each of the following 'areas'of thinking.

3   Much need for improvement
2   Moderate need for improvement
I   Slight need for improvement
0   No need for improvement

| *Skills* | *Your rating* |
|---|---|
| *Learning how not to think* | |
| Understanding the influence of my parents on how I prevent and manage problems. | _____ |
| Having an adequate conceptual framework with which to think through problems. | _____ |
| Understanding the influence of high anxiety on my thinking. | |
| Having insight into how I may sustain my deficient thinking skills. | _____ |
| | |
| *Owning responsibility for choosing* | |
| Being aware that I am always a chooser in my life. | _____ |
| Acknowledging personal responsibility for the authorship of my life. | _____ |
| Being fully aware of the inevitability of death and of the transient nature of life. | _____ |
| Being aware of my significant physical sensations. | |
| Being able to get in touch with my feelings. | _____ |
| | |
| *Using self-talk* | |
| Using 'I' self-talk that 'owns' my thoughts, feelings and actions. | _____ |
| Being able to identify my negative self-talk. | _____ |
| Using calming self-talk. | _____ |
| Using coaching self-talk. | _____ |
| Combining calming and coaching self-talk into coping self-talk. | _____ |
| | |
| *Choosing my personal rules* | |
| Being aware of my self-oppressing personal rules. | _____ |
| Disputing and reformulating my self-oppressing personal rules. | _____ |

Being aware of my self-oppressing pressurizer and inhibitor
directives. _____
Challenging and changing my self-oppressing directives. _____
Listening to and living up to my conscience. _____

*Choosing how I perceive.*
Monitoring and recording my upsetting perceptions. _____
Identifying my perceptual errors. _____
Generating and evaluating different perceptions. _____
Reality testing my perceptions by conducting appropriate
personal experiments. _____
Being aware of my negative self-labels. _____
Searching for and affirming my resources. _____
Being aware of my main defensive processes. _____
Letting go of my defensive processes. _____
Being aware that, on occasions, I may not perceive others
realistically. _____
Being able to correct my errors in perceiving others
realistically. _____

*Attributing cause*
Being aware of my misattributions about the causes of my personal
problems. _____
Being able to acknowledge accurately how I contribute to my personal
problems. _____
Being accurate about how I attribute cause for positive and
negative events. _____
Being accurate in how I attribute cause for my academic or work
successes and failures. _____

*Predicting and creating my future*
Making accurate predictions of risk. _____
Making accurate predictions of reward. _____
Knowing what my values are. _____
Having clear short-term, medium-term and long-term goals. _____

*Visualizing with my mind's eye*
Being aware of the power of visualizing. _____
Using visualizing to relax. _____
Using visualizing to manage anxiety. _____
Visualizing positive images to counteract negative feelings. _____
Using visualizing to perform specific tasks better. _____
Using visualizing to clarify my goals. _____
Using visualizing to enhance my relationships. _____
Using visualizing to avoid the negative consequences of giving in
to temptation. _____

*Making decisions*
Being aware of any self-oppressing decision-making styles I possess. _____

Knowing how to make rational decisions.         ————
Generating options and gathering information.     ————
Assessing the consequences of decision options.   ————
Being able to commit myself to a specific decision. ————
Planning the implementation of decisions.      ————
Evaluating the actual consequences of my decisions. ————
Being aware of thinking skills weaknesses that interfere with the quality of my decision-making.     ————

*Preventing and managing problems*
Using my thinking skills to prevent avoidable problems. ————
Confronting my problems.    ————
Fully describing problems that I want to work on. ————
Searching for thinking skill 'handles' on how I contribute to sustaining my problems. ————
Formulating working definitions of my problems. ————
Stating working goals to manage problems. ————
Developing plans to attain my working goals. ————
Evaluating my progress in managing my problems. ————

*Staying in control of my thinking*
Monitoring the adequacy of my thinking skills. ————
Possessing assertion skills. ————
Developing my thinking skills. ————
Having the courage to think for myself. ————

On the basis of your response to the above questionnaire, write out a summary statement of your thinking skills strengths and weaknesses. Then set yourself specific goals for improving your thinking skills.

## MAINTAINING YOUR THINKING SKILLS

How can you maintain your thinking skills? Effective thinking about your problems and decisions of living requires courage, inner strength and resilience. Human beings live in webs of fears and anxieties. You require the courage to confront your fears. You need to face up to and work on self-oppressing aspects of your thinking, however insidious they may be. You also require the courage to think for and define yourself, despite the fears and relationship skills weaknesses of those who prefer to define you on their terms. In brief, you need to assert yourself both inwardly and outwardly.

## Inner assertion

Inner assertion involves acknowledging and working on those aspects of your inner self that weaken your effectiveness. It entails delving behind your public mask to struggle with the fears, insecurities and anxieties that diminish you. It involves grappling with 'the enemy within' so as to avoid being 'your own worst enemy'. You are constantly being challenged by life to find answers to the problems and decisions of living.

There is no simple answer to how you can find the inner strength to stay in control of your thinking. However, below I indicate some self-talk that may encourage you to persist in asserting the constructive rather than the destructive tendencies within you.

- *'Good thinking skills require a daily struggle.'* You are born with the potential for both effective and ineffective thinking. Even people whom you consider to be outstandingly successful in managing their lives have to strive constantly to keep in control of their thinking. There is no easy way out. Human happiness and fulfilment comes from finding meaning in striving and not from the absence of challenge.

- *'Nobody's perfect.'* Vulnerability and fallibility are universal human character- istics. You may weaken yourself by possessing a mustabatory personal rule about your own need for perfection. Awareness of your vulnerability, though often painful, may be a sign of strength rather than of weakness. Weak people lack the courage to admit their fallibility. Where possible, be a friend to yourself and confront your thinking skills weaknesses, not in a spirit of self- blame, but in order to change them for the better.

- *'Changing my thinking skills may be difficult.'* Although it is not always the case, choosing to change how you think may be a long, hard process. You risk weakening your resolve if you expect it always to come easily. By the time you decide to change, you have probably got a long learning history of acquiring and sustaining your weaknesses. Ellis (1987) observes that many people sabotage themselves by thinking that changes *should* be quicker, more pro- found, easier and more continuous and 'so they settle for moderate rather than elegant emotional health' (p. 368).

- *'Maintaining my thinking skills involves practice.'* Like many skills, for instance, playing a musical instrument or sport, maintaining your thinking skills involves practice. Life is so full of problems and decisions that opportunities for practice are not hard to find. Consciously use these as opportunities to practise your skills. When you are faced with problems and decisions, remem- ber the self-instruction: 'stop . . . think . . . what are my thinking choices?'

- *'Using my thinking skills helps me.'* You are more likely to persist in using your thinking skills if you perceive them as bringing rewards. If you doubt whether it is worth the struggle of maintaining your thinking skills, ask yourself the following questions: 'What are the costs and consequences of maintaining my thinking skills?' and 'What are the costs and consequences of thinking like I used to?' Assuming that you genuinely do think more effectively, you are likely to find many more positive than negative consequences follow from maintaining your thinking skills. Self-support rewards, self-oppression hurts.

Many people find that they are able to discipline their thinking more if they make commitments that transcend what William James has called their 'convulsive little ego' (Gardner, 1965, p. 96). These commitments may be to loved ones, to sources of meaning in work and leisure, to helping others, to political and social change, and to religious faiths. The existential position heavily emphasizes that humans are meaning-seeking animals. Good thinking skills are likely to help you both to find and also to renew meaning in your life. This, in turn, contributes to your willingness and confidence to apply your thinking skills.

**Outer assertion**

> Tell the truth, and you will get your head bashed in.
> *Hungarian proverb*

Although having thoughts is a private activity, expressing your thoughts is a public or social activity. The distinction is not this simple since you may best develop some of your private thoughts in conjunction with others, or others may threaten you to the point where you inhibit some of your private thoughts. In this context, outer assertion means having the courage to assert what you think to others without counterproductive inhibition or aggression. You need to counteract not only the messages in yourself, but also the messages from others that put you off your thinking. Numerous books have been written about assertion skills (for example, Alberti & Emmons, 1986; Bower & Bower, 1976; Butler, 1981b; Steiner, 1981). Here my goal is to alert you to the importance of good assertion skills when expressing your thoughts. I will also indicate some of the ways in which others, intentionally or unintentionally, may try to dethink you. You need to look elsewhere for more detailed discussions of assertion skills.

*Stating what you think*

Good skills at stating what you think involve inner assertion, overcoming your mental barriers, as well as outer assertion, sending clear verbal, vocal and bodily messages to others. You seek to avoid the dangers of inhibition, 'bottling it up', and of either direct aggression, 'going over the top', or indirect aggression, 'letting it come out sideways'. Although you can choose to control your own behaviour, at most you can only influence how others behave. Consequently, although stating what you think assertively might increase the probability of your relating well to others, this cannot be guaranteed.

Briefly, some of the main component skills of assertively stating what you think are as follows.

- *Inner assertion skills.* You may need to work on thoughts that restrict your freedom of choice regarding defining and asserting yourself. These self-oppressing thoughts include: demands on yourself, for instance 'I must be nice, I must be liked and I must avoid conflict'; fears about others' reactions, for instance 'others might reject me, others might criticize me and others might think me unfeminine'; and fears about your reactions to others' reactions, for instance 'I can't handle conflict, I can't handle rejection and I can't handle causing pain'.

- *Verbal skills.* The words that you use to express your thoughts need to be simple and clear. They need to be stated as 'I' messages, indicating your ownership of your thoughts.

- *Vocal skills.* These are the messages that you send with your voice. They include loudness, pace, stress and enunciation. When stating your thoughts assertively you want to avoid being perceived as either weak or unnecessarily threatening. Therefore speak so you can be heard easily, at a pace that is comfortable to follow, with firmness that is appropriate to your message and with clear enunciation.

- *Body skills.* Your body language needs to match your verbal and vocal messages. You avoid signs of weakness, for instance absence of eye contact, and of unnecessary threat, for instance repetitive jabbing of your finger at another. You aim for eye contact, facial expression, gesture and posture that appropriately support you in communicating what you think.

*Counteracting dethinking messages*

There are many ways in which people may try to influence you not to think for yourself. These negative messages are verbal, vocal and bodily. Frequently they reflect the insecurities of those to whom you talk. What you say may challenge their picture of themselves and of you. They then export their fears and insecurities by threatening you. However, as all who have unwittingly allowed themselves to be seduced know, positive messages can also dethink you.

Below is a list of some of the ways in which others may put you off your thinking. These *dethinking messages* include the following.

- *Advising.* The message may be: 'I know what is best for you'.

- *Blaming.* Put simply, 'it's all your fault'.

- *Distracting*. Changing the subject. Fidgeting.

- *Flattering*. Trying to hook you by giving the message: 'wow, you're the greatest thing since sliced bread'.

- *Intellectualizing*. Using the intellect to talk around rather than to the point.

- *Intimidating*. Psychologically or physically threatening you.

- *Labelling*. Telling you how you are whether you want to be that way or not; for instance, 'Jane doesn't mind when I tease her, do you Jane?'

- *Playing stupid*. Deliberately not seeming to understand you.

- *Playing the victim*. Passive aggression designed to induce you to feel guilty; for instance, 'I'm so disappointed with you'.

- *Rule setting*. Defining the rules for handling a situation in ways unfavourable to you; for instance, 'children don't talk back to their parents'.

- *Talking down*. Being treated by another as inferior for reasons that may include your age, size, position in the family, gender, colour, status, financial position, etc.

This list of manipulations and power plays is far from exhaustive. Furthermore, it does not illustrate the many vocal and body messages that others can use to put you off your thinking. All these dethinking messages involve 'put-downs' of you of varying degrees of subtlety. They show a lack of respect for your right to express your options in an open and honest way. They may insidiously block your inner thinking in ways that alienate you from yourself.

How can you counteract attempts to put you off your thinking? This can be very difficult, especially when there are big differences in power in the relationship, such as between parents and dependent children or between bosses and employees. If possible, you avoid unnecessarily threatening people so that they are less likely to adopt dethinking tactics. *Preventive* assertion skills include using honest positives and making initial statements assertively.

- *Using honest positives*. Kassorla (1984) uses the term honest positives for positive feedback that you can honestly give to others. You may build an emotional climate whereby you are more likely to be listened to if you use this skill. Honest positives can be used before, during and after you have a problem involving another person.

- *Making initial statements assertively*. By aggressively stating your opinion it is very easy to set yourself up for someone to use dethinking tactics on you. The world is full of easily threatened people who are only too ready to punish themselves and you. This may happen anyway if you assertively state your opinions. However, why trigger others' defences unnecessarily by being aggressive?

There are a number of skills that you can use once confronted with dethinking tactics.

- *Awareness.* Awareness of others' manipulative tendencies involves realistic appraisal of their behaviour. Two risks here are *paranoia*, imagining dethinking tactics when they are not used, and *pollyannaism*, being blind to dethinking tactics when they are used. If you are aware that others are manipulating you, you then have a choice as to how to respond.

- *Calmly persisting in asserting what you think.* You may choose to keep asserting what you think at the same time as showing that you have understood another's position. Others may power play you because they expect you to give in. However, by having the courage of your convictions you may be able to get them to accept your thinking. Even if they do not, you are likely to feel better about yourself. This is because you have stated your thoughts and also because you have done so assertively rather than aggressively.

- *Confronting others with how you perceive their behaviour.* One option, if you think someone is trying to prevent you from doing your own thinking, is to point this out to them. Again, success cannot be guaranteed, but doing this assertively may improve the way you feel about yourself.

- *Using handling feedback skills.* You have a range of other skills you can use if you sense someone is using dethinking tactics against you. At the simplest level you can: assess whether the issue is worth bothering about; count to ten; relax yourself by regulating your breathing and using calming self-talk; and back-off. You may also choose to: gather more information about why he or she reacts negatively to your thoughts; clear up misperceptions and misunderstandings; agree to disagree; or try to work on the conflict between you. If all else fails, you can choose to seek more congenial company.

---

**Thinksheet 54    Maintaining your thinking skills**

*Instructions*

A    Inner assertion

1.   Write down the main ways in which you think you are at risk of not maintaining your thinking skills.

2.   Set yourself goals and develop a plan to combat these inner self-sabotaging tendencies.

B    Outer assertion

1.   To what extent do you consider that you have the courage to express your thoughts to others?

2.   Assess the extent to which you possess and use assertion skills.

3. To what extent and in what ways do you consider that you allow others, by using dethinking tactics, to put you off your thinking?

4. Set yourself goals and develop a plan to counter any weaknesses you may have in assertively expressing your thoughts.

---

## DEVELOPING YOUR THINKING SKILLS

The previous sections on monitoring and maintaining your thinking skills are also relevant to developing them. Below are some additional suggestions.

- *Working with another person.* You may choose to work with another person on a regular basis to improve both of your thinking skills. If you are in a relationship this other person may be your partner. One approach is for each of you to be available to support and help the other as and when you wish to think through a problem or decision. Another approach is to meet on a regular basis for, say, an hour a week. There are many ways that you can divide the time. The object is that each of you has 'air time' in which you can explore and work on your problems and decisions with the help of the other.

- *Developing a support network.* You can develop a support network of trusted people that you can turn to for thinking through your problems and decisions. These people may be relatives, friends, work colleagues, ministers of religion or helping service professionals, to mention but some. Where possible, they should have some insight into how people oppress rather than support themselves through ineffective thinking. Additionally, they should possess skills of helping you to do your own thinking rather than doing it for you. As well as receiving help, you may develop your own thinking skills by offering help to other members of your support network.

- *Peer support groups.* You may choose to meet on a regular basis with a group of similar people to work on your thinking skills. Here you have many people to give you support and feedback. Additionally, where you have effective thinkers in your group, you can learn from observing how they think through their problems. Alternatively, within the context of another focus, you can work on the thinking skills pertinent to the group's main task. Such peer support groups might focus on bereavement, living with spouses with Alzheimer's disease, being homosexual, overcoming alcohol or drug addiction, as well as on many other concerns.

- *Workshops and training courses.* Interest in an acknowledgement of the importance of thinking skills is rapidly increasing among helping service professionals and academics. Consequently, there is a growth in thinking skills training courses and workshops. Means of finding out about thinking skills training courses and workshops include: looking in the press; contact with educational institutions, personnel offices, counselling services and helping service agencies; and getting in touch with professional associations in psychology, counselling and social work. The message is 'buyer beware'. Before joining any training course or workshop, make enquiries about: its goals and training methods; the training and experience of the people running it; how large the group will be; the frequency and duration of the sessions; and what fees are involved. Since acquiring, maintaining and developing your thinking skills involves much work and practice, courses offering miracle cures should be avoided.

- *Counselling and psychotherapy.* Counselling and psychotherapy tend to be words that are used interchangeably. Some of you may consider that you need the service of a professional therapist to help you think through your problems and decisions more effectively. Therapists operate in different ways and some therapeutic approaches do not have a major focus on how people think. Adopting a 'cognitive approach' is the professional jargon term for focusing on a client's thinking. There is no single pre-eminent cognitive approach, but a range of cognitive therapies. If you wish to find a therapist who works roughly in accord with the philosophy of this book, look for someone who emphasizes helping you take more effective responsibility for your life by making better thinking, feeling and action choices. Be prepared to 'shop around' for a therapist with whom you will be comfortable, but not too comfortable! Good therapy involves being coached and challenged within the context of a caring and supportive relationship.

  Group therapy may be appropriate for some of you instead of, concurrently with, or after individual work. Therapy groups tend to be composed of a leader and around six to ten members. Their length and the duration of their sessions varies: for instance two-hour sessions may be held weekly for six months. Therapy groups, with their smaller numbers, provide a more intense opportunity for working on your thinking skills than that found in many training courses and workshops.

  You may not be immediately aware of a therapist you can go to. As with training courses and workshops, enquiries to helping service agencies, professionals and professional associations may bear fruit. Additionally, many therapists list their services in the phone book. Again, the message is 'buyer beware'.

- *Thinking skills reading.* Although there is no substitute for practice, you can learn much about thinking skills from reading relevant books and articles. In the bibliography at the end of this book I have marked with asterisks books likely to be of interest to the non-professional reader.

---

**Thinksheet 55   Developing your thinking skills**

*Instructions*
At the end of Thinksheet 53 you were asked to write out a summary statement of your thinking skills strengths and weaknesses for preventing and managing problems and making decisions. You were then asked to set yourself specific goals for developing your thinking skills. There are many different ways to develop your skills, including:

- inner assertion
- outer assertion
- working with another person
- developing a support network
- peer support groups
- training courses and workshops
- individual and/or group therapy
- thinking skills reading

Make a plan for developing at least one of your thinking skills. Write out the plan, specifying the following.

1.   Your goals.
2.   The methods that you intend to use to achieve each goal.
3.   A realistic time schedule.
4.   How you intend to monitor and evaluate your progress.

---

## THE COURAGE TO THINK FOR YOURSELF

Life only demands from you the strength you possess. Only one feat is possible—not to have run away.

*Dag Hammarskjöld*

The thinking skills described in this book do not require intelligence so much as courage and integrity. Based on his experience in Nazi concentration camps, Frankl (1959) observed: 'From all this we may learn that there are two races of men in this world, but only these two—the "race" of the decent man and the "race" of the indecent man' (p. 137). Another way of putting Frankl's statement is that humans fall into two broad categories: those who are aware of the fallibility of their thinking and strive to think rationally and those who are psychologically toxic because they do not.

Those who strive to think rationally possess some insight into their vulnerability as human beings. They seek to affirm themselves without damaging others. They attach as much, if not more, importance to giving as to receiving love. They are committed to meaningful activities. Those afraid to think rationally are preoccupied with themselves. They are psychological children who do not possess the courage to confront their vulnerability when faced with problems and decisions. Much of their thinking avoids rather than assumes their personal responsibility for their lives. Lacking insight and self-respect, they may seek to damage others by attacking them if these others do not agree with their fantasies about themselves.

Most people fall at varying points between the two extremes mentioned above. However, beyond the problem of preventing and managing problems is the problem of personal excellence. This is a problem that faces people whatever their gender, socioeconomic status and race. It is not a matter of recognition of outer achievements, but of the inner achievement of continuously striving to think constructively. You require the courage to choose to assert your inner freedom to think for yourself. You do not demand perfection and you do not run away.

Where do you stand? The courage to think for yourself requires a lifelong commitment. It is one thing to read about thinking skills and another to apply them conscientiously in your daily life, even when nobody's looking. The world is a beautiful place filled with much ugliness. If the human race is going to fulfil its potential, more and more people are going to have to commit themselves to the inner struggle to think for themselves. As the Berkeley, California, street poster of the 1960s said: 'To make a better world, make yourself a better person'.

## CHAPTER HIGHLIGHTS

Monitoring your thinking skills can help you to identify and work on weaknesses.

Maintaining your thinking skills requires inner assertion, confronting your own fears and anxieties, and outer assertion, being able assertively to express your thoughts despite others' fears and anxieties.

There are many ways in which others may try to put you off your thinking.

Skills for counteracting dethinking tactics include: using honest positives; making initial statements assertively; awareness of when you are being manipulated; calmly persisting in asserting what you think; confronting others with how you perceive their behaviour; and using handling feedback skills.

Ways of developing your thinking skills include: working with another person; developing a support network; peer support groups; training courses and workshops; counselling and psychotherapy; and reading about thinking skills.

Thinking skills for facing problems and decisions require courage and integrity more than intelligence.

The courage to think for yourself requires a lifelong commitment.

# Bibliography

References likely to be of special interest to the self-help reader are indicated with an asterisk.

Abramson, L. Y., Seligman, M. E. P. & Teasdale, J. D. (1978). Learned helplessness in humans: critique and reformulation. *Journal of Abnormal Psychology*, **87**, 49–74.

* Alberti, E. E. & Emmons, M. L. (1986). *Your Perfect Right: a Guide to Assertive Living* (5th edn). San Luis Obispo, CA: Impact Press.

Argyle, N. (1988). The nature of cognitions in panic disorder. *Behaviour Research and Therapy*, **26**, 261–4.

Arroba, T. (1977). Styles of decision making and their use: an empirical study. *British Journal of Guidance and Counselling*, **5**, 149–58.

Bandura, A. (1977). *Social Learning Theory*. Englewood Cliffs, NJ: Prentice Hall.

Barnard, M. E. (1986) *Staying Rational in an Irrational World*. Melbourne: McCulloch Publishing.

Beck, A. T. (1976). *Cognitive Therapy and the Emotional Disorders*. New York: New American Library.

Beck, A. T. (1987). Cognitive models of depression. *Journal of Cognitive Psychotherapy*, **1**, 5–37.

Beck, A. T. & Emery, G. (1985). *Anxiety Disorders and Phobias: a Cognitive Perspective*. New York: Basic Books.

* Beck, A. T. & Greenberg, R. L. (1974). *Coping with Depression*. New York: Institute for Rational Living.

Beck, A. T., Laude, R. & Bohnert, M. (1974). Ideational components of anxiety neurosis. *Archives of General Psychiatry*, **31**, 319–25.

Beck, A. T., Rush, A. J., Shaw, B. F. & Emery, G. (1979). *Cognitive Therapy of Depression*. New York: John Wiley.

* Berne, E. (1964). *Games People Play*. New York: Grove Press.

* Berne, E. (1972). *What Do You Say after You Say Hello?* London: Corgi Books.

* Bower, S. A. & Bower, G. H. (1976). *Asserting Yourself: a Practical Guide for Positive Change*. Reading, MA: Addison-Wesley.

Brewin, C. R. (1986). Internal attribution and self-esteem in depression: a theoretical note. *Cognitive Therapy and Research*, **10**, 469–75.

Brewin, C. R. & Furnham, A. (1987). Dependency, self-criticism and depressive attributional style. *British Journal of Clinical Psychology*, **26**, 225–6.

* Bry, A. (1978). *Visualization: Directing the Movies of Your Mind*. New York: Harper & Row.

Burns, D., Shaw, B. F. & Croker, W. (1987). Thinking styles and coping strategies of depressed women: an empirical investigation. *Behaviour Research and Therapy*, **25**, 223–5.

* Butler, P. E. (1981a). *Talking to Yourself: Learning the Language of Self-Support*. New York: Harper & Row.

* Butler, P. E. (1981b). *Self-assertion for Women* (2nd edn). San Francisco: Harper & Row.

Camper, P. M., Jacobson, N. S., Holtzworth-Munroe, A. & Schmaling, K. B. (1988). Causal attributions for interactional behaviours in married couples. *Cognitive Therapy and Research*, **12**, 195–209.

Carkhuff, R. R. (1973). *The Art of Problem Solving*. Amherst, MA: Human Resource Development Press.

Cautela, J. (1967). Covert sensitization. *Psychological Reports*, **20**, 459–68.

Clark, D. M. (1986). A cognitive approach to panic. *Behaviour Research and Therapy*, **24**, 461–70.

Dryden, W. & Ellis, A. (1986). Rational-emotive therapy (RET). In W. Dryden & W. Golden (eds), *Cognitive-behavioural Approaches to Psychotherapy*, pp. 129–68. London: Harper & Row.

Dyer, W. W. (1976). *Your Erroneous Zones*. London: Sphere.

D'Zurilla, T. J. & Goldfried, M. R. (1971). Problem solving and behaviour modification. *Journal of Abnormal Psychology*, **78**, 107–26.

D'Zurilla, T. J. & Nezu, A. (1980). A study of the generation-of-alternatives process in social problem solving. *Cognitive Therapy and Research*, **4**, 67–72.

Egan, G. (1986). *The Skilled Helper* (3rd edn). Monterey, CA: Brooks/Cole.

Eidelson. R. J. & Epstein, N. (1982). Cognition and relationship maladjustment: development of a measure of dysfunctional relationship beliefs. *Journal of Consulting and Clinical Psychology*, **50**, 721–6.

Ellis, A. (1962). *Reason and Emotion in Psychotherapy*. New York: Lyle Stuart.

Ellis, A. (1980). Overview of the clinical theory of rational-emotive therapy. In R. Grieger & J. Boyd (eds), *Rational-emotive Therapy: a Skills Based Approach*, pp. 1–31. New York: Van Nostrand Reinhold.

Ellis, A. (1985). *Rational Humorous Songs*. New York: Institute for Rational-Emotive Therapy.

Ellis, A. (1987). The impossibility of achieving consistently good mental health. *American Psychologist*, **42**, 364–75.

* Ellis, A. & Harper, R. A. (1975). *A New Guide to Rational Living*. Hollywood: Wilshire.

* Emery, G. (1982). *Own Your Own Life*. New York: New American Library.

Fincham, F. D. (1985). Attribution processes in distressed and nondistressed couples: 2. Responsibility for marital problems. *Journal of Abnormal Psychology*, **94**, 183–90.

Fincham, F. D., Beach, S. & Nelson, G. (1987). Attribution processes in distressed and nondistressed couples: 3. Causal and responsibility attributions for spouse behavior. *Cognitive Therapy and Research*, **11**, 71–86.

Flavell, J. H. (1985). *Cognitive Development* (2nd edn). Englewood Cliffs, NJ: Prentice Hall.

* Frankl, V. E. (1959). *Man's Search for Meaning*. New York: Washington Square Press.
  Frankl, V. E. (1969). *The Doctor and the Soul*. Harmondsworth: Penguin Books.
  Fricker, P. (1987). Quoted in an anonymous article, 'The will to win'. *Australian Weekend Magazine* 11–12 July, 1–2.
* Friedman, M. & Rosenman, R. H. (1974). *Type A Behavior and Your Heart*. New York: Alfred Knopf.
  Fuqua, D., Seaworth, T. B. & Newman, J. L. (1987). The relationship of career indecision and anxiety: a multivariate examination. *Journal of Vocational Behavior*, **30**, 175–86.
  Gardner, J. (1965). *Self-renewal: the Individual and the Innovative Society*. New York: Harper & Row.
  Gendlin, E. T. (1981). *Focusing* (2nd edn). New York: Bantam Books.
  Glasser, W. (1984). *Control Theory*. New York: Harper & Row.
  Goldfried, M. R., Decenteceo, E. T. & Weinberg, L. (1974). Systematic rational restructuring as a self-control technique. *Behavior Therapy*, **5**, 247–54.
* Gordon, T. (1970). *Parent Effectiveness Training*. New York: Wyden.
* Howe, M. A. (1986). *Imaging*. Melbourne: Spiral.
  Ivey, A. E., Ivey, M. B. & Simek-Downing, L. (1987). *Counseling and Psychotherapy: Integrating Skills, Theory and Practice* (2nd edn). Englewood Cliffs, NJ: Prentice Hall.
  Jacobson, E. (1938). *Progressive Relaxation* (2nd edn). Chicago: University of Chicago Press.
  Jacobson, N. S., McDonald, D.W., Follette, W. C. & Berley, R. A. (1985). Attributional processes in distressed and nondistressed married couples. *Cognitive Therapy and Research*, **9**, 35–50.
  Janis, I. L. (1982). *Counseling on Personal Decisions*. New Haven, CT: Yale University Press.
  Janis, I. L. & Mann, L. (1977). *Decision Making: a Psychological Analysis of Conflict, Choice and Commitment*. New York: The Free Press.
  Jarrett, R. B. & Nelson, R. O. (1987). Mechanisms of change in cognitive therapy of depression. *Behavior Therapy*, **18**, 227–41.
  Kassorla, I. C. (1984). *Go for It!* New York: Dell.
  Kelly. G. A. (1955a). *The Psychology of Personal Constructs*. New York: Norton.
  Kelly, G. A. (1955b). *A Theory of Personality*. New York: Norton.
  Kinnier, R. T. (1987). Development of a values conflict resolution assessment. *Journal of Counseling Psychology*, **34**, 31–7.
  Kohlberg, L. & Gilligan, C. (1971). The adolescent as philosopher: the discovery of the self in a postconventional world. *Daedalus*, **100**, 1051–86.
  Kulik, J. A. & Mahler, H. I. M. (1987). Health status, perceptions of risk, and prevention interest for health and nonhealth problems. *Health Psychology*, **6**, 15–27.
  Laing, R. D. (1969). *The Politics of the Family*. London: Tavistock Publications.
  Lang, P. J. (1977). Imagery in therapy: an information processing analysis of fear. *Behavior Therapy*, **8**, 862–86.
* Lazarus, A. (1977). *In the Mind's Eye*. New York: The Guilford Press.
  Leong, S. L., Leong, F.T. & Hoffman, M. A. (1987). Counseling expectations of rational, intuitive and dependent decision makers. *Journal of Counseling Psychology*, **34**, 261–5.
* Lewisohn, P. M., Munoz, R. F., Youngren, M. A. & Zeiss, A. M., (1986). *Control Your Depression*. New York: Prentice Hall.
  Lopez, F.G. & Thurman, C.W. (1986). A cognitive behavioral investigation of anger among college students. *Cognitive Therapy and Research*, **10**, 245–56.

Lucock, M. P. & Salkovskis, P. M. (1988). Cognitive factors in social anxiety and its treatment. *Behaviour Research and Therapy*, 26, 297–302.

Marsh, H. W. (1986). Self-serving effect (bias?) in academic attributions: its relation to academic achievement and self-concept. *Journal of Educational Psychology*, 78, 190–200.

Maslow, A. H. (1962). *Toward a Psychology of Being*. New York: Van Nostrand.

Maslow, A. H. (1970) *Motivation and Personality* (2nd edn). New York: Harper & Row.

Maslow, A. H. (1971). *The Farther Reaches of Human Nature*. Harmondsworth: Penguin Books.

May, R. (1953). *Man's Search for Himself*. New York: Norton.

Meichenbaum, D. (1977). *Cognitive-behavior Modification*. New York: Plenum.

* Meichenbaum, D. (1983). *Coping with Stress*. London: Century Publishing.

Meichenbaum, D. (1985). *Stress Inoculation Training*. New York: Pergamon Press.

Meichenbaum, D. (1986). Cognitive-behavior modification. In F. H. Kanfer & A. P. Goldstein (eds), *Helping People Change* (3rd edn), pp. 346–80. New York: Pergamon Press.

Mitchell, L. K. & Krumboltz, J. D. (1987). The effects of cognitive restructuring and decision-making on career indecision. *Journal of Counseling and Development*, 66, 171–4.

Moon, J. R. & Eisler, R. M. (1983). Anger control: an experimental comparison of three behavioral treatments. *Behavior Therapy*, 14, 493–505.

Mowrer, O. H. (1964). *The New Group Therapy*. Princeton: Van Nostrand.

Nelson-Jones, R. (1984). *Personal Responsibility Counselling and Therapy*. London & Sydney: Harper & Row; New York: Hemisphere.

Nelson-Jones, R. (1988). Choice therapy. *Counselling Psychology Quarterly*, 1, 41–53.

Nezu, A. M. & Ronan, G. F. (1988). Social problem solving as a moderator of stress-related depressive symptoms: a prospective analysis. *Journal of Counseling Psychology*, 35, 134–8.

Novaco, R. W, (1977). Stress inoculation: a cognitive therapy for anger and its application to a case of depression. *Journal of Consulting and Clinical Psychology*, 45, 600–88.

Peale, N. V. (1953). *The Power of Positive Thinking*. Kingswood, Surrey: World's Work.

Perry, W. G. (1970). *Forms of Intellectual and Ethical Development in the College Years*. New York: Holt, Rinehart & Winston.

Peterson, C., Semmel, A., von Baeyer, C., Abramson, L., Metalsky, G. I. & Seligman, M. E. P. (1982). The Attributional Style Questionnaire. *Cognitive Therapy and Research*, 6, 287–300.

Peterson, C., Villanova, P. & Raps, C. S. (1985). Depression and attributions: factors responsible for inconsistent results in the published literature. *Journal of Abnormal Psychology*, 94, 165–8.

Piaget, J. (1970). Piaget's theory. In P. H. Mussen (ed.), *Carmichael's Manual of Child Psychology* (3rd edn, vol. 1), pp. 703–32. New York: John Wiley.

Pietromonaco, P. R. & Rooks, K.S. (1987). Decision style in depression: the contribution of perceived risks versus benefits. *Journal of Personality and Social Psychology*, 52, 399–408.

Platt, J. J., Pout, M. F. & Metzger, D. S. (1986). Interpersonal cognitive problem solving therapy (ICPS). In W. Dryden & W. Golden (eds), *Cognitive-behavioural Approaches to Psychotherapy*, pp. 261–89. London: Harper & Row.

* Rogers, C. R. (1961). *On Becoming a Person*. Boston: Houghton Mifflin.

* Rogers, C. R. (1980). *A Way of Being*. Boston: Houghton Mifflin.

Ross, S. M., Gottfredson, D. K., Christensen, P. & Weaver, R. (1986). Cognitive self-statements in depression: findings across clinical populations. *Cognitive Therapy and Research*, **10**, 159–66.

Sanford, N. (1962). Developmental status of the entering freshman. In N. Sanford (ed.), *The American College*, pp. 253–82. New York: John Wiley.

Sartre, J. P. (1956). *Being and Nothingness*. New York: Philosophical Library.

Schulman, P., Seligman, M. E. P. & Amsterdam, D. (1987). The attributional style questionnaire is not transparent. *Behaviour Research and Therapy*, **25**, 391–5.

Seligman, M. E. P., Abramson, L. Y., Semmel, A. & von Baeyer, C (1979). Depressive attributional style. *Journal of Abnormal Psychology*, **88**, 242–7.

* Simonton, O. C., Matthews-Simonton, S. & Creighton, J. L. (1978). *Getting Well Again*. New York: Bantam Books.

Skovolt, T. M. & Hoenninger, R. W. (1974). Guided fantasy in career development. *Personnel and Guidance Journal*, **52**, 693–6.

Skovolt, T. M. & Thoen, G. A. (1987). Mental imagery and parenthood decision-making. *Journal of Counseling and Development*, **65**, 315–16.

* Steiner, C. M. (1974). *Scripts People Live*. New York: Bantam Books.

ᵗ Steiner, C. M. (1981). *The Other Side of Power*. New York: Grove Press.

Szasz, T. S. (1973). *The Second Sin*. London: Routledge and Kegan Paul.

Teasdale, J. D. & Dent, J. (1987). Cognitive vulnerability to depression: an investigation of two hypotheses. *British Journal of Clinical Psychology*, **26**, 113–26.

Tillich, P. (1952). *The Courage to Be*. New Haven: Yale University Press.

Tresemer, D. W. (1977). *Fear of Success*. New York: Plenum Press.

Ward. C. H. & Eisler, R. M. (1987). Type A achievement striving and failure to achieve personal goals. *Cognitive Therapy and Research*, **11**, 463–71,

Warren, R., McLellarn, R. & Ponzoha, C. (1988). Rational-emotive therapy vs general cognitive-behaviour therapy in the treatment of low self-esteem and related emotional disturbances. *Cognitive Therapy and Research*, **12**, 21–38.

Watson, J. (1986). Parental attributions of emotional disturbance and their relation to the outcome of therapy: preliminary findings. *Australian Psychologist*, **21**, 271–82.

Weiner, B. & Kukla, A. (1970). An attributional analysis of achievement motivation. *Journal of Personality and Social Psychology*, **15**, 1–20.

Weinstein, N. D. (1980). Unrealistic optimism about future life events. *Journal of Personality and Social Psychology*, **39**, 806–20.

Weinstein, N. D. (1984). Why it won't happen to me: perceptions of risk factors and susceptibility. *Heath Psychology*, **3**, 431–57.

Wessler, R. L. & Hankin-Wessler, S. W. R. (1986). Cognitive appraisal therapy (CAT). In W. Dryden & W. Golden (eds), *Cognitive-behavioural Approaches to Psychotherapy*, pp. 196–223. London: Harper & Row.

Witmer, J. M. & Young, M. E. (1985). The silent partner: uses of imagery in counseling. *Journal of Counseling and Development*, **64**, 187–90.

Wolpe, J. E. (1982). *The Practice of Behavior Therapy* (2nd edn). New York: Pergamon.

Woolfolk. R. L., Parish, M. W. & Murphy, S. M. (1985). The effects of positive and negative imagery on motor skill performance. *Cognitive Therapy and Research*, **3**, 335–41.

Yalom, I. D. (1980). *Existential Psychotherapy*. New York: Basic Books.

Young, R. A. (1986). Counseling the unemployed: attributional issues. *Journal of Counseling and Development*, **64**, 374–8.

# Index